Understanding
Social Work Research

SAGE has been part of the global academic community since 1965, supporting high quality research and learning that transforms society and our understanding of individuals, groups, and cultures. SAGE is the independent, innovative, natural home for authors, editors and societies who share our commitment and passion for the social sciences.

Find out more at: **www.sagepublications.com**

Understanding
Social Work Research

Second Edition

Hugh McLaughlin

Los Angeles | London | New Delhi
Singapore | Washington DC

First edition published 2007
This edition first published 2012

SAGE Publications Ltd
1 Oliver's Yard
55 City Road
London EC1Y 1SP

SAGE Publications Inc.
2455 Teller Road
Thousand Oaks, California 91320

SAGE Publications India Pvt Ltd
B 1/I 1 Mohan Cooperative Industrial Area
Mathura Road
New Delhi 110 044

SAGE Publications Asia-Pacific Pte Ltd
3 Church Street
#10-04 Samsung Hub
Singapore 049483

Library of Congress Control Number: 2011929787

British Library Cataloguing in Publication data

A catalogue record for this book is available from the British Library

ISBN 978-0-85702-871-6
ISBN 978-0-85702-872-3 (pbk)

Typeset by C&M Digitals (P) Ltd, Chennai, India
Printed and bound by CPI Group (UK) Ltd, Croydon, CR0 4YY
Printed on paper from sustainable resources

Contents

About the Author

Hugh is a registered social worker and is currently Professor of Social Work at Manchester Metropolitan University. Hugh was born and brought up in Carrickfergus, Northern Ireland. He is married to Catherine and they have two grown up children, James and Eleanor, of whom they are very proud.

Before moving into academia, he was a practising social worker, team leader, area manager, service manager and assistant director in local authority children and family services. During this time he maintained a keen interest in research for social work practice undertaking his PhD, MPhil, MSc and MA (Econ) part-time. Following 22 years in practice he moved to the University of Salford developing his research interests and publications to include the meaningful involvement and limitations of service users in evaluating/researching social care provision, developing a research informed social work practice, child care practice and the development of learning organisations. Hugh retains a keen interest in practice and is chair of the trustee board for After Adoption, a member of the trustee board for the National Children's Bureau (NCB), the advisory group for Involve (NIHR) and a member of SCIE's Partner Council.

When Hugh is not working or writing he likes to run, go to the theatre and scuba dive – preferably in warmer waters than the UK!

1 Why Research for Social Work?

Introduction

This book seeks to identify research as an underused but essential tool for the busy social worker in undertaking their difficult, demanding and often contradictory tasks within society. For too long research has been ignored by social workers or at best been relegated to an add-on or luxury. There are many reasons why this has been so and some of these will be explored in later chapters. Social workers work with people often at their most vulnerable – children who have been abused, those who have been subject to domestic violence or those suffering chronic mental ill health. Each of these deserves the highest professional expertise from their social workers and this book argues that this is not possible without also including a research-minded perspective. Research can help social workers deliver their practice agenda and in many ways good research and good social work are synonymous. D'Cruz and Jones (2004: 2) write that:

> We teach research to social work students because we believe that social work practice is more likely to be effective when social workers are able to draw on and evaluate previous research.

As a social worker, or social work student, you will want to know whether your interventions are making a difference, either positively or negatively. Social work is not a neutral activity. Social work can lead to a positive outcome for the service user or the social worker or it may lead to a negative outcome for one or both of them. To this end it is imperative for social workers to be in a continuous reflective relationship with their practice seeking to find evidence and answers that help them to identify whether their intervention is effective or mere interference. As such the social worker may have to ask:

- Will the care package I commission enable Mr and Mrs Jones to live independently in their own home?
- Is the Council's policy on personalisation working?
- What does the research evidence say about effective residential provision?
- Is there a link between domestic violence and child abuse?

As a social worker there is a need to be able to ask these and similar questions at the individual, your own caseload, the agency and the policy level. The policy level may be both at local service delivery and national in terms of government policy and its impact on practice.

The Notion of the Social Worker and Social Work

The notion of a social worker has been defined in a number of different ways over the years. In 1982 following a series of child abuse tragedies and inquiries, the then UK Conservative Government commissioned Peter Barclay to review the role and function of social workers. In the prelude to the report, Barclay noted:

> Too much is expected of social workers. We load them with unrealistic expectations and then complain when they do not live up to them. Social work is a relatively young profession. It has grown rapidly as the flow of legislation has greatly increased the range and complexity of its work. (Barclay, 1982: vii)

Payne (2005) describes three major differing approaches to how we conceptualise social work. These are:

- *Individualism–reformism:* this refers to social work as an activity that aims to meet social welfare needs on an individualised basis.
- *Socialist-collectives:* this approach focuses on promoting cooperation within society in order that the most oppressed and disadvantaged can gain power and take control of their own lives.
- *Reflexive–therapeutic:* this approach is focused on promoting and facilitating personal growth so that people are enabled to deal with the suffering and disadvantage that they experience.

Reflexive Questions

What do you consider social work to be? Is it what social workers do, or is it based on some other ideas about values and skills? What do you consider to be the core of social work? Can only social workers undertake social work? You may want to keep a copy of your answers for consideration later.

Throughout the book you will see reflexive questions like those above. These questions are there to help you to consider, reflect and develop your own views on some of the key issues facing social workers in coming to terms with research and research evidence. You may also want to consider writing your answers down to the different questions in a notebook to keep with this book to act as a reminder of your original thoughts and to see how they develop or change.

The International Association of the Schools of Social Work (IASSW) and the International Federation of Social Work (IFSW) have agreed on the following definition of social work as they have sought to transcend national boundaries and identify social work within a global economy:

> The social work profession promotes social change, problem solving in human relationships, and the empowerment and liberation of people to enhance well-being. Utilising theories of human behaviour and social systems, social work intervenes at points where people interact with their environments. Principles of human rights and social justice are fundamental to social work. (IASSW and IFSW, 2004: 4)

Whilst this is the agreed definition by the different international social work associations, their members do accept that how it will be interpreted will vary between nations and contexts. A respondent to the consultation from Hong Kong proposed additions including an acknowledgement of responsibility and the importance of the collective. This internationalisation of the definition of social work raises questions as to how 'international' social work can be. As Hugman (2010: 150) recognises, this perspective has resulted in two extreme views between those who regard social work as a single entity whose values, skills and knowledge remain the same irrespective of the national context and those who regard social work as being shaped inextricably by the local national context in terms of its legal mandate, culture and welfare system. Social work is now recognised in 90 countries and the truth probably lies within the two extremes. There are obviously international issues that social work is concerned with including – refugees, human trafficking, famine and drought, natural disasters and poverty – and social workers should consider enhancing their local practice by developing a more international perspective.

Horner (2006) criticises the internationally agreed definition of social work for failing to acknowledge the controlling aspects of social work involving the use of statutory powers to intervene to protect vulnerable children and older people. It is notable that the IFSW website acknowledges that social work in the twenty-first century is dynamic and evolving, and that the definition should not be considered exhaustive (IFSW, 2011).

The important point here is that the most widely accepted definition of social work is not written on tablets of stone and is likely to change as society changes. This is not to suggest an 'anything goes' mentality but to be realistic that changes in wider society will result in changes in social work practice. Social work is not a fixed entity. Therefore, what you and I consider to be representative of social work today may not be the position in the future. You might like to keep your answer to the first reflective exercise above and keep it somewhere safe to look at again not only as you finish this book but in a couple of years' time to see whether your view has changed.

What is important for our future discussions is that social work is neither a neutral nor a static activity, it is dynamic and can have positive and/or negative consequences for service users and social workers alike, as such social work represents a value-driven form of welfare practice.

Social Work and the Modernisation Agenda

Within the British context social service departments were created following the introduction of the Local Authority Social Services Act 1970. This brought together the three separate local council departments – children, mental health and welfare – into a single unitary social work department headed up by a Director of Social Services. Initially, social work was viewed as a generic activity but has become increasingly specialist and fragmented ever since.

Major structural changes occurred in the early 1990s signalled by the introduction of the Children Act 1989 and the NHS and Community Care Act 1990. These two Acts pushed many authorities into separating children and adult services. The Children Act 1989 was one of the first major pieces of social services legislation to be explicitly informed by research (Parker et al., 1991). The introduction of these two Acts increased the fragmentation of the service and subjected it (albeit unevenly) to the disciplines of the mixed economy of welfare. This involved redefining the role of social services from that of provider of services to that of 'enabler', 'commissioner' or 'purchaser' or services. The government also sought to promote a mixed economy of care whereby the 'commissioners' and 'purchasers' of service were expected to commission or purchase services less from the local authority and more from a mix of public, private and voluntary providers. Included within this was also a broad intention to transform the nature of social services from a welfare agency run by professionals, allegedly too much in their own interests, to a customer-centred organisation run by professional managers. Adams sums up this trend as 'new managerialism' whereby 'managerialism' is the term used to describe styles of management that put managers in the central role of the organisation. 'New managerialism' (Adams, 1998: 44) is the term used to describe management approaches in the public services that were imported from the private sector in the early 1980s, with decisions based on the criteria of economy, efficiency and effectiveness (Adams, 2002: 176).

The Labour Party came to power in 1997 and far from retreating on the reformation of local government moved it onto a new level. The Labour government's big idea can be summed up in the discourse of modernisation. Modernisation has permeated all aspects of central and local government, including social services and health services (Department of the Environment, Transport and the Regions (DETR), 1998; Cabinet Office, 1990; Department of Health (DH), 1998b) as the necessary process for updating services to match the expectations of modern-day consumers. Modernisation emphasises partnership (Balloch and Taylor, 2001; Glendinning et al., 2002) and joined-up thinking (Frost, 2005), whereby traditional boundaries that have been seen as barriers to meeting service users' needs are now addressed by workers working together in partnerships or joint teams. This emphasis on partnerships and joined-up thinking accepted that traditional uni-professional ways of working were not going to address society's 'wicked' problems (Glasby and Dickinson, 2008) like poverty and social exclusion (see Chapter 9 for a fuller discussion on interprofessional practice). Accompanying this was a growth in professional accountability to government through performance indicators and the Performance Assessment Framework (PAF) that covered key indicators for all aspects of social service performance.

Besides these developments there has also been an increasing government support for practice based on research evidence particularly visible since the Children Act 1989. Besides individually funding research projects, the Department of Health has also developed a number of research overviews summarised for practitioners and managers including: *Patterns and Outcomes in Child Placements* (1991); *Child Protection: Messages from Research* (1995); and *Caring for Children Away from Home: Messages from Research* (1998b). In recent years this has also spread into other research dissemination activity, including: conferences; the support of Research in Practice (RiP); Making Research Count (MRC); the launch of the Social Care Institute for Excellence (SCIE) (SCIE, 2011) in England; and the Institute of Research and Innovation in Social Services (IRISS) (IRISS, 2011) in Scotland. SCIE is an independent company and charity partly funded by government. SCIE is committed to developing and promoting knowledge about good practice in social care and is very much a part of the government's drive to modernise social care. SCIE and IRISS reviews can be downloaded free from the Web addresses listed in the References at the end of the book (IRISS, 2011; SCIE, 2011). SCIE Knowledge Review No. 3 identified the *Types and Quality of Knowledge in Social Care* (Pawson et al., 2003). Pawson and his colleagues produced a five-part classificatory framework for understanding knowledge in social work and social care:

> *Organisational knowledge:* knowledge gained from the governance and regulation activities involved in organising social care.
>
> *Practitioner knowledge:* knowledge gained by practitioners in their day-to-day work that tends to be personal, tacit and context-specific.
>
> *User knowledge:* knowledge gained from the experience of using social care services; again this is often tacit and is explored further in Chapter 6.
>
> *Research knowledge:* knowledge gathered systematically within a planned strategy; such knowledge is mostly explicit and available in reports, evaluations, books and articles.
>
> *Policy community knowledge:* knowledge that is gained from the wider policy context and may include knowledge in the civil service, think tanks and agencies.

This book is primarily interested in the use of research knowledge, but as the reader will realise, although Pawson et al. (2003) have identified a conceptually distinct framework, there are often overlaps. In particular we will also look at practitioner knowledge and service user knowledge, but will also be aware of the potential for organisational knowledge and policy community knowledge to impact upon social work research.

The accessibility of research for students in social work has led Butler (2003) to comment wryly that:

> It is rare to complete a student placement visit to a social services department without at least coming across one of the several Department of Health (DH) 'Messages from Research' (e.g. DH, 2001a) or 'Quality Protects' (e.g. DH, RiP and MRC, 2002) briefings that seek to influence social work practice with children and families through the use of research findings. Central government is actively involved in other ways too: not just in funding and disseminating research but also in various forms of its governance and ordering. It is difficult to remember a time when interest in social work research was so widespread, so urgent and so apparently full of possibilities. (Butler, 2003: 19)

What Butler doesn't tell us is whether these documents were being actively read or whether they were merely available and gathering dust on bookshelves or desks.

At this point it is worthwhile clarifying the distinction between social care and social work, although in many places the terms are now used interchangeably. In this book, social workers refer to those with a professional social work qualification and in the UK context are registered with their national regulatory body. Whilst this group are also part of the wider social care workforce, they represent only a small part, as this is primarily made up of unqualified staff, many of whom work part-time. Skills for Care (Eborall, 2010) estimate that there were 1.75 million jobs in adult social care in 2009 whilst the Children's Workforce Development Council (CWDC, 2008) estimated that there were approximately 168,340 social care staff in 2007 in occupations covered by the CWDC. Estimating the total of those who work in social care has become increasingly difficult as the boundaries between those who provide social care services in the statutory, private and voluntary sector merge and split and include those who work in their own homes, other people's homes, care homes, day care, hospitals and the wider community. However, the point here is that social care is a major provider of employment in England and the UK in general. In 2009, the General Social Care Council (GSCC) (GSCC, 2010) had over 83,000 registered social workers listed – although not all of these are working as social workers, some will not be employed in social work, some will be taking a career break or are people like myself, social work academics. The number of qualified social workers is a small subset of all those who work in social care. Of this English subset 77 per cent were female, 70 per cent white and 77 per cent took their qualification in the UK. It is this group of registered social workers working in statutory, voluntary and private social care services that we refer to as 'social workers' in this book.

In the UK, the General Social Care Council (England), the Care Council for Wales, the Scottish Social Services Council and the Northern Ireland Social Care Council have been tasked to register and regulate the activities of all social care workers, beginning with qualified and student social workers. Also from April 2005, it became illegal to use the title of 'social worker' unless someone has an approved social work qualification and is registered with the appropriate regulatory body. In many other countries like America, Australia and Germany, social workers already have protection of title and a governing registration body.

Social work in the UK is presently at a point of contradiction, social work is now an all-graduate profession (with an increasing move towards more and more postgraduate qualifying provision), and the title of social worker is protected for those registered with the requisite care council, with a requirement for continuing professional development to reregister. Alongside these developments, in England the Social Work Taskforce (SWTF) – an expert group set up by the Department of Health and the Department for Children, Schools and Families to undertake a comprehensive review of frontline social work practice – reported in 2009, and amongst its stated ambitions was the wish to secure 'a reliable supply of confident, high quality, adaptable professionals into the workforce' and the desire to see a greater use of research and continuing professional development to inform frontline practice (SWTF, 2009: 6).

These aspirations have since been delegated to the Social Work Reform Board to implement and it is too early to see if any of these changes are making any impact upon practice. It will also be interesting to see how the commitment to research will be operationalised as this is yet unclear; but the report's admonishment of academics is not hopeful:

> Educators need to share in the real challenges posed in service delivery and avoid any temptation to criticise from the sidelines. (SWTF, 2009: 1.25)

It is rather insulting to suggest that social work educators are not concerned with the 'real challenges' of service delivery and that they should suspend their critical faculties when researching or discussing these with social workers or social work students. It is surely the research and critical analysis of educators in dialogue with social work staff, social work students and service users that can help to identify where service delivery is proving effective or not, and can help ensure the best possible outcomes for service users and carers.

At the same time as these potentially positive moves, we have experienced the fragmentation and dismantling of standalone social service departments, previously the main employment opportunity for social workers. These standalone social service departments have been replaced by new local authority configurations of education and children's social services, representing a split from adult social services. These arrangements have been further complicated where social service personnel have been merged with health personnel to form mental health and learning disability trusts. In some parts of the country, children's social services staff along with education department personnel and health colleagues are being combined to form children's trusts. It is also interesting to note that a number of social service departments have since recombined their adults and children's services in recognition that the artificial split was causing more structural difficulties than it solved (see Chapter 9). Today, social workers are employed in an increasingly wide range of non-statutory social care agencies. These include those in the private and voluntary sector, multiagency teams, Sure Start, Connexions, Youth Offending Teams, Drug and Alcohol Teams, Mental Health Trusts, Children and Family Court Advice and Support Services (CAFCASS) and an ever-growing number of recruitment agencies. For many of these organisations, social work will not be the major profession or social care the dominant discipline. The majority of social workers in the future may not be employed in monolithic social service departments but in a mosaic or tapestry of welfare provision.

The above relates particularly to England, but England is only one part of the four nations that make up the UK. All four nations organise their social work services slightly differently. In Scotland, the term 'social work services' is used to describe the full range of services, including criminal justice as well as child and adult services. Criminal justice is separate in the rest of the UK. Northern Ireland's social services have developed against a backdrop of a contested nation and civil unrest. 'The Troubles' and political uncertainty have resulted in social services being located under the direction of the Department of Health and Social Services and managed as an integrated service with health by Health and Social Services Boards since 1973. Wales, since devolution, has seen a great deal of policy activity and a divergence from the English context, including a decision not to promote the development of Children's Trusts. A particular issue within the Welsh context has been the promotion of the Welsh language and the need to promote Welsh-speaking services for those whose first language is Welsh. (For a fuller discussion on social work in the British Isles see Payne and Shardlow, 2002.)

This has been a rather long introduction into the state of social work in the UK and its international context. However, this provides the background to how social work research is expected to operate and promote research-minded practice.

> You might like to consider what type of setting you work in or would ideally wish to work in?
>
> Why, have you chosen this type of setting? If you have not chosen the 'traditional' local authority department, why have you done so? If you have chosen local authority social work, what do you see as the advantages of such a system?

 Reflexive Questions

What is Research?

Up until now it has been assumed that we all have a shared understanding about what research is. The stereotypical image of the researcher emphasises what one might call the manipulative aspects of the role – designing questionnaires or engaging in statistical analysis, writing incomprehensible reports, detached from reality and living in an ivory tower. Within such a perspective, social work practitioners may experience research as irrelevant and inaccessible and at worst as the process of being manipulated for the researcher's career enhancement.

> What is your image of the researcher?
>
> How do you define research?
>
> Who undertakes research?
>
> Which organisations undertake research?

Reflexive Questions

As Hughes (1990) notes, research is carried out to discover something about the world and is an activity that many of us engage in daily as we seek to find out something that we did not previously know. What makes research different from other ways of finding out is its processes that are characterised as systematic and disciplined. As Becker and Bryman (2004: 14) observe, for something to count as research:

> the enquiry must be done in a systematic, disciplined and rigorous way, making use of the most appropriate research methods and designs to answer specific research questions.

This technical definition ignores the value-driven nature of social work. At one level this does not matter and that research should be seen as standing objectively outside the practice milieu. However, to do so would be to privilege the researcher's perspective of the world. Research, like social work, is value-driven. As Rosen has noted:

> The selection of a research topic and corresponding method are in many ways a life choice. They are indicative of what the researcher believes as important to 'see' in the world, to investigate and to know. An individual choice of topic and method corresponds to his or her ontological vision, his or her model of being. (Rosen, 1991: 21)

The question of which topic to research is not purely a technical question, but also a philosophical one. In deciding upon a topic to research and the resultant research methodology, the researcher is making a statement about human nature, society and the relationship between the two. Likewise, we need to acknowledge that research sponsors and funders will target funding on particular aspects of social life and organisations and will only allow access to particular aspects of their organisations. It is more likely to be easier to gain access to research how social workers could become more efficient and effective, as opposed to similarly examining the impact of senior managers, lead councillors or management boards.

Coupled with this, there is also the vested interest in organisations to ensure that research reports reflect a positive view of the organisation. Recently I was 'invited' to meet with an assistant director immediately prior to a research report being agreed for publication. The local authority did not like what the report said about their management team or style and felt that the report was too sympathetic and accepting of the views of their frontline staff. The local authority wanted the final pages of the report rewritten before they would agree to their organisation's data being included in the report. Following long and torturous negotiations, a compromise was agreed that allowed both parties to retain their integrity. This can become even more invidious when research commissioners block publication because they do not want the results of the research to be in the public arena. Such checks and balances can be helpful in ensuring accuracy in research, but at the extreme they can also result in compromising and undermining the veracity of the research process and any contributions to knowledge the research may make. Researchers and organisational commissioners need to be clear at the beginning of the research process to identify the parameters around publication. These need to ensure that research publications do not become blocked because the results are not positive whilst researchers also need to be able to convince organisations of their political awareness, accuracy and honesty of their work. This topic is dealt with in greater detail in Chapter 7.

Research Mindedness

In order to address these difficulties, Everitt et al. (1992) identified 'research mindedness' as a means of enhancing good social work practices. They also suggested that social work and social work research could be conceptualised as interrelated processes. In order to achieve this they identified three principles of 'research mindedness':

- A participatory/developmental rather than a social control model of social work.
- Anti-oppressive values are applied.
- Genuine partnerships are established with those whom social work serves.

These principles are in keeping with our previous discussions on the ethical nature of social work. It emphasises that research subjects are valued in their own right and not purely viewed as objects to be exploited for the further advancement of the researcher. This view recognises that the basis of 'knowing' is shared and should be made explicit between researcher, informant and the research audience. They also argue that subjectivity viewed as personal experience, or worldview, is valued and is seen as integral to the research experience. Everitt et al. (1992) did not make a claim for a definitive methodology but rather some tentative approximations and provisional suggestions.

Social Work Research: A Different Type of Research?

Having identified the nature of social work, research and research mindedness, it is important to question whether there is a distinct form of research that can be termed 'social work research'.

What do you think? Is there a distinct form of research that can be termed 'social work research'? If so, how would you identify whether a research project constituted social work research or just social research?

It is clear that we have social work academics that conduct social research into social work problems. It is also clear that others, who are not social workers, also research many of these issues, like domestic violence, child protection or disability. It is thus worth asking what makes the difference between a social work researcher and a non-social work researcher? Dominelli (2005) argues that there is a distinctive research approach that can be defined as social work research. In particular she identifies the following key features Dominelli (2005: 230):

- A change orientation.
- A more egalitarian relationship between themselves and those who are the objects of their research.

- Accountability to 'clients'/service users for the products of their work.
- A holistic engagement with the different aspects of the problem(s) of people they are investigating.

None of the above can be viewed as purely exclusive to social work. However, when they are combined they can be viewed as typifying the nature and scope of social work. Social work research thus aims not only to support practice but also to transform it. As Orme and Shemmings (2010: 17) recognise, social work research 'can be *for* social work, *on* social work, *or from* social work that is *by* social workers' (italics in original). Lyons (2000) suggests that the distinctiveness of social work research can be identified by its contribution to knowledge production, knowledge transmission and knowledge application. In other words, social work research's contribution to the social sciences knowledge base, its contribution to social work teaching and learning and, most importantly, its contribution to practice.

Shaw (2007: 663) challenges the focus on the distinctiveness of social work research, suggesting that social work research will be poorer if we overemphasise its distinctiveness and instead challenges us to focus less on 'what makes social work distinctive' and more on 'what might make it distinctively good?' It is the challenge of this book, to help you the reader, to be able to appreciate and utilise how research can help you to become a more effective social worker. Integral to this is how to become a research-minded social worker in order to maximise the benefits of social work research to support critically your practice and to generate potential research questions for the future.

Chapter Summary

The future of social work is both uncertain and exciting. The previous certainties have been stripped away whilst the future remains in the balance. It has been argued that social work and social work research are value-driven activities, which are both contested and contestable. This is why it is so important for you as a social worker to become research minded if you wish to be able to engage in debates about the effectiveness of your practice, to demonstrate the impact of government policies on your cases or to advocate on behalf of some of the most disadvantaged groups within our society. As a social worker it will not be enough to say that you believe something to be true, you need to be able to explain the evidence for your belief whether this is in a contested childcare case or an accommodation review for a service user with a physical disability.

The Organisation of the Book

The book seeks to place social work research within a framework for research-minded practitioners who are able to see the challenges and opportunities provided by a better understanding of research and its potential. Whilst the book is written with a clear direction and format, it can be read from beginning to end or each chapter individually as each is self-contained, focusing on specific aspects of social work research. The reader should use the book in whatever way best suits their purpose – writing an assignment, inquisitiveness or trying to find out some specific piece of information – whilst remembering that the positions taken by the author in this book are just that: positions that the author believes are justifiable but that you the reader are invited to challenge and to critique in order to develop your own position. Research-minded practitioners don't just accept something because it is written in a book but because the supporting evidence justifies the conclusion(s).

The book seeks to ground social work research in practice, its context, concepts and key issues. In order to maximise the benefit of each of the following chapter's, readers should regularly reflect on the following key questions:

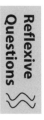

How does this help my understanding of social work and research?

What are the implications of this for my practice?

How might I become more research minded?

How do we develop a research mindedness within our team and/or service?

Chapter 2 begins by locating social work as a practice discipline and examines the business of social work research. This lays the foundation for Chapter 3 concerning 'The Philosophy of Social Research' and in particular its major paradigms and how these impact upon research design and the research question. Chapter 4 then returns to the 'Ethical Issues in Social Work Research', part of which we have begun to discuss in this chapter. This chapter explores whether social work research can be seen to have a specific research code and identifies the major ethical issues before, during and after a research project.

The book then moves onto identifying key issues in social work research, beginning in Chapter 5 with a focus on 'Research and Anti-Oppressive Practice', highlighting research considerations in relation to sites of oppression whilst seeking to develop an anti-oppressive research practice. Chapter 6 examines the nature of 'Evidence-Based Practice'. Evidence-based practice is defined and explored from a medical model perspective before assessing its applicability to probation and social work. The politicisation of evidence-based social work is investigated along with the claims for a hierarchical evidence-base. The next chapter, Chapter 7, considers the growing importance given to 'Getting Research into Practice' and the barriers and drivers in relation to this.

Chapter 8, titled 'Service Users and Research', investigates the trend towards involving service users in research and identifies some of the practical and ethical problems for doing this whilst also seeking to identify when this would be appropriate and when it would not. The chapter also begins to identify when such an approach should be used and begins to examine what are its costs and benefits. Chapter 9, titled 'Interdisciplinary Contributions to Social Work and Social Work Research', identifies the growing importance of interprofessional practice and interprofessional research, especially as this is now an integral part of the requirements for the new social work award. The final chapter, Chapter 10, 'Whither Social Work Research', provides a summary of the previous chapters and then examines the future for social work research.

Suggested Reading

D'Cruz, H. and Jones, M. (2004) *Social Work Research: Ethical and Political Contexts*. London: Sage.
A very readable introduction, grounded in the belief of improving social work practice through the application of research.

Orme, J. and Shemmings, D. (2010) *Developing Research-Based Social Work Practice*. Basingstoke: Palgrave Macmillan.
A very useful introduction into how research can improve the quality of research and the encouragement of 'reflective research practitioners'.

2　The Research Business

Introduction

This chapter begins by considering how research is funded and the process by which research becomes published. This then leads into a discussion on the contributory knowledge streams to social work and the nature of social work as a discipline and to suggest that research is an underused tool in the social worker's toolbox.

Why Bother with Research?

The first question to ask is why should we bother with research?

> Before going any further, you might want to write down the reasons why you believe that we should undertake research.
>
> Second, you might like to consider who benefits from research?

Reflexive Questions

On the surface this may appear a rather trivial question, but the answer is very important as it helps us to understand what we expect of research, and in particular what we expect social work research to deliver. Your list may have included some of the following reasons:

- To answer questions that we did not know the answer to.
- To find out 'what works'.
- To inform decision-making.
- To justify a particular intervention.
- To further the careers of researchers.
- To evaluate whether new interventions work.
- To make money.
- To win a Nobel Prize.

- For intellectual stimulation.
- To prove that something doesn't work.
- To obtain the evidence to justify a change.
- For the completion of a dissertation.
- To enhance the reputation of social work as a serious discipline.
- For submission to the Research Excellence Framework (REF).

As can be seen from the above, there are a wide variety of reasons why research gets undertaken. Some of these reasons focus on the intellectual desire to develop new knowledge in terms of answering the 'questions we do not know the answer to' or 'to evaluate new interventions'. It is not unusual for a sponsor of research to commission research in order to obtain external evidence that something is working so that they can use the results with potential funders. This could be the case for a homeless charity that is dependent on local authority funding and wants to convince commissioners that they provide a service with added value. This has become all the more prevalent with the increasing auditing of services in a period of reduced funding and the emphasis placed upon 'best value'. It may also happen that research is commissioned in order to prove that something is not working so as to provide an external impetus for change. Easterby-Smith et al. (1991) suggest that managers and workers may be more willing to hear such messages about the shortcomings of their service from 'neutral' researchers rather than from their own senior managers' delivered the messages.

In our list of reasons, there were also the reasons concerned with furthering or developing the researcher's career or enhancing social work as a research discipline, including submissions to the **Research Excellence Framework (REF)** exercise which has replaced the Research Assessment Exercise (RAE), of which more will be said later, or, even winning a Nobel Prize! There is also the pragmatic response in terms of completion of an academic dissertation or module. It should be noted that the choice of one reason does not necessarily exclude others, so that you may be undertaking research to obtain an academic award but may also be genuinely interested in evaluating whether or not a new intervention works. Or, as a researcher, you may be wanting to answer a question that you do not know the answer to whilst also seeking to produce an internationally peer-reviewed article to help promote your career.

In terms of social work, the instrumental reasons listed above take on a moral dimension when we remember that social work service users are amongst the most vulnerable in society. For the social worker, either using research or acting as a practitioner researcher there are also ethical dimensions to these questions (this will be discussed more fully in Chapter 4). It was noted in Chapter 1 that a distinctive feature of social work was its value-driven nature and that social work research needed to reflect this. This is not to say that any research that does not reflect these values will not be of use to social workers. Patently, such a position would be absurd. As we have already shown, social work is a complex activity with a set of contested meanings. It does suggest, though, that a social work researcher will adopt a particular stance in relation to the world, to the methods that they use and as to how service users and other research respondents will be treated in the research process.

The Research Business

Social work research is funded in a number of different ways. These include the funding that universities receive via the Higher Education Funding Council (HEFCE), competitive bidding to the research councils, government departments, charities or local social service providers. Researchers may also be directly approached by organisations to undertake research and lastly, there is unfunded research. This latter case may come about because of the particular interest of a researcher or for the completion of a higher degree or post-qualifying course. Unfunded research probably reflects the majority of practitioner research.

Not all research is undertaken in universities or by university staff. There are a growing number of independent research agencies or consultancies and also a few local authorities and voluntary agencies that have their own research staff. However, at present, the majority of social work research is undertaken within a university framework.

University research funding was influenced by the outcome of the last Research Assessment Exercise (RAE), which has been replaced with the Research Excellence Framework (REF). Each university submits researchers to units of assessment, for example social work, administration and social policy, for which it is then graded and receives money accordingly. This money is then given to the university to disperse in the way that it feels is most appropriate.

The second area of funding identified was the research council. There are currently eight research councils of which the Economics and Social Research Council (ESRC) is the most important for social work. The ESRC is a non-government publicly funded body whose mission includes the promotion and support of world class research and promotion of public understanding of the value of the social sciences. In 2009–10 it provided £134 million to support social scientific research (ESRC, 2010b). Peer reviewers assess all applications for council grants. Shaw et al. (2004) undertook a review of the ESRC funding of social work and social care and found that researchers did not consider that social work research, with its applied nature, was very attractive to the ESRC.

Third, research may be commissioned by government through competitive application, as was the case in relation to research on the outcomes of the new social work degree or the Sure Start programme. There is then research funded by charities, including the Joseph Rowntree Foundation, Nuffield Foundation and Leverhulme Trust Foundation, which all support research in social work. These foundations often have thematic approaches with competitive bidding processes alongside researcher-generated research proposals.

Fourth, research is also commissioned by local authorities and charities to focus on a specific issue. Often these relate to service evaluations, for example an evaluation of the care planning approach in mental health or the effectiveness of direct payments to people with disabilities. These agencies may advertise the research contract or contact specific preferred researchers or research centres.

Last, the researcher may provide their own funding to research an issue that is of particular interest to them. Such research is often related to the attainment of a higher degree, but is not purely restricted to this. Practitioners and academics often undertake such research. Practitioners will probably focus on areas of particular interest that may be supported by their employers. This support may include some or all of the following: paying for a higher degree, allowing the staff member time to undertake the research, rearranging their work schedule or providing access to research subjects within their organisation. Where social work organisations are supporting staff they may also wish to influence the research. This works best when both the interests of the staff member and their employer are coterminous.

Social work academics, unlike academics in the many other academic subject areas, often do not have a PhD at their point of recruitment. Social work academics, in my experience, are primarily recruited from practice where a PhD or research experience is not a requirement and may in some cases be viewed as a handicap. This results in social work academics being appointed on the basis of their practice and teaching expertise and not for having a proven research track record. In many universities, social work lecturers are recruited on the basis of their potential ability to become research active. Even with the increased numbers of professional doctorate opportunities for applied disciplines, health professionals have been much quicker to take up these opportunities than social work professionals. This has particular consequences for social work research as it seeks to establish a credible research mass and culture whilst also competing with the more traditional academic departments as well as other applied disciplines. Mills et al.'s (2006) demographic review of the UK social sciences noted that social science academics tended to be older than their natural or physical sciences counterparts, that social work had the highest percentage (47 per cent) of staff aged between 50 and 55 years and was one of seven areas highlighted as in need of greatest attention for capacity building.

It is also worth considering the funding position between health and social care that are often located in same faculty in many universities. Marsh and Fisher (2005: ix) graphically illustrate this when they note that:

> The overall spend per workforce member stands at about £25 in social care compared with £3,400 in health. Using the more specific comparison with primary care, the annual R&D spend per social worker is about £60, compared with £1,466 per general practitioner (GP); annual university research income from the Higher Education Funding Council (HEFC) Quality-related research (QR) is £8,650 per social work researcher and £26,343 per primary care researcher.

The UK Government has established an aspiration for the knowledge economy that 2.5 per cent of gross domestic product should be invested in research and development by 2014. This target is already met by health spending but would require an eightfold increase in funding for social work and social care. These disparities, Marsh and Fisher (2005: ix) suggest, reduce the potential for social work research to deliver social welfare and 'hinders the modernisation of social care'.

This section has sought to show that the funding for research, limited as it is, comes from a diverse set of directions. It is also suggested that although the government is heavily involved in supporting research, either directly or indirectly, more still needs to be done for social work research to become fully effective. Each of the identified funding streams also has their own particular views on what and which research priorities they are willing to support and what they will not.

How many social work journals can you name? How many of these have you read more than one article from? Why is this?

Reflexive Questions

Social Work Publications

Once the research has been completed there then needs to be a knowledge transfer and dissemination process. Traditionally research has been published in peer-reviewed journals. In UK social work there is an ever-increasing number of these, including the following:

- *British Journal of Social Work*
- *Child Abuse Review*
- *Child and Family Social Work*
- *Ethics and Social Welfare*
- *European Journal of Social Work*
- *International Journal of Social Work*
- *Journal of Social Work*

- *Practice*
- *Qualitative Social Work*
- *Research, Policy and Planning*
- *Social Work Education*
- *Social Work and Social Sciences Review*

There are also a growing number of social science journals that are not purely social work but cover an interprofessional or related social work areas. These include journals like:

- *Age and Ageing*
- *British Journal of Criminology*
- *Critical Social Policy*
- *Disability and Society*
- *Health and Social Care*
- *Journal of Interprofessional Care*
- *Journal of Social Policy*
- *Sociological Research Online*

There is thus a diverse range of outlets for social work research. It should be remembered, though, that the research reported in journals has often taken place two to three years previously. This takes into account the time to complete the research report, write the article, submit it to a journal for peer review, receive the article back with amendments to be made concerning any reviewers comments, resubmit the article, the article to be accepted and then to await its turn for publication. Some journals, like the *British Journal of Social Work* and *Social Work Education,* are now providing an advance access to papers online before the journal is published due to the large number of accepted articles waiting their turn to be published. Most of the journals above are also published electronically; it is also likely that in the future all journals will be published online. There are also journals, like *Sociological Research Online* and *Social Work and Society* (see References) that are solely published online.

Books are dealt with quite differently. Any book proposal is also peer reviewed but the difference here is not whether the work is good science or meets the required academic standards, but whether it will sell. Books, unlike journal articles are peer reviewed at the proposal stage and then again after the book has been written. A social work book may be the most innovative research ever printed about a particular assessment technique or intervention, but if it is believed that there is no market for it, in all likelihood it will not be published. Like journals, books are increasingly being produced electronically and most libraries are now building up stocks of electronic books. In recent years, we have also seen the emergence of the electronic reader like the Kindle and how this will impact upon our buying of books and reading habits is yet to be determined.

One other aspect of books that is worth noting has been the tendency for authors and editors to term books as health and social care. The first aspect of this is that health almost always goes first and that some of these are more health than social care. Two examples are an edited book on ethics by Long and Johnson (2007) and another on user participation by Nolan et al. (2007). The first of these alleging to cover health and social care ethics contained no social work or social care authors, which helps to explain why some of the comments on social work are inaccurate. Nolan et al. (2007) contains 28 authors, of whom two come from a social work background and 20 from a health background. This tendency to over-claim on social work or social care relevance can be seen as either a commercial decision by publishers and authors to sell more books, or as a dangerous step towards the colonisation of social work. You may thus like to check whether books that claim to cover both health and social care in their title actually do so.

Social work also has a number of regularly published 'trade magazines': *Community Care* and *Professional Social Work* being the most important in the UK. These trade journals contain job adverts, news items and short articles. Many of the articles, besides containing commentaries on policy initiatives or current events, will also report research findings.

Social workers and students are increasingly expected to be able to access the World Wide Web (WWW) or the Internet. The Internet grew out of the (Advanced Research Projects Agency Network (ARPANET), which was commissioned by the US Department of Defense for research into computer networking (Hewson et al., 2003). The amount of material available on the Internet is unfathomable and social worker, student or researcher need to be careful to draw down materials of a high quality. Among the sites that you may want to use or select as favourites are: government sites, for example www.dfe.gov.uk or www.dh.gov.uk; social work research dissemination sites such as www.rip.org.uk and the Joseph Rowntree Fellowship section on research findings www.jrf.org.uk; and social work portals such as www.scie.org.uk including its searchable database social care online. There is a temptation for some students to go straight to Wikipedia and whilst this online dictionary may have useful information, it cannot always be assumed to be correct or up to date and students should only use it with caution.

Besides the Internet, local authorities, trusts and many of the larger voluntary and independent agencies also have their own intranet system. Intranet systems usually only contain information accessible to that agency's employees and will cover the agency's major policies and procedures, key documentation and often other information of interest to employees. This is potentially a rich source of information for the social work researcher.

These various publishing outlets represent the major sources of written social work research, although there is also an increasing use of podcasts, vodcasts and videos/CDs of research material and poster presentations at conferences.

The Discipline of Social Work

Before reading any further, I would like you to write down whether you believe that social work is a discipline or not? Why do you think that this is the case? What subject disciplines like physics or history inform our understanding of social work.

It is contestable whether social work can be considered to be a discipline or not. It can be argued that social work is not a discipline in its own right but an important area of activity studied from a variety of disciplines. Alternatively, it could be argued that it is unclear what a university discipline is in the first place. At its most basic level, a discipline could be defined as any individual subject area that a university wishes to define as a separate discipline. At the university level, social work is located in a wide variety of departmental arrangements. For example, social work is located in the School for Policy Studies at the University of Bristol, in the School of Social Relations at the University of Keele, School of Social Sciences at the University of Bangor, the Department of Applied Social Studies at Lancaster University. This is not to say that there are no examples of social work being in the title of university departments, for example at Queens University Belfast, the University of Glasgow or Manchester Metropolitan University.

This may in part be explained by the difficulty in describing a distinctive social work discipline that does not include a range of other disciplines to add insight into the process. For example, at the start of this section you were asked to identify all the academic disciplines that you could identify that helped to inform social work. Your list probably has a number of the following academic subject areas:

- Social policy
- Social Anthropology
- Sociology
- Psychology
- Social Psychology
- Law
- Philosophy
- Counselling
- Management

- Education
- Economics
- History
- Politics

It is also possible to add computing, given the increasing amount of time that social workers spend in front of computers and the electronic nature of social work records. Similarly, you may have also added mathematics, given that social workers have had to be increasingly aware of the cost of residential placements or packages of personalised care and the balancing of budgets. Social work may thus be viewed as a value-driven activity in which aspects of a number of differing social sciences are brought to bear on the object of study, which is social work. This, however, does not identify how differing concerns from the differing disciplines, for example, from psychology with its emphasis on understanding individual or group behaviour as opposed to sociology with its emphasis on society.

At one level it is possible to argue that social work is a university discipline – there are groups of students studying at departments that have social work in the title. On the other hand, it is difficult to conceptualise a distinctive subject area that is social work studies that is not informed by the other social sciences. This topic is discussed further in Chapter 8.

Summary

This chapter has covered a wide terrain generally subsumed under the notion of the business of research. The purpose of the chapter was to identify parts of the research process that are usually left unsaid in research textbooks.

In particular we highlighted how research was funded, the disparity between health and social work research funding, research publication outlets and the disciplines that help to inform social work practice and research.

3 The Philosophy of Social Research

Introduction

This chapter explores ontology, epistemology and the major paradigms or ways of making knowledge claims about the social world. The major paradigms explored consist of positivism and interpretivism with an analysis of their associated research methods, strengths and weaknesses. The chapter also introduces the development of pragmatism and participatory research approaches.

Ontology

Ontology is the science or study of being. Snape and Spencer (2003) identify three key questions to examine the nature of existence and what there is to know about the world. In particular:

- Whether or not social reality exists independently of human conceptions and interpretations.
- Whether there is a common, shared, social reality or just multiple context specific realities.
- Whether or not social behaviour is governed by 'laws' that can be seen as immutable or generalisable. (Snape and Spencer, 2003: 11)

These points identify key ontological debates, including whether there is a captive social reality and how it should be constructed. In response to these questions there are two major positions, realism and idealism. Realism is based on the perspective that there is an external reality that exists independently of our views or understanding about it. Macquarrie (1973: 57) observes that:

> If there were no human beings, there might still be galaxies, trees, rocks and so on – and doubtless there were in those long stretches of time before the evolution of *Homo sapiens* or any other human species that may have existed on earth. (Italics in original)

Idealism, on the other hand asserts that reality is only knowable through the human mind and through socially constructed meanings. What is real is only 'ideas' that are confined to what is in the mind. Crotty (2003) comments on Macquarrie's observation that although it is conceivable to consider the existence of a world that is independent of our consciousness that this is not the same as saying that meaning exists independently of consciousness. Or as Crotty (2003: 10–11) explains it:

> The existence of a world without a mind is conceivable. Meaning without mind is not.

Whilst realism and idealism represent the two extreme positions, there have been a number of attempts to modify these, including critical realism (Bhaskar, 1979) and subtle realism (Hammersley, 1992) as variants of the realist position but influenced by idealism. In these positions it is accepted that there is an external reality but that reality is only knowable through the human mind and socially constructed representations. There are similar representations within idealism such as subtle idealism and relativism. Subtle realism recognises that reality is only knowable socially constructed meanings, but that these meanings are shared allowing the creation of a collective meaning. Relativism similarly claims that reality is only knowable through socially constructed meanings but that there is no single reality, only multiple realities (Crotty, 2003).

> Where do you stand in this debate – are you a realist, idealist or one of the variants in between? How do you think that this might impact on how you might view the world and the different types of knowledge claims that you might make and the different types of methods that you might want to use?
>
> Reflexive Questions

Having looked at ontological versions of 'what is' the structure of reality, we now move on to epistemology or the 'nature of knowledge' (Crotty, 2003). Epistemology refers to how we philosophically ground what we can know about the world, the types of knowledge claims that we can make about the world and how we can then assure the credibility of such claims. In particular we will focus on positivism and interpretivism and then on different types of research methods and highlight pragmatism and participatory approaches.

Positivism

Positivism has a long intellectual history dating back at least to Bacon (1551–1626) and Descartes (1595–1650). Auguste Comte (1798–1857) is often considered the first self-conscious voice proclaiming positivism. He argued that society, or the social world, could be studied using the same logic of enquiry as that employed in the natural sciences. Phenomena in both the natural and the social world were subject to invariant laws. The differences between them occurred because of their respective subject matters, which were little more than irritants to overcome by developing appropriate research techniques and methods. Importantly, such a view suggests a deterministic conception of the human race and society by effectively underplaying those factors regarded as uniquely human: free will, choice, morality, emotions and the like. In this approach the pursuit of knowledge is achieved through the process of deduction that leads to experimentation, verification, explanation and finally to prediction.

Giddens (1977: 28–9) identified four major claims made by positivists:

- Reality consists of what is available to the senses.
- Science is the primary discipline.
- The natural and social sciences share a common unity of method.
- There is a fundamental distinction between fact and value.

The fourth of these factors suggests that facts, being the product of science, are superior, whilst values represent an entirely different and inferior order of phenomena.

Associated with the positivist's view of classification is that of measurement. Accordingly, there have been great efforts to scale all kinds of variables in order to achieve an exactness and precision characteristic of natural sciences. It is possible to see this in many forms of psychology and sociology with their focus on stress, attitudinal scales or criminal behaviour.

Positivists believe that the basis of science lies in the theoretically neutral observation language, which is both ontologically and epistemologically primary. As Delanty and Strydom (2003) note, neither of theses terms can be seen as unequivocal. It is generally accepted, though, that ontology relates to what is the essence of things that make up the world or the theory of the nature of the world. Epistemology, on the other hand, relates to what is the character of our knowledge of the world and what is to count as facts. Both concepts are linked in that claims about what exists in the world almost inevitably lead to questions about how what exists in the world and how it is made known (Delanty and Strydom, 2003).

Statements made in the theoretically neutral observation language are directly verifiable as true or false by looking at the 'facts' of the world. This represents a correspondence theory of truth, in which the truth of a statement is confirmed by the correspondence with the facts. If it corresponds with the facts, it is true, if not, it is false. Language and the facts 'would speak for themselves'. This form of empiricism can best be seen in the popular TV series *CSI* in which Grisholm, a crime scene investigator examines all the evidence, in minute detail, to ascertain the facts of the death and to discover whether it was murder and if so who the murderer was. Grisholm famously encouraged his team to let the 'facts speak for themselves'.

Similarly, positivist statements would be directly verifiable as true or false by their correspondence with the facts. The beliefs we hold or the values we subscribe to are as factually 'brute' as atoms, velocities or simple harmonic motion. If social scientists or social workers would only use carefully constructed apparatus – questionnaires, Likert scales and the like – inner mental states could, in principle, be researched empirically. Standardised lists could be developed; all social phenomena could be classified, correlated and measured. Hypotheses could be formulated and tested with a view to proving whether they were true or false. As such, the world would become predictable and with predictability comes the potential for control. This would provide the social worker with the opportunity to intervene in social situations knowing that their interventions would result in positive outcomes; children would be safeguarded, people with disabilities would be empowered and the elderly supported to live their lives independently.

Falsification and Popper

Karl Popper (1902–94), a philosopher, was a key figure in the development of positivism. Popper was particularly concerned not with how to verify a theory, which he believed was impossible, but how to refute one. Popper grudgingly admitted that metaphysical ideas may have helped with the development of science but that the primary purpose of empirical science is to draw a line between the empirical and the metaphysical, science and pseudoscience. He developed the idea of deductivism or hypothetico-deductivism. In it he contends that a scientific theory can never be accorded more than provisional acceptance (Popper, 1980). Popper gave the example of white swans to demonstrate his point. If our concept of a swan includes the notion of them being white, then we only need to see one black swan to falsify our previously held theory of what it is to be a swan. Popper was able to show that although deductivism was not able to prove a universal statement, all statements were in principle refutable:

> There can be no ultimate statements in science: there can be no statements that cannot be tested, and therefore none that cannot in principle be refuted, by falsifying some of the conclusions that can be deduced from them. (Popper, 1980: 47, underlining in original)

Popper thus revised the orthodox positivist conception of science; no longer was the object of science to infer from specific instances to generalisations but to search for ways of refuting what he called 'conjectural hypotheses'. Science thus becomes not a body of accumulated and accumulating true theories but a series of series of conjectures or hypotheses that are yet to be refuted (Hughes, 1990). The best theories will provide very precise predictions across a range of spheres, allowing for empirical testing and opportunities for refutations. As such this suggests an almost evolutionary survival of the fittest.

Popper's contribution of post-positivism emphasises that theory acceptance must always be tentative can be challenged on both theoretical and practical grounds. On theoretical grounds, if theory acceptance is always tentative, then how can theory rejection be decisive when observation statements are by their very nature theory dependent and fallible? On the practical level, Popper suggests that social scientists should set to disprove their theories, to find the 'black swan'. How realistic this is, is open to debate. From my own experience of researchers, they often start with the opposite viewpoint and set out to prove what they already believe to be true. May (2001) also makes the point that if our empirical evidence falsifies a theory, is this sufficient reason for rejecting it? We may just have found a deviant case or a new result that is yet to be built into the overall theory.

Reflexive Questions

At this point you should write down what you consider to be the key tenets of positivism and Popper's development of positivism. Can you identify in what ways positivist assumptions are used in your practice?

The Interpretivist Reaction

Like the positivist tradition, the interpretive tradition has its roots in the seventeenth century with Vico (1668–1744), who stressed that you could not study humans and society in the same way that you studied inanimate nature. The former implied subjective understanding and thus required a wholly different method of inquiry to that of the natural sciences. Society – a product of the human mind – was not only intellectually different, but also subjective and emotional, requiring different models of explanation.

Thus developed an alternative evolving framework stressing 'humanistic' or 'interpretive' approaches. These alternative approaches rejected the view that the scientific method could be applied to the study of social life and instead emphasised the importance of interpretation and understanding as the only legitimate ways of gaining understanding. The term 'interpretivism' is being used here as an umbrella for a range of approaches, including ethnomethodology (Garfinkel, 1967) phenomenology (Schutz, 1973), symbolic interactionism (Goffman, 1961), interpretive interactionism (Denzin, 1989), new paradigm inquiry (Reason and Rowan, 1981), and social constructionism (Berger and Luckman, 1979). In this section it is impossible to cover all of the nuances of the different approaches, nor would all of the proponents of the different approaches necessarily agree with this articulation of their position.

The interpretivist tradition does not set out to gather facts or to measure the frequency of occurrences. In fact, one of their major criticisms of the positivist is that they analysed out, or reduced to a set of statistics, those unique features that make social life a distinctive human experience. What exactly is left out is open to debate but may include: choice, moral and political concerns, emotions, values or the self.

Schutz (1978), an important interpretivist, expresses the difference between the natural and social sciences like this:

> The worlds of nature, as explored by the natural scientist, does not 'mean' anything to the molecules atoms and electrons therein. The observational field of the social scientist, however, namely a social reality, has a specific meaning and relevance structure for the human beings living, acting and thinking therein. (Schutz, 1978: 31)

Thus one of the key differences between positivism and interpretivism can be seen to be the ability of the subjects of social life to create their own common-sense structures and to be able to interpret their own experiences. In other words, unlike atoms or molecules, social actors can talk about, explain to others or justify their actions. Knowledge is then not something 'out there' to be discovered, but something derived and created from the experiences of the social actors.

This highlighting of meaning and the describing of actions leads the researcher to impute motives of one sort or another. The analytic force of motives and reasons lie not so much in their being 'internal' but in their being tantamount to rules for governing behaviour. This behaviour though can often be explained in a variety of ways. Thus it is possible for a social worker with a 'nod' to communicate to a service user that they wish them to continue with what they are saying, to indicate that they agree with what is being said, to indicate that they disagree with what is being said or to indicate to a colleague that they want to leave. The same movement can in various circumstances and with various intentions constitute any of these actions; it could also be argued that as a result of this it constitutes none of them. The observer cannot see directly into the minds of the observed to inspect their motives. Nonetheless if certain particulars of the context are supplied, an interpretation, of greater or lesser value, can be attempted.

Positivists developed their version of social reality by drawing a distinction between identifiable acts, structures and institutions as 'brute' facts, on the one hand, and beliefs, values and attitudes, on the other. These two orders of reality were then correlated in order to derive generalisations or regularities that then become the substance of social life. The 'brute' facts are considered as objective whilst the values, beliefs and attitudes are considered as a subjective reality, an inferior status. The elements of meaning were thus relegated to secondary versions of reality. For the interpretivist reality cannot be identified apart from the language in which it is embedded. Social realities are constructed, reconstructed, negotiated and renegotiated in and through meanings. Meaning is thus not only about grammatical rules, but also about social interaction. Language and the importance of language is critical in this tradition. The reality of the natural or social sciences cannot be known independently of the concepts available in language. Second, meanings are not totally idiosyncratic, otherwise it would be impossible to communicate. This is not to deny that there are differences in the way that black and white people, women and men, the disabled and non-disabled or children and adults all experience the world. Meanings are therefore not finitely specific, but achieve meaning from their background, context and the interpretations of the language speakers and receivers. Finally, disputes about meaning do not necessarily stem from deficiencies or inadequacies of natural language but may represent inherent features of social reality.

Interpretivism and Relativism

The interpretivist cannot help but be continuously engaged with his/her own subject matter. This poses the eternal problem for the social researcher in how they can maintain that their reality or interpretation is more accurate and valid than that of the subjects of the study. This is particularly the case when we remember that both use the layperson's world as their reference point and share the same resources.

Hammersley (1995) identifies relativism as the key stumbling block for interpretivists. Whilst accepting that there is no universally agreed definition of relativism, what appears to be central to the notion is a view of knowledge as paradigm dependent. Paradigms are discussed later, but it is useful to think of them here as a worldview containing a set of assumptions that go beyond rational explanation. When someone makes a knowledge claim, we can ask by what criteria she or he judges her or his knowledge claim to be true. Then, when the criteria are presented we can ask on what basis this set of criteria is believed to be valid. When that basis is identified we can then ask why that is believed to be true. This argument becomes increasingly circular, with no definitive endpoint. The interpretivist becomes hoisted by their own petard, not only is a relativist position false – when viewed from other positions – but also when viewed within the framework of interpretivist assumptions.

In the end we need to recognise that absolute certainty is not available, and that attempts to produce absolute knowledge by sense data are bound for failure. Such a view is in danger of sinking into total relativism wherein anything can be true in some framework, if not our own. To avoid this position, Hammersley

(1995) invokes Pierce's 'commonsensism', where assumptions are relied on until subject to genuine doubt. This potentially produces more questions than it answers, as there is often nothing common about commonsense. One group's taken-for-granted assumptions do not necessarily transfer to any other group. In the 1990s, Oliver (1990, 1993) argued that people with disabilities should not take part in research unless it was informed by the social model of disability as their experience of able-bodied researchers' commonsense understandings were experienced as oppressive and discriminatory. We next move onto research methods or the tools that researchers use to help them make sense of their data.

Having read this section on interpretivism, you should write down what you consider to be the key tenets of interpretivism and its critique. Can you identify in what ways interpretivist assumptions are used in your practice?

Having looked at both the interpretivist and positivist approaches, which do you favour, and why?

Research Tools

Having read the preceding sections, you will have noted that both positivism and interpretivism make different assumptions about how the world can be known. Before we look at some of the well-known research methods, it is important to note that new research methods are continually under development and that there are a wide range of both qualitative and quantitative methods that social work researchers could use, including: documentary analysis, discourse analysis, narratives, biographical methods, increasingly complex statistical quantitative methods as well as making use of the opportunities provided by the digital media and computers. These methods are beyond this textbook and you are now invited to consider which of the identified methods are associated with which philosophical approach.

Can you identify which of the following you would associate with a positivist position?

1. Participant observation.
2. Questionnaires.
3. Surveys.
4. Interviews.

What reasons did you give for your view?

Traditionally, research methods are split between quantitative and qualitative approaches. Positivist researchers are often associated with quantitative methods, including random control trials, surveys and questionnaires. It is important first to clarify what we mean by quantitative:

> Quantitative methods (normally using deductive logic) seek regularities in human lives, by separating the social world into empirical components called variables which can be represented numerically as frequencies or rates, whose associations with each other can be explored by statistical techniques, and accessed through researcher-introduced stimuli and systematic measurement. (Payne and Payne, 2004: 180)

'Quantitative methods' is an umbrella term and covers a wide range of methods that have been informed by positivist assumptions. At it's simplest it involves counting how frequently things happen (e.g. the number of GCSEs that looked-after children attain as compared with children in the wider population) and the presentation of these frequencies in tables and graphs. This is then often extended to look at whether two or more factors are associated, related or can even be seen to be causal. In the example given above, Jackson (1987, 1994) and Heath et al., (1994) have both demonstrated that being accommodated is associated with poor educational attainment that is also associated with poor life chances.

Payne and Payne (2004) identify the common features shared by almost all forms of quantitative research.

- The core concern is to describe and account for regularities in social behaviour.
- Patterns of behaviour can be separated into variables, and represented by numbers.
- Explanations are expressed as *associations (usually statistical) between variables,* ideally in a form that enables prediction of outcomes from known regularities.
- Social phenomena is explored through *systematic, repeated and controlled measurements.*
- They are based on the assumption that *social processes exist outside of individual actor's comprehension,* constraining individual actions, and accessible to researchers by virtue of their prior theoretical and empirical knowledge. (Payne and Payne, 2004: 181–2, italics in original)

In seeking to explain quantitative research methods I would like to examine random controlled trials, surveys and questionnaires.

Random Controlled Trials: 'The Gold Standard'

The random controlled trial (RCT) is most closely associated with medical research, but it is possible to undertake RCTs in other knowledge domains. Sheldon (2000) has consistently advocated that social work needs more RCTs.

The RCT is often cited as the 'gold standard' method of assessing the efficacy of treatment methods (Reynolds, 2000). The central feature of an RCT is the random allocation of potential participants to an experimental or control group. The intention is to eliminate bias by ensuring that all conditions are randomised, including the preferences and expectations of patients and doctors. Randomisation does not necessarily ensure that groups are identical but what it does is ensure that any differences that arise do so as the result of chance. In some of these trials, the treatment group will be further divided with one half of the group receiving the treatment and the other half a placebo. Ideally this is done as a 'double blind', where neither the patient nor the doctor are aware of who is receiving the treatment and who the placebo. As MacDonald and Popay (2010) acknowledge, knowing a respondent's allocation may influence the observations made and judgements inferred. For similar reasons, whoever is evaluating the clinical outcomes should not be aware of who has and who has not been treated.

RCTs then follow up their patients in order to identify the relative outcomes for the control and experimental group with a view to establishing whether the results are clinically important or not. Clinical importance is often used to replace statistical significance. Clinical importance may refer to the speed of recovery of the patient, whether the patient has suffered side-effects, required re-admission to hospital or even whether the patient survived the treatment or not. Clinical importance though may be identified differently by the anaesthetist: the patient survived the operation; the surgeon: the patient was discharged from hospital; the GP: the patient was still alive and survived six months after the operation; and the patient whose quality of life had improved.

Surveys: 'Would You Mind if I Asked You a Couple of Questions?'

All of us will have experienced being stopped in the street by someone holding a clipboard who then asked us a number of questions about which adverts we watched, drinks we drank or foods we ate. During this process, the researcher would be ticking boxes in response to our answers. While this is market research, the use of surveys is also a central part of social research. Surveys are one of the most frequently employed methods in social research. Governments, academic researchers and campaigning organisations alike, use surveys (May and Williams, 2001).

Ackroyd and Hughes (1981) have characterised surveys under four different headings:

- The factual or social survey aimed at eliciting general facts, rather than opinions or attitudes, about the conditions and the organisation of whole societies.

- Attitude surveying which focuses on the attitudes people hold as a means to seek to explain and potentially predict their behaviour. This represents a move away from factual surveying to public opinions.
- Social psychological surveying which is more explanation and theory oriented and seeks to investigate personality via various types of attitude measurement techniques.
- Explanatory surveys designed to test some theoretical explanation.

The first two of these were designed to achieve practical as opposed to theoretical ends, although it could be claimed that they all seek to provide or contribute some degree of explanation.

Payne and Payne (2004: 219) note that surveys have typically three types of characteristics:

> They *collect data in a standardised way* from a *sample* of respondents, enabling the data to be *codified, normally into a quantitative form.* (Italics in original)

There are an increasing range of surveys and these include face-to-face interviewing, telephone, postal, email, Web-based or texted surveys. As can be seen, some of these survey types require the interviewer to be present and others are self-completion. Where the interviewer is not present it is very important for the questions to be clear and unambiguous. Preferably a survey will be piloted to pre-test the questions for their ease and clarity of operation, to check whether they are addressing the research question(s) and whether they provide a means of differentiating between different respondent groups.

The survey questions are usually contained in a questionnaire, which starts with a set of classificatory questions contained in the 'personal' section of the questionnaire; these may include questions about age, gender, ethnicity, occupation, salary and so on. The researcher must also make a judgement about whether to use open or closed questions. Open questions allow the interviewee greater freedom to respond to the question in a way that suits their interpretation. Closed questions limit the number of possible answers, allowing for easier and cheaper analysis.

Surveys very rarely report a 100 per cent response rate, for example people move home, go on holiday, cannot be traced or die. Generally, 70 per cent is seen as an adequate response rate for face-to-face interviews. In self-completion and postal surveys, 33 per cent is seen as more typical.

Easterby-Smith and Thorpe (1996) describe the benefits of quantitative methods in general and of surveys in particular as:

> They can provide wide coverage of the range of situations; they can be fast and economical; and, particularly when statistics are aggregated from large samples, they may

be of considerable relevance to policy decisions. On the debit side, these methods tend to be rather inflexible and artificial; they are not very effective in understanding the processes or the significances that people attach to actions, they are not very helpful in generalising theories. (Easterby-Smith and Thorpe, 1996: 32)

Qualitative Methods

The preceding two research tools methods were primarily associated with quantitative methods. The next three are primarily associated with qualitative. Qualitative methods are linked to the interpretivist perspective of philosophy. Silverman (1993: 170) has stated that qualitative methods are 'especially interested in how ordinary people observe and describe their lives'. As such, Payne and Payne (2004: 175) describe qualitative methods in the following way:

> Qualitative methods produce detailed and non-quantitative accounts of small groups, seeking to interpret the meanings people make of their lives in natural settings, on the assumption that social interactions form an integrated set of relationships best understood by inductive processes.

Qualitative, like quantitative, is an umbrella term. Qualitative methods refer to a set of approaches that share common features. Qualitative methods:

- Focus on seeking out and interpreting the meanings that people ascribe to their own actions.
- Actions are seen as contextualised, holistic and part of a social process.
- Seek to encounter social phenomena as they naturally occur.
- They work with smaller samples looking for depth and detail of meaning with a less general and abstracted level of explanation.
- They use inductive as opposed to deductive logic allowing ideas to emerge as they explore the data. (Payne and Payne, 2004)

Thus the qualitative methods focus on individuals, their interactions, emphasising interpretation and meaning and the ways in which mutual understandings are negotiated. This alternative research direction requires a different set of methods than that of the quantitative researcher.

Qualitative methods have the ability to look at change processes over time, to understand people's meanings, to adjust to new issues and ideas as they emerge. They also contribute to the evolution of new theories and are seen as 'natural' rather than as 'artificial'. In particular we are going to focus on participant observation, ethnography and interviewing.

Participant Observation

Participant observation requires the researcher to immerse themselves in the lives of those being studied. Participant observation thus requires the researcher to engage in a number of activities, including looking, listening, enquiring and recording. May (2001) comments that the apparent naturalness of this approach leads those new to social research to assume that they can undertake this approach with ease. On the contrary, it is probably one of the most personally demanding and analytically difficult methods of social research to undertake. Depending on the aims of the study, the researcher may be required to spend a great deal of time in unfamiliar surroundings, building and maintaining relationships with people whom they have little personal affinity, making copious notes on what to others would appear to be mundane happenings, putting themselves at a degree of personal risk and then spending months analysing the data after the fieldwork has been completed.

There are two main types of participant observer, the researcher as 'complete participant' and the researcher as 'participant-as-observer'. In the 'complete participant' role, the researcher becomes a fullfledged member of the group under study, the purpose of the research being concealed from this group. There have been a number of such studies in the past, including one where a social work lecturer caused a major stir by living in a council estate in Glasgow whilst she observed and wrote down her views on the resident's lifestyle. Following publication of her views, some of the residents were very disparaging about her comments and felt let down that she had written such comments about them. In this type of approach, the residents were not aware that they were being observed nor of the value judgements that were being made about them and the way they lived.

The more common approach is of 'participant-as-observer', wherein both the researched and the researcher are aware that theirs is a fieldwork relationship. Since the research relationship is not concealed the researcher is able to use other methods, for example interviewing to complement their research. This type of research has been used with teenage gangs, drug users and in residential settings.

Participant observers may work in teams, but more often they work alone. In the process of observing, they witness how their research subjects interact with their social environment, continually interpreting and applying new knowledge. The researcher or ethnographer is the instrument of data collection. The ethnographer enters the research subject's social universe and using a range of techniques that could include: 'living among people', interviews or life histories. Researchers accept that they will 'contaminate' the situation although in doing ethnography this engagement is used to an advantage. In this process, ethnographers draw upon their own experience and biography to help understand the research process. This use of the researcher's own cultural equipment is used reflexively to make sense of social action in context. Reflexivity thus implies that 'knowledge is made rather than revealed' (Taylor and White, 2000: 199). Ethnography thus requires us to consider how power is exercised in the research process and the implications of this for what does and does not constitute knowledge.

Focus Groups

In recent years, there has been an explosion in the use of focus groups for all sorts of activities, including the market testing of new products, voting intentions and within a wide range of social care activities where service user perceptions are wanted to help inform service provision. Focus groups allow us to collect a large amount of research data for relatively little financial cost or just as importantly the researcher's time (Hardwick and Worsley, 2011). Cronin (2001: 165) defines a focus group as a group interview:

> A focus group consists of a small group of individuals, usually numbering between six and ten people, who met together to express views about a particular topic defined by the researchers. A **facilitator**, or **moderator**, leads the group and guides the discussion between the participants. In general, focus groups last one-and-a-half to two hours and are tape-recorded. (Bold type in original)

Focus groups are thus managed discussions that are organised to explore a specific set of issues that involve some kind of group activity. Focus groups are particularly useful when the researcher wants to explore people's experiences, opinions and concerns. What sets them apart is that focus group participants, unlike individual interviews or questionnaires, engage in discussion with each other, creating an interactive and dynamic process led by a moderator or facilitator.

There are at least four advantages of using focus groups:

- They provide an opportunity to observe and collect a large amount of data and interaction over a short period of time.
- Discussions should provide rich data as participants present and defend their own views whilst challenging the views of others.
- This very process may help participants clarify their own views but also open them up to alternative views that they would not have considered.
- Focus groups encourage theorisation and elaboration.

On the negative side, the data that focus groups generate is limited in its generalisability. This is because focus groups do not generally consist of randomly selected individuals and those who are willing to participate in a focus group may be different from those who are not. There is also an issue of interviewer bias whereby the researcher is required to be both reflective and reflexive in order to minimise the impact of their role. Due to these difficulties, focus groups are often included as part of a research strategy although they can be used and justified in their own terms.

Research Techniques can be Both Quantitative and Qualitative

In this section I would like to look at a major research tool that can be both quantitative and qualitative. The importance of this method is that it is closely related to the key social work skill of interviewing. Traditionally the worlds of the social worker and the researcher have been seen as mutually exclusive and esoteric activities. One sat in an ivory tower theorising about the world whilst the other had to grapple with the wicked problems and messy business of the world. Both, though, may have more in common than is usually acknowledged. I would like to suggest that interviewing is a central technique for both. Kadushin (1972: 8), in a classic text on interviewing, described the essential features of an interview as:

> a specialised form of communication. A communication interchange in the interview involves two people, each of whom possesses a receiving system, a processing system and a transmitting system. The receiving system consists of the five senses, the receptors. Communication in the interview involves primarily the use of two sense receptors – the eyes and the ears. Having received the incoming signal, one processes it; this involves making sense of the received message, giving it meaning. The processing activity consists of recalling stored information, relating related information to the message, thinking about the message, evaluating the message, translating it so the message is coherent with the receiver's frame of reference. As receivers we select certain items from the incoming message, ignore others, and rearrange what we hear into interpretable patterns. We then typically formulate a response.

Interviewing aims at establishing a framework for future evaluation and enquiry in both spheres. Both probe and must be continually aware of the conditions under which information is generated. The difference occurs at a later stage when social workers use the data from the interview to assess a situation and to decide whether an intervention is required, and if so, what type of intervention. This does not mean that social workers eschew theoretical considerations or give up their analytical powers but that their priorities are different. It should also be remembered that researchers do not necessarily stop at the theoretical, but may wish to see their work established as current practice or result in a change of policy.

At this point it could be suggested that interviews could be seen as a qualitative tool, given their negotiative and social constructivist agenda. As the reader will already be aware, such distinctions are not always as clear-cut as we would first believe. It is possible for an interview to be quantitative, qualitative or both. What decides whether it is one or the other is the nature of the questions being asked. When we discussed surveys, we noted that the questions could be open or closed. Quantitative interviews would use closed questions and qualitative interviews open questions. One would be asking the respondent to identify a pre-designed response whilst the other would use a much more discursive approach, possibly probing answers to elicit deeper and more meaningful understandings.

An interview is neither inherently qualitative nor quantitative, although we normally associate it with qualitative approaches. Interviews also regularly use schedules to help direct the researcher to the question areas in which they want a response. Within the social sciences, semi-structured interviews are very common which include both closed (quantitative) and open (qualitative) questions. The closed questions may be seeking to gain comparative views of a particular policy or implementation strategy and the open questioning trying to construct or understand the reasoning behind that view. The closed questions may focus on outcomes, but without the open questions they suffer the severe limitation that they do not tell us what these outcomes were outcomes of.

In the last two sections we looked at some examples of qualitative and quantitative research methods. At one level it has been possible to associate different methods with different research epistemologies. However, a commitment to qualitative approaches does not necessarily imply innumeracy as qualitative methods often include statements about sample proportions and analysis of field notes may include content counting. It has also been possible to show that research methods can be both quantitative and qualitative, or even both at the same time. At this point it would be useful to explore the notion of a paradigm and how this impacts on how the world can be known.

Paradigms: As Worldviews

It is often presented that the positivist and interpretive perspectives on the world represent incommensurate paradigms of how we understand the world. Kuhn (1970: 175), a historian, discussed how natural scientists engage in debates about the phenomena that they study and how they move from one major theory to another and in so doing defined paradigms as:

> The entire constellation of beliefs, values, techniques and so on shared by members of a given community.

As such, paradigms are the worldviews or theories, which define legitimate areas for research questions, methods and solutions for a scientific community. While

Kuhn's views were developed in response to the natural sciences, they were also viewed as very pertinent to the social sciences. As Gilbert (2001) acknowledges, social research – and we can also include social work research in this – is situated within a 'paradigm', a scientific tradition. Any new research project is linked into what has gone before. The problems that many social work researchers tackle are derived from previous social work research, they will have been discussed in the relevant journals and the methods used will have been honed by previous researchers. Evidence of the linking between new research to previous ideas and concepts is an important function of the literature review and references sprinkled throughout the article or book. These references not only acknowledge previous work, but also borrow their authority and that of the author to legitimate their own work.

Gilbert (2001) suggests that knowledge is constructed and linked to a particular professional knowledge community. This links back to Kuhn (1970), who suggested that during periods of 'normal science' the focus is on: first, clarifying the facts of the within the paradigm; second, comparing the facts with predictions from the paradigm; and third, articulating and fleshing out the paradigm. During this period of normal science, if results do not fit the theory then they are overlooked, suppressed or explained away as a novelty. With time these novelties come to be seen as more than just another puzzle requiring a solution. These novelties become too great to be ignored and there begins a transition to crisis and abnormal science when the very foundations of the science are challenged.

This creates the conditions for a change in paradigm choice. Kuhn (1970) claims that the choice of a paradigm is not a rational process and can never be settled unequivocally just by logic or experimental evidence. The new paradigm is not a special case of the old one, but is incompatible and incommensurate with what has gone on before.

Paradigms and Incommensurability

A critical concept in relation to paradigms is the notion of incommensurability. The traditional view of incommensurability is that rival positions, or paradigms, are irreconcilable. It is not possible to believe in both positions at the same time, to believe in one is to deny the other. The second aspect of incommensurability relates to the relationship between paradigm and method. As previously noted in this chapter, both positivism and interpretivism help to inform particular social research methods. Research incorporating quantitative methods presupposes certain beliefs about what the world is and how it can be known. Likewise, research with qualitative methods makes different competing and antithetical assumptions. Paley (2000) questions whether this relationship is either logical or preordained. In order to make his point Paley uses maps as a metaphor. An Ordnance Survey map is more detailed and complete than a motorway map. But, for the motorist the fact that a motorway map does not include every bridle path or footpath does not mean that it is incomplete. Indeed, for the motorist it is the fact that the map is not to scale that is a benefit, otherwise it would be impossible to see the roads! This he suggests is a matter of function, and methods like maps are dictated not by inherent philosophical positions but by particular functions. Both maps are tools and are only suitable for particular purposes and tasks. What then should drive a choice of method is not a philosophical standpoint position but a question as to what is the most appropriate tool for the task in hand. This leads us into the issue of mixed methods approaches and pragmatism.

Mixed Methods Approaches

Since writing the first edition of this book the increasing acceptance and development of pragmatism has been a key change within the social work research landscape. This is not to mean that mixed methods were not used before, but when they were they were often viewed as 'less than perfect' research. More recently we have seen the growth of publications in this field and the acceptance of mixed methods and pragmatism as a paradigm in its own right. Cresswell (2003) notes that pragmatism has its roots in the works of John Dewey (1859–1952) and Margaret Mead (1901–1978) and its key features are:

- Pragmatism is not committed to any one system of philosophy.
- Individual members have a freedom of choice to choose which methods, techniques or procedures best meet their needs.
- Pragmatists do not see the world as an absolute entity.
- Truth is what works at the time.
- Pragmatist researchers look to the 'what' and 'how' of research based on its intended consequences. Mixed methods researchers need to establish a purpose for their 'mixing'.
- Pragmatist researchers agree that research always occurs in social, hierarchal, political and other contexts.
- Pragmatists believe that we need to stop asking questions about reality and the laws of nature. (Creswell, 2003: 12)

Certainly the viewpoint of this book is that it is more important to ensure a suitable fit between the research question and the method(s) being adopted than to achieve a form of epistemological and methodological purity. This also opens up the possibility of being able to use different methods in the same study – the motorway map of the survey approach to gain a broad brush understanding of a particular issue, for example the characteristics of children in residential care including their age on admission, reason for admission, length of time in care, number of placements and so on. This could then be followed up with an ethnographic study to examine the meaning of being looked after as experienced by young people, their carers and their parents. As Ritchie (2003: 43) observes:

> When using qualitative and quantitative research in harness, it is important to recognise that each offers a different way of knowing about the world. Although they may well be addressing the same research issue, they will provide a different 'reading' or form of calibration on that issue. As a consequence, it should not be expected that the evidence generated from the two approaches will replicate each other. Instead the purpose of interlocking qualitative and quantitative data is to achieve an extended understanding that neither method alone can offer.

Thus when adopting a mixed methods approach, it is important to recognise that not only does each method have a different way of knowing about the world but that they will also approach the question differently and provide a different answer. As a consequence, it is imperative for researchers who use mixed methods approaches to explain why the data and their 'meanings' are different and to avoid the situation where one approach becomes the dominant one and conflicts between the data become hidden. ˎ

Triangulation is potentially important here; triangulation originated from quantitative research and the 'multiple operationalism' of Campbell and Fiske (1959), whereby multiple measures are used to ensure that the variance reflected is that of the trait or treatment and not associated with any other measure. Triangulation has also come to mean 'convergence' between researchers and convergence amongst theories. To achieve this it is generally accepted that the researcher should pick triangulation sources that have different biases and different strengths so that they can complement one another. Triangulation thus involves the use of different methods and sources to check the data's integrity and/or to extend the inferences that can be drawn from the data.

We should not just assume, though, that by using multiple methods, or by using triangulation, that our research will automatically result in sounder conclusions. Shaw (2003: 110) approvingly quotes Trend's classic account of an evaluation of a USA programme evaluating the effectiveness of direct payment of housing allowances to low income families. Trend concluded:

> The complementarity is not always apparent. Simply using different perspectives, with the expectation that they will validate each other, does not tell us what to do if the pieces do not fit. (Trend, 1979: 110)

Using multiple methods and triangulation does not remove the responsibility from the researcher in order to ensure that these methods work together in such a way that they provide additionality and address the research question. Using triangulation does not remove the responsibility for ensuring that generated data is analysed rigorously and methodically, identifying both areas of correspondence and dispute.

MacDonald (1999: 98) argues that if there is to be a rapprochement of quantitative and qualitative approaches then four principles will need to be conserved:

- As far as possible, researchers should make explicit the assumptions and values underpinning the questions they ask and the methods they deploy.
- The methods should both be internally and externally robust and valid.
- The methods employed should neither be oppressive to the researcher or the researched.
- That the research should be oriented towards knowledge that can be used by users themselves.

Whilst the first two principles would appear to be supportive of Paley's position, the second two are of a different order. The last two principles could be seen as particularly important to ethically driven professions such as social work, with a value base and commitment to service user empowerment.

Paley's perspective is not universally accepted and D'Cruz and Jones (2004) argue that you cannot ignore that methods have a relationship to the philosophical positions in which they have their roots. They do argue, though, for a more hardheaded approach to method choice to ensure that powerful groups will engage with the results and not just seek to attack the methodology. In so doing, they note that discussions about the relationship between paradigms and methods has become more relevant as knowledge and social research has challenged the previously unseen positivistic, scientific, white, Western male perspectives. Feminist, postmodern, poststructural and post-colonial perspectives have all served to reinforce the positioning of the knower as essential in the creation of knowledge and given marginal groups a voice. This leads us onto participatory knowledge claims.

Participatory Knowledge Claims

Both positivism and interpretivist approaches can be criticised for their acceptance of the status quo and by implication their conservative stances. Positivist perspectives impose structural laws and theories that reduce minority or marginalised groups' experience to numbers whilst failing to address issues of social justice. Interpretivist approaches are criticised for not going far enough to support marginalised groups (Cresswell, 2003). In response to these criticisms there has developed an alternative advocacy or participatory approach influenced by the works of Marx, Friere and Habermas. Cresswell (2003: 11) identifies four key tenets of this approach:

- Participatory action is recursive or dialectical and is focused on bringing about change in practice.
- It is focused on helping individuals free themselves from constraints found in the media, in language, in work procedures and in relations of power in educational settings.
- It is emancipatory in that it helps unshackle people from the constraints of irrational and unjust structures that limit self-development and self-determination.
- It is practical and collaborative because it is inquiry completed 'with' others rather than 'on' or 'to' others. In this spirit advocacy/participatory authors engage the participants as active collaborators in their inquiries.

From the characteristics identified above it is easily seen why such approaches are often favoured by social work researchers and are discussed further in Chapters 5 and 8. Research within this approach is not just a process but also contains an inherent agenda to address social injustice, challenge oppression, promote empowerment and challenge inequality at individual group or societal levels. As Glasby and Beresford (2006) assert, research only becomes justified when it is accompanied by change. The participatory approach has a history of being developed from feminist perspectives, racialised discourses, critical theory, queer theory and disability inquiry that have all tended to favour social models of explanation and sought to challenge accepted and dominant discourses.

This research approach has also suggested that the choice of research methods is not just an issue of the appropriate tool for the task, but also a statement concerning how the researcher positions themselves and how they consider the world can be known. This does not mean that we should adopt an incommensurate or different paradigm position, but demands that we make clear the intellectual, ethical and methodological assumptions with which we are working. D'Cruz and Jones, (2004: 57) express their position well:

> as social workers, we must be aware of the political and ethical processes of knowledge construction. Social work research is just one of these aspects. If we are to achieve social change as social workers, we are immediately positioned both politically and ethically in relation to social issues and social problems. Therefore we cannot escape our personal or professional assumptions or goals.

At this point it is important to understand where the writer locates himself. I am a white, middle-class (at least by occupation, if not by birth) male, married with two children, brought up in Northern Ireland during 'The Troubles', but who has not lived there since finishing his first degree. Politically, I adopt a critical perspective and see the world as an unequal place both within the four nations and between the 'developed' and 'majority' worlds. As a social worker, or social work manager, for most of my career I have struggled with the contradictions and ambiguities of social work practice as I strived to steer a course in which service users could be empowered, or at worst, be no worse off after than before my contact. As I have predominately worked in childcare, this has created difficulties with the sometimes conflicting needs of children and parents. On occasions, this has also included differences of interests between brothers and sisters and mothers and fathers, I believe that social work can make a difference, but is in danger of becoming overly managerial and bureaucratised, losing the human connection, creativity and 'subversive' nature that gives it its critical edge.

Ontologically, I tend to favour the 'subtle realism' of Hammersley (1992), whereby I accept that there is a world independent of individual subjective understanding, but that that world is only accessible through the understandings of research respondents, including that of the researcher. Individual research respondent's interpretations are thus critical; different vantage points will yield different explanations and experiences, but these do not necessarily contradict the notion of an external reality. I hope that this will help the reader to begin to identify some of my biases and be able to read this book with the knowledge of where the writer is located and ask themselves how would a writer located in a different standpoint respond to the issues identified in this book.

How would you locate yourself?

How does this impact on how you see the world?

How does this relate to why you want to be a social worker?

How does this impact on the area of social work that you want to follow?

Reflexive Questions

Summary

This chapter has raised a number of important philosophical issues that you may feel the need to re-read in order to begin to understand them fully. Often social workers and researchers find philosophy difficult, preferring to be 'doers' rather than 'thinkers'. But, as I hope, you now appreciate, both concepts are linked and how you think impacts on what you do and vice versa. In particular the chapter has highlighted two of the major paradigms of social research – positivism and interpretivism, identifying some of their key assumptions and claims to knowledge and identifying how both approaches represent different versions of how the world can be understood. Different research approaches were identified and it was shown how they relate to some of the key social research methods and different paradigms. This was followed by a discussion on the nature of paradigms, their incommensurability and whether this incommensurability also relates to method. In response to this, we noted the growth of pragmatism and mixed methods and their view that it is the nature of the research question that should drive the chosen research method. Alongside these differing perspectives, it was also suggested that the researcher needs to reflect on how their own standpoint will affect what methods are chosen and how they are combined.

Suggested Reading

Cresswell, J.W. (2009) *Research Design: Qualitative, Quantitative and Mixed Methods Approaches*, 3rd edn. London: Sage.
Particularly useful for its explanation and justification of mixed methods.

D'Cruz, H. and Jones, M. (2004) *Social Work Research: Ethical and Political Contexts*. London: Sage.
This is a well-written easy-to-read book that was also identified in Chapter 1.

Hughes, J. (1990) *The Philosophy of Social Research*, 2nd edn. London: Longman.
A challenging but engaging introduction to the philosophy of social research.

4 Ethical Issues in Social Work Research

Introduction

This chapter examines the ethical issues surrounding the undertaking of social work research. The chapter begins by identifying the rationale for ethical research behaviour and then discusses the nature of ethics and social work as a basis for a social work and social care ethical research code. This is then followed by a discussion of ethical issues as related to the research process and is divided into issues that arise before the research commences, during the research and after the research has been completed. This chapter takes the perspective that ethics is not a 'bolt-on' but an inherent, demanding and ongoing aspect of the research process (Humphries and Martin, 2000).

Ethics, in its grandest form, may be recognised as a philosophical discipline of which its primary concern is the science of morality. Ethics though takes on a more distinctive form when applied to social research. Here ethics refers to the standards established within the social research profession for the conduct of its members (Homan, 1991). It is with the conduct of social work researchers that this chapter is concerned with.

The Rationale for Ethical Research

It could be argued that there should be no concern about the nature of ethics of social work researchers as many are registered social workers for whom ethical issues are integrally entwined at the heart of social work practice. We have already discussed the nature of research and noted that it is neither intrinsically neutral nor inherently beneficial. This is most graphically displayed in medical research. In New Zealand, women with pre-cancer symptoms were assigned to one of two groups without their consent. One group received treatment and the other did not (Smith, 1999). Public funding in America funded the testing of AZT, an anti-viral HIV drug, against placebos in Asian, African and Caribbean countries. Plomer (2005) suggests that the testing of AZT was governed by ethical standards that would not have been accepted in the United States and resulted in the needless death of several thousand non-United States children. More recently, in the UK there has also been the organ retention scandal at Alder Hey Hospital (DH, 2001d) where organs from dead babies were kept for biomedical research without the prior consent of their parents, all of whom thought that they had already buried their children. These examples not only highlight issues of power but also challenge the ethical stance and commitment of researchers.

Whilst the challenges and excesses of biomedical research have been a major driver for ethical governance in the social sciences, it would be wrong to think those researched by social worker researchers were not exposed to potential harm. As Orme and Shemmings (2010) observe, just because social work researchers are not administering drugs or medical interventions their actions can still result in obvious harm.

> The risks associated with social work research are more subtle, in that engagement with those who are experiencing disadvantaged and poor social conditions can lead to raising the hopes of those with whom the researcher is in touch. Social work research also often involves making contact with those who for a variety of reasons are isolated and excluded. This can lead to unrealistic expectations of the research relationship. (Orme and Shemmings, 2010: 47–8)

In response to these concerns about ethical research practices differing professions have developed their own 'code of ethics'. These include the Social Research Association (www.the-sra.org.uk), the British Psychological Association (www.bps.org.uk), and the British Sociological Association (www.britsoc.co.uk). The ESRC (ESRC, 2010a) also has its own ethical framework that applicants for the research council's funds would be ill-advised not to consider in their applications. Butler (2002) has made the argument for a distinctive code of social work and social care research. He recognises that any such code is a form of professional claims-making and represents a measure of self-interest and as such the relationship between those who wish to be included in the code can be as important as the code itself. It is thus important that ethical codes are contextualised and situated. This leads us to two important implications. First, codes of ethics, like the moral principles on which they are based, are normative. Second, such codes can never be morally and ethically neutral. They inevitably reflect and articulate the occupation's ideological and moral aspirations (Butler, 2002).

If social work research is to claim its own distinctive ethical research code, it can only do so by claiming disciplinary or occupational distinctiveness. As such, this argument proposes that social work and social work research occupy the same discursive site and generally serve the same audiences and fields of interest:

Social work research is about social workers, what they think, what they believe, what knowledge they claim and what they do with it, and its primary (but not its only) audience will be social workers, service users and those who determine who falls into which category for the purposes of public policy. If this is so, then the ethics of social work research must logically be at least compatible if not coterminous with the ethics of social work generally. (Butler, 2002: 241)

As Butler (2002) admits, such a proposition is not without its difficulties; terms like 'social work' and 'social worker' are contested and contestable and are located within particular temporal and spatial contexts.

Second, this characterisation of social work research may be interpreted as implying that only social workers can undertake social work research. Given the recruitment criteria for employing social work academics and researchers, this is likely to be true but is not necessarily so. Of more interest is the case of other professional groups, for example psychologists or management researchers undertaking social work research into, for example, the levels of stress of front-line social workers or into the effectiveness of residential care management. In these cases, should their research be rooted in the ethics of social work research? Butler (2002) argues that the answer is 'probably not' if the research was related to their own fields of interest, discourses and usual audiences. However, he does not identify when it should be rooted in social work's ethical code. Of the two examples identified, it could be argued that if psychologists were studying staff stress levels using questionnaires and neither researchers nor workers ever met face to face, then the acceptance of a social work code of ethics would not be necessary. The psychologists' own code of ethics would be suitable to safeguard staff in this situation. The second example is potentially less straightforward. Let us say that the management researchers were examining management effectiveness in a therapeutic community of young children. As such, they wanted to undertake participant observation of managers and workers *in situ* and also wanted to interview the young people concerning their experiences of different management styles.

Any therapeutic community commissioning such research is likely only to commission researchers who are sympathetic to their aims, are aware of the impact of others on the dynamics of the therapeutic relationship, are aware of child safeguarding issues and are able to communicate with young people in a range of mediums. It is also likely that they would want to see some acceptance and willingness to abide by an ethical code informed by social work principles. However, it is unlikely that the management researchers' own code of ethics is likely to have covered these issues in sufficient detail. It is not being suggested that social work cannot benefit from alternative disciplinary research or that social work researchers cannot undertake worthwhile research in other disciplinary realms. Such a position would be patently untenable. What is being suggested is that we need to be careful and begin to differentiate as to when social work questions, problems, issues and research strategies require the acceptance of a social work ethical code as opposed to an alternative disciplinary and/or occupational code.

There is one other issue raised by the management example and Butler's exposition; social work researchers are not in a position to claim ethical superiority. Other researchers cannot be assumed to be unethical nor driven by ethical frameworks that can be assumed to be morally inferior to social works. This is important as each ethical code represents a degree of self-interest for that profession and is contextually and temporally situated.

The Ethics of Social Work

England (1986) argues that the choice for social workers is not whether their actions have an ethical dimension or not, but whether this dimension is made explicit and open to question. As Hugman and Smith (1995: 1) rightly point out, ethical issues are at the heart of social work:

> Herein lies the crux of the problem, because value statements, being views about what is desirable in society, are highly contentious. They say 'what *ought* to be the case' (Shardlow, 1989: 3), and so open up the potential for disagreement between individuals on grounds of belief and perception (for example of politics, culture or religion). Not only does this mean that an activity like social work will always reflect values, because it is required to intervene in important aspects of everyday life, but that it will often be disputed because the goals of social work may not necessarily be equally acceptable to every member of society.

Reflexive Questions

List what you consider to be the important values that you hold as a social worker. (Keep these safe; you will need them again later in the chapter.)

Compare these values with those identified by Biestek below. What were the major differences between your values and those of Biestek?

Why do you think this was so?

Social work has a long history of engaging with ethical issues and various attempts have been made to classify the principles of social work practice. Probably the most famous and one of the most influential of these has been the work of Biestek, an American Catholic priest who identified the 'seven principles of casework'. These principles were:

- Individualisation concerns the recognition of each client as unique.
- The purposeful expression of feeling.
- Controlled emotional involvement.
- Acceptance – unconditional acceptance of the client as a person.
- Non-judgemental attitude.
- User self-determination.
- Confidentiality.

(Biestek, 1961)

These principles have been surprisingly influential, given that they were not initially developed as social work principles. Second, Biestek's emphasis is on the voluntary one-to-one casework relationship of the client and caseworker. In this type of relationship, the client voluntarily contacts the agency and relates individually to the caseworker. Many social workers today will find this form of relationship far removed from the complexity of their day-to-day experience. Banks (1995) compared a number of social work ethical codes and came to the conclusion that they were similar to Biestek's with the Kantian key theme of respect of persons. Downie and Telfer (1969) suggest that respect for persons highlights the notion of persons as being capable of rational thought and able to act with intent. Respect, in this context represents an 'active sympathy' or love towards another human being. Respect for persons can be criticised for its failure to take into account the position of children who may yet have not reached the stage to be able to act in a rational way, although it could be argued that they could be considered as 'potential persons'. Similarly, how are we to consider those suffering from a chronic mental illness or Alzheimer's disease; are they to be considered as 'lapsed persons'? The notions of 'potential persons' or 'lapsed persons' potentially allows both of these groups to be treated to a different and lesser standard than that of other members of society. Respect for persons is seen as important as it reminds us that we should treat others as beings who have ends, and are not merely objects or means to an end. The individual is seen as worthy and deserving of our respect simply because he or she is a person. This respect is unconditional.

In the 1980s, many social work commentators moved away from the 'list approach'. The 'list approach' was seen as inadequate, for example Banks (1995: 29) suggests that 'self-determination can mean "all things to all people"'. Second, there is little indication given as to the status of the different principles. Some of these appear to be methods for effective practice (purposeful expression of feelings), whilst others may be regarded as standards for professional practice (confidentiality), and others as general moral principles (self-determination).

Third, how does the code help us to decide which principle to give priority when two of them come into conflict? What criteria are we to use when deciding whether we should promote a client's self-determination and in so doing reveal confidential information?

These principles were also criticised in the 1970s and 1980s for their focus on the individual casework relationship. During this period, there was a growing awareness of the need to avoid pathologising service users whereby an individual's problems, such as poverty, homelessness or crime, were conceptualised as individual inadequacies resulting in 'blaming the victims' for society's inequalities. A body of writing, which can be loosely termed 'radical social work', took the view that social work ethics could only be grasped from the perspective of what actually happened in practice. The framing of ethical questions, and therefore their answers can only be arrived at from the class positions of those involved, can be seen in the work of Bailey and Brake (1975) or Corrigan and Leonard (1978). This body of work was informed by Marxist perspectives and was critical of the notion of 'individualisation' that was viewed as taking the individual out of their social and political context. This is in contradiction to the Marxist approaches that emphasise a materialist framework, locating human individuality as being formed by the divisions within society and in particular instanced by divisions of social class.

Banks (1995) does not consider that this literature has had a direct impact on social work values, nor would it have been intended to, as one of its key themes is 'praxis' the notion of 'committed action'. This views values, theories and practice as integrally related and it would make no sense in the Marxist approach to separate them. This helped to create a deeper understanding of oppression and to inform later critiques as developed by the feminist and anti-racist movements and has now found its way into mainstream social work values (Dominelli and McLeod, 1989; Shah, 1989; Ahmad, 1990 and Day, 1993). Whilst this body of work is often critical of the Marxist-inspired writings, their work can be seen to have grown out of, and alongside, the 'radical social work' tradition. A concern for anti-oppressive practices was later incorporated into the list of values produced by a previous regulatory, body the Central Council for the Education and Training of Social Workers (CCETSW, 1991a) (see Chapter 5 for a fuller discussion).

Banks (1995) has traced the influences of the Kantian, radical and utilitarian perspectives influence on social work ethics and then compared 15 national social work codes of ethics. From this national comparison she came to the conclusion that there was a significant degree of congruence. There was, though, a degree of variance between the codes as to the extent in which they acknowledged societal and agency contexts. She also identified differences in their impact on practice and practical guidance over such things as charging fees or user access to records. Congruence was identified in the shared values underpinning social work and included:

- Respect for the individual person.
- Promotion of user self-determination.
- Promotion of social justice.
- Working for the interests of users.

(Banks, 1995: 92)

Looking back at your list of ethical principles, are there any changes that you would like to make?

How does your new list compare with Banks's view above?

Can you see any conflicts between the principles?

All four of these shared values are multifarious and can mean different things to different people, but they do reflect the complexities of social work and begin to allow us to glimpse a value base.

The professional capability framework as identified by the Social Work Reform Board (2010) acknowledges the importance of values and ethics to guiding professional practice. The report is, however, light on what the nature of these values and ethics are. These are more explicit in the benchmark statements for graduate social work students in the UK that states that:

Social work is a moral activity that requires practitioners to recognise the dignity of the individual, but also to make and implement difficult decisions (including restriction of liberty) in human situations that involve the potential for benefit or harm.

Honours degree programmes in social work therefore involve the study, application of, and critical reflection upon, ethical principles and dilemmas. (Quality Assurance Agency (QAA), 2008: 4.6)

These are later translated into subject knowledge and skills for ethics and values that include:

- The nature, historical evolution and application of social work values.
- The moral concepts of rights, responsibility, freedom, authority and power inherent in the practice of social workers as moral and statutory agents.
- The complex relationships between justice, care and control in social welfare and the practical and ethical implications of these, including roles as statutory agents and in upholding the law in respect of discrimination.
- Aspects of philosophical ethics relevant to the understanding and resolution of value dilemmas and conflicts in both interpersonal and professional contexts.
- The conceptual links between codes defining ethical practice, the regulation of professional conduct and the management of potential conflicts generated by the codes held by different professional groups. (QAA, 2008: 5.1.3)

These statements from the Quality Assurance Agency for Higher Education (QAA) in the UK, although useful, highlight the difficulties that any attempt to state universal principles are bound to fail. As Mackie (1977: 15) noted, 'There are no objective values'. Universal ethical principles cannot help but fail; they cannot refer to a shared general conception of social and moral good, such a view is inherently contestable. Hugman and Smith (1995) point to the work of MacIntyre (1985) to avoid the danger of descending into a spiral of relativism. McIntyre refers to the eighteenth-century Enlightenment for a conception of ethics that saw moral authority and its principles rooted in a particular society at a particular point of time. Ethical principles can thus never be finished but are always open to debate and disagreement and are by their very nature situated and impermanent. However, this does not mean that we cannot begin to identify what is good social work or what are the virtues of a good social worker or social work researcher. In particular, McIntyre argues that in contradiction to the Enlightenment way of thinking, in certain circumstances, it is possible to infer 'ought' from 'is'. Thus when we speak of a 'good' farmer, nurse or social worker, we have some idea of what a farmer, nurse or social worker ought to be. This notion goes beyond mere 'competency' and brings to the fore the specific virtues of each calling. Husband's (1995) account of the 'morally active practitioner' is helpful here and easily transferable to the notion of the 'ethically active researcher' in articulating this struggle to achieve professional ethical guidelines that can never be irreducible to routinised statements.

Given these conditions and an awareness of the limitations of ethical codes, Butler (2002) identifies an ethical framework for social work research. His code was formally adopted by the Joint University Council's Social Work Education Committee (JUC SWEC) and has also been incorporated into the British Association of Social Workers *Code of Ethics for Social Work* (BASW, 2002). This model is based on the principles of respect for autonomy, beneficence, non-malevolence, justice and 'scope'. 'Scope' relates to the process for deciding 'to whom and in what circumstances the moral obligation applies' (Butler, 2002: 243).

'Respect for autonomy' refers to the moral obligation to respect the autonomy of each individual in so far as that it does not interfere with the autonomy of others. Like respecting persons, it implies the need to treat people as ends in themselves and not simply as means. Respect for autonomy thus begins to identify the need to secure informed consent, preserve confidentiality and to act as to avoid wilful deceit. 'Beneficence' and 'non-malevolence' at their most simple, mean 'doing good' and 'avoiding doing harm'. These terms in the world of medicine can be reduced to a rational calculation as to the costs and benefits to a patient. If the costs are greater than the benefits then the treatment or intervention should not take place. 'Justice', the fourth of the principles, refers to the need to deal fairly in the face of competing claims. As such, justice requires the researcher not to further his or her own interests at the expense of other people's legitimate interests, for example in using scarce resources for unprofitable ends, favouring ones' own community of interest and disapproval of the moral choices of others.

Butler (2002) cites Gillon (1994: 186) as to how these principles can be combined to identify other moral obligations, for example the empowerment of others is essentially a combination beneficence and respect for autonomy whereby the researcher is obliged not only to respect the patient's autonomy but also to enhance it. The application of these moral principles represents the 'scope' or space in which individual researchers can act in accordance with their own moral conscience. This requires the 'morally active researcher' to consider which principle is to take precedence under which circumstances and to be in continuous engagement with their research project.

Social work and the health services have an often strained relationship, but the four principles and 'scope' are very much in line with Banks's (1995) review of other social work codes of ethics and the four key principles that she identified as underlying international codes. In many ways Banks's four principles could be substituted as social works' four principles with the addition of 'scope'.

Butler has attempted to use these principles in order to identify a code of ethics for social work and social care research and offers them, hesitantly, on the assumption that there exists a body of morally active social work researchers 'to contest it and develop it'(Butler, 2002: 245). The code of ethics for social work practice is a major step forward for social work research in the UK. Such a code can be seen as an attempt to contribute to the establishment, maintenance and professionalisation of social work researchers. It can also be viewed as providing guidance for practitioners on how to act and as a means to protect research subjects from malpractice or abuse. In recent years there has also been an interest in virtue ethics or the ethics of character that Hugman (2010: 151) characterises as doing 'what is right is encountered in the qualities of the person acting'. Orme and Shemmings (2010) claim that it is virtue ethics that has been most prevalent in discussions about social work research where the research is undertaken by those with a commitment to the social work profession and its value base.

Codes, though, do have certain limitations. Homan (1991) recognised that a code implies some means of obligation to behave in a particular way, which in turn implies that the professional group is identifiable and a clear line demarcates members from outsiders. In some occupational groups, maybe medicine, this is achievable but the notion as to who is and who is not a social work researcher is more difficult to police. This becomes even more problematic when we consider the growth of service user involvement in research (as discussed in Chapter 8). There is also the question as to what teeth such a code has, especially as at present there is no single regulatory body for social work researchers, although those social work researchers who are also members of their national association like the

British Association of Social Workers (BASW) or national registration body could be expelled or de-registered from these organisations. However, not all countries have either national bodies or national registration requirements.

Butler (2002), in his criticism of other codes, has already identified an inherent weakness of any code in that it cannot be the final word on ethical matters and will therefore need reviewing and updating. There is also a danger that the code will invite practitioners to find loopholes and to 'play the system' when their research does not fit easily into the code. This might happen when researchers justify the use of deception in order to obtain their data. A final and fundamental concern is that any code will not be able to cover all eventualities. Social life does not fit easily into a commodification of rules of behaviour. Every social work research encounter is likely to be unique and it is therefore not helpful to have a code of behaviour that is slavishly followed that fails to acknowledge the nuances, dilemmas and contradictions of social work research practice.

Having examined the underpinning of social work research ethics, the chapter now discusses a number of the key ethical issues associated with the research process. In particular it will focus on ethical issues before the research commences, during the research and after the research is completed. It would be naive to suggest that research is a straightforwardly sequential process whereby one stage leads neatly into the next: as researchers know, research can often be a messy and disjointed affair. It is, however, conceptually helpful to divide the research process into a series of stages even if it is acknowledged that it is unlikely to pan out like this in practice.

Ethical Issues Before the Research Commences

Research Governance Framework

Prior to any research being undertaken it will need to be appraised and approved by an ethics or research governance committee. Ethics and/or research governance committees are constituted to regulate research and to quality assure research proposals and check that the proposed research is ethical. These committees are well established in universities and cover both staff and student proposals. They are also well established in the NHS but have only in recent times become a serious issue for social services departments. In order to address this gap, the UK government introduced the *Research Governance Framework for Health and Social Care* (DH, 2001a). The central purpose of the framework was to ensure that 'participants are protected from the risks associated with research' (DH, 2004: 1.1.3). The framework also sought to ensure the integrity of the research and the establishment of transparent systems.

In order to achieve their aims the government has established the responsibilities of a research sponsor, who in most cases is also likely to be the research funder. The research sponsor is expected to ensure that the research is worthy of being undertaken and in particular that:

- The research proposal is worthwhile. Of high scientific quality and represents good value for money.
- The principal investigator, and other key researchers, have the necessary expertise and experience and have access to the resources needed to conduct the proposed research successfully.
- The arrangements and resources proposed will allow the collection of high quality, accurate data and the systems and resources being proposed are those required to allow appropriate data analysis and data protection.
- Intellectual property rights and their management are appropriately addressed in research contracts or terms of grant awards.
- Organisations and individuals involved in the research all agree the division of responsibilities between them.
- Arrangements are proposed for disseminating the findings.
- All scientific judgements made by the sponsor in relation to the responsibilities set out here are based on independent and expert advice. (DH, 2001a: 3.8.6)

Whilst this is a very helpful list there is a problem as to how, or whether, the requirements of a research sponsor can be enforced by the Department of Health. Also, as Lewis (2002) points out, what would happen where a sponsor could fulfil all the requirements bar one? Would this require the research proposal to be turned down?

The guidance recognises that there are important differences in research in health and social care. Medical research may involve life-threatening conditions requiring very invasive interventions. The threats to individuals in social work research are likely to be of a different order and are more likely to relate to emotional or psychological harm. This may result in differing governance mechanisms, but research governance in both realms should still achieve the same standard. In particular, the Research Governance Framework (RGF) focuses on achieving key standards in five domains in order to ensure good research governance:

- Ethics: ensuring the dignity, rights, safety and well-being of research participants.
- Science: ensuring that the design and methods of research are subject to independent review by relevant researchers.
- Information: ensuring full and free public access to information on research and its findings.
- Health and safety: ensuring at all times the safety of research participants, researchers and other staff.
- Finance: ensuring financial probity and compliance with the law in the conduct of research. (DH, 2004)

The Department of Health's initial introduction of research governance was to cover both children and adult's services but with the move of children's services to the Department of Children, Schools and Families there was no requirement for local authority children's services to adopt the adult services model. McLaughlin and Shardlow (2009) and Department of Health et al. (2010) identified a range of differing research governance arrangements in local authorities:

- Adult social services only covered.
- Adult and children's social services covered.
- Adult and children's services covered.
- Corporate – involving all council services.
- Multi-council – same arrangements apply across two or more local authorities.
- Multi-agency – where two or more agencies, including at least one local authority have adopted the same arrangements.

What is clear from the above is that although adult service users, carers and staff are subject to research governance arrangements, this is not necessarily the same for those in children's services. Although the initial draft of the Department of Health's (2004) research governance resource pack was supported as good practice by both the Association of Directors of Children's Services and the Department of Children's Schools and Families, the 2010 version was not. In December 2010, Boddy and Oliver undertook a scoping exercise for children's services that reiterated the wide variety of arrangements between local authorities and also acknowledged that the increasingly integrated children's services had resulted in a blurring of boundaries and that there were particular issues in relation to children's services, including access to children and consent:

> However, the main conclusion from this work is clear. To develop a coherent and transparent system of research governance – a system that can be applied across the diverse, and increasingly integrated climate of children's services – necessitates a simple, and flexible, approach. The approach must be based on clear principles, whilst being flexible in its implementation around key minimum standards. (Boddy and Oliver, 2010: 6)

Whilst such an approach awaits new guidance, children are not afforded the same protection as their adult counterparts and the ethical approval of research services remains largely open to the whims of different authorities. The author is aware from discussing children's research projects with local authority research governance officers that there are examples of researchers when finding out that their proposal will be subject to research governance assessment withdrawing their request and reapplying to authorities where such arrangements are not in place.

It will be interesting to see how, if at all, these proposed new arrangements affect the research undertaken in social work and social care and whether the format of external review undertaken by local authorities will reflect that undertaken by the

NHS that Lewis (2002), amongst others, views as relatively unsympathetic towards qualitative research proposals. Furedi (2002) has also suggested that research ethics committees are more concerned with protective paternalism and act as bureaucratic gatekeepers using ethics as the new managerial ideology. There is also the potential for researchers, engaged in multiagency studies, having to present their research proposals to a number of such committees, each of which may require minor adjustments to the research process that when all taken together may result in changing the nature of the research. An example of this would be an academic researcher undertaking research in mental health services where university, health service and local authority approval may all be required separately. Whilst guidance suggests the avoidance of duplication, a system of passporting approvals is yet to be agreed.

In relation to ethics/research governance committees, they have the power and responsibility to veto an application where it is not up to standard. However, it should also be remembered that gaining ethical committee/research governance committee approval does not mean that the researcher can stop thinking ethically. As most researchers realise, although there are clearly ethical dimensions to research design, the difficult ethical issues often arise once the research has gotten underway. Ethical approval within the RGF is conceptualised as a one-off event but research is a process, and as we identified earlier, the researcher needs to be continually engaged in reflecting upon the ethical dimensions of their research and adopting the stance of a morally active researcher.

Informed Consent

Imagine that you have been invited to take part in a research study.

What would you want to know about the study before you agreed to take part?

When would you want to know this and in what format would you want this information?

Under what circumstances might you decline the invitation?

What could the researcher do to alleviate these fears?

Reflexive Questions

A central issue of research ethics that is covered in all research textbooks and all ethical research codes is the need for informed consent. Informed consent implies that all human participants should be fully informed about a research project before they agree to take part. This means that all participants should be provided with information about the purpose of the study, what participation is required of them, who the sponsors are and who the researchers are who make up the research team. This information is also likely to cover what subjects they may be asked, whether participants will be identified or comments attributed to them in the report, whether and if so, how participants will be able to find out the results of the study. The participants should also be informed that they have the right to exit the study at any time without prejudice. This information may also provide details on how to make a complaint and may request a signed declaration from the participants to say that they understand what they have been told and that they wish to continue with the research.

Informed consent should also clearly identify that participation is voluntary. This issue is of particular importance when people who have a professional relationship with the research participants carry out the research. Under such circumstances, research participants may feel an obligation of gratitude towards the researcher and provide overly positive results. At the other end of the spectrum, participants may fear that they will receive a poorer service or that services will be removed if they do not take part.

The notion of informed consent is not without its difficulties, for example it begs the question, how informed is informed? There is a balance to be struck here as too much information may curtail involvement unnecessarily or curb spontaneous views. However, as Lewis (2003) comments, there is nothing to be gained from participants who are inadequately prepared. There are potential difficulties for participants in hierarchical work structures when they are asked to comment about the organisation's management style unless the participants are convinced that senior management approves of their involvement and that their comments will not be personally identifiable. Informed consent becomes particularly important where there is a possibility of adverse consequences for the participant.

Having gained informed consent, the researcher needs to decide how they will evidence this. This may be in the form of an oral or written agreement. The difficulty with an oral agreement is that in any dispute it will be one person's word against another's. Personally written or recorded consent is preferable.

Covert Methods

In relation to informed consent it is important to consider the ethical issue of covert methods and their place within social work research. Covert methods involve the concealment of the researcher within an otherwise acceptable social role (Homan, 1991). Covert research usually involves participant observation, but may also include the use of new technology to 'bug' using video or digital recorders. The question though remains as to whether covert methods are ever justifiable?

Homan (1991: 109–13) identifies thirteen arguments against the use of covert methods:

- Covert methods flout the principle of informed consent.
- Covert methods help erode personal liberty.
- Covert methods betray trust.
- Covert methods pollute the research environment.
- Covert methods are bad for the reputation of social research.
- Covert methods discriminate against the defenceless and powerless.
- Covert methods may damage the behaviour or interests of subjects.
- Covert methods may become habitual in the everyday life of the person doing the research.
- The habit of deception may spread to other spheres of human interaction.
- Covert methods are invisibly reactive.
- Covert methods are seldom necessary.
- Covert methods have the effect of confining the scope of the research.
- The covert researcher suffers excessive strain in maintaining the cover.

This is a very long and compelling list and suggests that covert methods are at best highly controversial and problematic – if ever justifiable.

Humphries and Martin (2000) cite the case of Davidson (Davidson and Layder, 1994) as a defence of an invasion of privacy. Davidson and Layder studied power and control in the interactions between a sex-worker (Desiree) and her clients. In order to conduct participant observation research Davidson took on a number of roles, including acting as the sex-worker's receptionist. Davidson listened into conversations between the 'punters' and Desiree and also discussed the sexual preferences of her punters with her. Davidson defended this covert research strategy by stating that the clients remained totally anonymous to her and that Desiree had willingly offered the information. It was also very clear that the researcher had little time for Desiree's 'punters':

> I have a professional obligation to preserve and protect their anonymity and to ensure they are not harmed by my research, but I feel no qualms about being less than frank with them, and no obligation to allow them to choose whether or not their actions are recorded. (Davidson and Layder, 1994: 215)

Davidson and Layder (1994) then suggest that virtually all social research is exploitive and intrusive to some degree. Social research, and this is also true of social work research, is rarely undertaken at the bequest of its human subjects nor without due regard to the career of the researcher. This example ably demonstrates that the ownership of information is not always a straightforward manner. It could be argued that the researcher behaved ethically towards Desiree, who participated with informed consent whereas the 'punters' may understandably feel aggrieved that they were duped and that their information was illegally and unethically obtained without their consent. As Punch (1998: 179) observes, 'where you stand will doubtless help to determine not only what you will research but also how you will research it'.

Accompanying covert methods is also the use of deception, of which Homan (1991) identified four types: concealment, misrepresentation, camouflage and the acquisition of confidential documents, which are then used to contact potential respondents.

Homan (1991) argues that where covert methods have been used, the researcher has claimed that the end justifies the means. As the above example shows, this can be a highly ambiguous and contentious argument. Most research codes prohibit covert research and the deceit inherent in it, although they may contain a rider suggesting that it could be justified in an exceptional case. Butler (2002) provides such a rider when, in point eight of the code of ethics for social work and social care research, he proposes three conditions before deception or concealment can be used. These conditions are that there should be no alternative feasible strategy, no harm can be foreseen to the research subject and that 'the greater good is self-evidently served'. Any social work researcher considering covert methods would seriously need to consider these ethical dimensions of their research and should also expect a major challenge from their ethics and research governance committee and from their peers if the research enters the public arena.

Anonymity and Confidentiality

Anonymity and confidentiality are sometimes confused in research. Anonymity means that those outside the research team will not know the identity of participants. This may become compromised where participation is arranged through a third party, like an employer, or in case studies where there is structural linkage between samples (Lewis, 2003). In these situations, absolute guarantees cannot be given and research respondents should be made aware of this before they agree to participate.

Confidentiality refers to ensuring that the attribution of comments in reports, presentations or externally published works cannot be linked to individual participants. This includes both direct attribution, where comments are linked to a name or specific role, and indirect attribution, where a collection of characteristics may make it possible to identify an individual or small group. It needs to be remembered that if the organisation has singleton roles, for example director or staff development manager, any comments from these roles, or about these roles, will be identifiable to those who know the organisation being described. Indirect attribution needs to be carefully scrutinised for if the detail given about an individual or group is too distinctive, then that individual or group will become identifiable. In order to avoid this situation, the researcher may have to restrict the amount of contextual detail that is given.

Ethical Issues During the Research

It is during this phase of the research process that there is the closest interaction between the researcher and the researched. Such interaction inevitably generates ethical issues that may not have been identified in the original research proposal. In social work research this may result in a young person identifying that they have been abused, or are using illegal substances or planning to break the law. When situations like this occur, the researcher needs to remind themselves that they are acting as a researcher and not as a social worker (even if they are professionally qualified and registered). In these circumstances, they need to be able to refer these issues on to those who can deal with them appropriately, having originally identified any limitations to the participant's confidentiality in undertaking the informed consent. It is also interesting to speculate whether a researcher who is a qualified social worker would be deemed to be in breach of their professional code of conduct if they did nothing in such circumstances?

One key area, which raises significant ethical issues during research, is that of recording data. Focus groups, unstructured interviews and semi-structured interviews are generally digitally recorded. Videotaping is sometimes used, and does have the advantage of being able to record physical gestures, facial expressions and bodily postures but may be intimidating to research participants. Note-taking, though, is generally insufficient for ensuring the accuracy of recording and the actual words spoken, let alone the often important emphases and silences in question responses. A researcher taking notes is also less able to concentrate fully on the research interview, as they will be concerned about ensuring that responses are written down legibly rather than understanding what the respondent is telling them. Where researchers wish to include video or digital-recording, they need to ensure that the reason for this is explained and that this is included in the information provided in securing informed consent. This should also include information as to who will listen or view the recording, where such data will be stored, for how long and what the procedure is for destroying the recording. Recordings and transcripts should not be labelled in such a way that it would compromise anonymity and identifying information like sampling documents or frames should be stored separately.

Researchers also need to bear in mind that a digital recorder may appear quite threatening to a participant. To help overcome this, the researcher may wish to let the participant hear her/himself before officially starting the interview and place the microphone where the participant can turn it off.

The Right of Respondents to End their Involvement in the Research

Oliver argues that it is:

> arguably part of the principles of freedom and autonomy inherent in taking part in research that the participants should feel free to withdraw at any time. Even when participants give their informed consent, they cannot necessarily be expected to anticipate their feelings about participation. ... They should not have to give any notice about withdrawal, and they should not have to provide any explanation. (Oliver, 2003: 47)

Oliver highlights the ethical imperative that respondents have the right to withdraw their involvement in the research at any time and without prejudice. This is particularly important, as one of the key principles of respondent involvement was that it should be voluntary. This can be difficult for researchers to accept as should all their respondents withdraw they would not be able to complete the research!

There are though a number of reasons why a respondent might withdraw their cooperation. No matter how clear a researcher has thought that they have been in informing a participant about the research, the participant may not have fully understood what was required of them and it was only once they began answering the questions that it all became clear. Similarly, it is not always possible to plan every aspect of the research and changes of detail need to be renegotiated and this may also include the participant's participation. It may also be that the research raises painful issues for the participant that they are not willing to acknowledge, or are too painful, and they thus decide to withdraw their consent.

Protecting Participants from Harm

Reflexive Questions

Imagine that you are a researcher undertaking a study to understand why those suffering domestic violence regularly return to their violent partner before telling anyone. What practical considerations might you need to take into account before interviewing those who have been physically assaulted and emotionally abused by their partners.

How might these arrangements differ if you were interviewing the violent partner? How would you justify this?

In any research study, it is important to consider from the outset whether it is likely that taking part may be harmful to individual respondents, and if so to take alternative action or plan contingencies. This may arise directly as in studies on sensitive topics or indirectly when sensitive subjects are raised in relation to otherwise non-sensitive material.

Where subjects are asked to participate in a research study known to cover sensitive material, the potential respondent should have been advised of this when their consent was being sought. Lewis (2003) offers the advice that sensitive topics or issues are best addressed through clear and direct questions, so that ambiguity can be avoided and respondents are not drawn unwittingly into areas that they would prefer to avoid. The researcher also needs to be sensitive to the respondent's discomfort, and to check whether the participant is willing to carry on. It may on occasions be necessary to stop an interview in order to allow a respondent to regain their composure before asking them whether they wish to continue or revisit previous answers.

Researchers must also guard against 'mere voyeurism' and be able to justify clearly why certain questions are being asked and how they are essential to the study and contribute to knowledge development. Any subject area is potentially sensitive to someone. This is irrespective if the question is about family composition or health status, never mind issues like underage sex, euthanasia or domestic violence.

In the example given above you might need to consider the interview venue – somewhere that the abused person feels safe – whether they need to be accompanied by a friend and whether there needs to a be a counsellor on hand should the interviewee become distressed. You will also need to advise the respondent about what types of information can remain confidential and what types of information cannot. This could include information about his or her own abuse but might also involve clarifying that any ongoing abuse of a child or vulnerable adult would be reported.

In relation to research with an 'abuser', you will also need to consider where to interview and how this is likely to impact on the information given. This interview is more likely to take place at a neutral venue. If it is decided to interview in the abuser's home you will need to consider the possibility of being accompanied, for example by a colleague or probation officer, although this is likely to impact on the quality of the data collected. It is also good practice for researchers to ensure that another member of the research team is aware of where they are when undertaking home interviews. Health and safety issues are major considerations in both cases and will by necessity impact on how welcoming and open the interview process is likely to be. The researcher should also consider what their response would be if the abuser should admit further abuse to another partner or request help with their behaviour.

As can be seen, the responses to both interviewees are very similar, although the degree to which the researcher takes cognisance of the relevant issues varies. Both interviewees deserve respect as people, even if the actions of one of them is abhorrent to the researcher. It would be just as bad for a researcher to over-identify and sympathise with the abused as it would be to vilify the abuser. Besides suggesting that right and wrong are simplistic categories, such views would be reflected in the study, distorting the potential for knowledge development. This does not mean that the researcher should not have a view on such issues, but it does mean that they should be aware of what it is, be clear to any reader about what that view is and to seek to reduce the bias that their view results in. This way the reader is able to make their own assessment as to the impact of researchers' views on the results produced.

As mentioned before, it is not only sensitive subjects that are likely to bring forward difficult ethical issues, these are also likely to emerge in apparently non-sensitive subject areas. In these cases, seemingly 'non-sensitive questions' may raise distressing responses. It is not uncommon for researchers to be faced with the ethical dilemma of being told very sensitive personal material to a question that did not require such a response. One colleague recently was asking a young person about their educational experience, only to be told that she had been sexually abused. The young person wanted to share this information and have it recorded before the interview could progress. This can be very difficult for any researcher and particularly for a researcher who is uncomfortable in dealing with such emotionally charged matters.

Reflexive Questions

At this point consider your position as a researcher if you have told the interviewee that everything they tell you is confidential. Are you able to break this confidentiality? If yes, under what circumstances would this be done? How would this vary depending on the age and maturity of the respondent, or is it inviolate?

This leads onto an important point: the researcher's role is not to be confused with that of adviser, counsellor or social worker. The researcher should avoid giving advice, commenting favourably or unfavourably on participant's decisions. The researcher, if they are researching a known sensitive subject area, should have identified as part of their research plan competent professionals who could offer appropriate support and advice should a respondent become distressed. This is not a role that they should take on themselves. As part of the research plan for 'non-sensitive' subject areas, they should also consider what they should do and whom they could refer participants to should such a situation as the one identified above occur. In such circumstances, the researcher may be required to call a halt to the interview and advise the young person that they are dutybound to advise the local children's services department. This may seem an obvious action to take, but it does present clear difficulties. To pass on information without the participant's consent is a profound loss of control for the informant. The consequences of passing on information may be hazardous for the participant and raise the likelihood of further harm. However, this may be dependent on other factors like the age or maturity of the young person, or where they are currently living and with whom. Certainly the situation of a mature 18-year-old living away at university may be treated differently to an immature 10-year-old living with the perpetrator of the abuse. Even so, as Lewis (2003) acknowledges, this judgement of the degree of risk is likely to involve some subjectivity and may not be one that is shared by those being interviewed.

Protection of Researchers from Harm

It is not only those who are researched who may be at risk of harm but also those who conduct the research. Thought should be given at the start of the research as to the necessary arrangements to minimise any foreseen risk. Risk arises in different ways and may include the travel arrangements to a public place or interviews in private homes.

In public places this may include the funding of appropriate modes of transport and the prior identification of appropriate meeting places at mutually acceptable times. All of this may indicate the need for interviewers to work in pairs, either conducting the interview together or one escorting the other to promote safety.

Lewis (2003) reminds us that, although fieldwork often takes place in private places, it is a public engagement. Others should know where the researcher is and this is likely to offer a degree of protection to the researcher. Risk will always be present no matter how carefully planned and where possible the potential risk factors need to be identified, reduced and managed.

Researchers may also be at risk due to the nature of the interview or the questions included in the interview. When entering private homes, or unfamiliar buildings to interview, researchers should make themselves aware of an 'escape route' from the building should one be needed. Researchers need to be continually monitoring the emotional level of the interview and be aware that they might need to stop the interview should they feel threatened or worried about their own welfare. It may also be prudent to agree to contact a colleague after the interview, not merely for debriefing but to confirm that you are safe and well. Opportunities for debriefing and providing support to researchers need to be built into the process. All these actions may cost money and should be budgeted for at the design stage of the original research budget application.

Ethical Issues after the Data Collection has Been Completed

Sharing the Data

The researcher's ethical responsibilities do not end once the data collection has been completed. Respondents may wish to check the accuracy of their information and may request a copy of their questionnaire or interview. Respondents, though, do not have a right to other respondents' views.

Respondents may be sufficiently interested to find out the conclusions of the research. If this is the case, they may need to wait until the research is in the public domain in the shape of a published report or article. However, if the original research contract notes that the intellectual rights of the research report is the research sponsor's it will not be within the gift of the researcher to share the report without previously gaining the sponsor's permission. Where possible researchers should advise respondents where they will be able to gain access to the research results and this should have been an issue included in the original ethical approval application.

Publication of the Research Results

For the researcher the end of the research may well be the publication of the results in a book or an article. This too is not without its ethical quandaries. Researchers need to discuss publication as part of the original research agreement with the research sponsor and this should also have been discussed with informants and any cooperating organisations prior to the research beginning. Homan (1991) suggests, and I would agree, that possibly the biggest irritant for a social researcher is the requirement by a research sponsor to approve all forms of publication prior to their submission. This can include not only the final research report, but also any articles or conference presentations derived from the research.

In relation to the final research report, the research sponsors may not like what has been written about them or their organisation. There are a number of issues here. It is only right that a research sponsor should be able to see what is written and be able to correct any factual inaccuracies. Even with the most scrupulous of sponsors, there may be difficulties where the sponsor finds it problematical to distinguish between requesting a change because of an inaccuracy as opposed to the findings being inconvenient or not the desired outcome. This is particularly the case when there is disagreement about an interpretation. Often, but not always, a compromise can be reached without jeopardising the integrity of the material or the researcher.

Many researchers will also have faced the situation where the sponsor does not want staff members' responses reported. This might be because the report does not reflect what the manager wants to reflect, the research undermines a favoured policy or practice or the research reflects badly on the manager. This type of situation can be very difficult for a researcher to manage ethically and raises the thorny question of academic freedom:

> Within the research community the most persistent concern is for the maintenance of academic freedom because it is supposed that the quality and validity of research are dependent upon it. Government investment in research, it is feared, too often has the motive of legitimising intended policy and is too seldom open to findings that would contradict or embarrass policy intentions. Academic freedom is a principle that espouses the discovery of truth without fear or favour. (Homan, 1991:137)

It is quite possible to substitute any research sponsor or commissioner for the government in the above quotation. The pursuit of academic freedom is undertaken against a background of competition, often between research commissioners particularly in service evaluations and competition between researchers for research contracts in order to develop research careers. Under conditions like these there is always a danger that the principle of academic freedom will be compromised.

Authorship

Imagine that you have just completed your dissertation or PhD and have written an article of 5,000 words from your work. On showing this to your supervisor they make some changes and suggest where you should publish. At the bottom of their page of comments they request that their name should be added to the work, how does this make you feel? Do you think that it is fair or not?

Authorship can be a tricky ethical matter. Butler (2002: 247) suggests that all publications of social work findings 'should properly and in proportion to their contribution, acknowledge the part played by all participants'. There is an immediate difficulty here to define what is meant by 'properly and in proportion to their contribution'. At one level this opens the door to different types of contributions, say around sharing and developing ideas, critiquing work and helping to structure the research. What it does not do is help identify how much of this needs to go on before someone should be considered a joint author. It also raises the difficult issue of how much help a supervisor can provide a dissertation or PhD student before the work is no longer that of the student.

For the student's part, they may feel aggrieved for being put in this difficult position. On the one hand, they may not see any valid reason to agree to the request. They are the ones that have completed the research and it is they who have written both the dissertation/PhD and the article. Also, is not the supervisor employed to offer this help and that should surely be reward enough? On the other hand, they may feel that they cannot say 'no' as the supervisor is in a hierarchically powerful role in comparison to them. On the positive side the supervisor may have helped with the planning of the research, contributed a critical eye to the analysis, read and commented on earlier drafts and supported the student when the going got tough. It certainly would not be easy to refuse such a request. Oliver (2003) suggests that in trying to arbitrate in such a situation we need to consider the different elements of a research article, which includes the academic content and the writing of the article. In looking back at the example above it would appear that the student did most of the writing except for some minor proofreading. The supervisor will automatically have contributed to the research design, although this was part of the original dissertation/PhD design. In this type of case, it would seem that the major work is that of the student's and that may be what should happen is that a note should be added at the end of the article thanking the supervisor for their support in the completion of the research, which was the basis of the article. This would represent a proper acknowledgement of their efforts on behalf of the student.

The example above also raises the ethical issue of the exercise of undue influence by the supervisor. It was they who made the request and it is rather difficult to separate this from the issue of power and authority that comes from the role of supervisor. Whilst it is expected that students will listen and act on their supervisor's suggestions, it is also expected that supervisors will not act to abuse their position of authority (Oliver, 2003).

Confidentiality and Publication

It is usual for respondents to be given a guarantee, or contractual agreement, that they will not be identified in the report or any subsequent publication. Confidentiality is offered as a condition of informed consent. Pragmatically, confidentiality may not only assist respondents to be more truthful about their views as they cannot be identified, but it may also help to guard against a 'halo effect' as there is no purpose in presenting a good impression. One aspect of this, less open to control, is how to ensure that neither harm nor embarrassment comes to those who have been researched or to those undertaking research after the report and its findings have become known. Kimmel (1988) reported long-term negative consequences of those involved in the Cambridge Somerville Youth Study 30 years after the original project. Punch (1998) also argues that it is important to avoid the sense of betrayal felt by some interviewees when they find that their information has been used for purposes that were unclear or unknown about at the start of the process. Once published, it is very difficult to predict what uses one's research might be put to. Thus, whilst it is possible to give a guarantee of confidentiality, there is no guarantee that once published the work will not incur negative effects on those involved nor that respondents will feel angry about how their data has been used.

Summary

Ethics are integral both to social work practice and to social work research. This chapter began by identifying some of the abuses in the name of research demonstrating why ethical research is so important. Having established the need for ethical research, the chapter then argued that if there were to be a claim for a distinct social work research ethics this would be related to the ethical nature of social work and social workers. There then followed a discussion of social work ethics, starting from the work of Biestek. From this it was established that social work ethics were situational and contextual, and although not fixed, there was a congruence of an international social work ethical position around the principles of respect for persons, honouring diversity and challenging injustice. This was then related to the nature of social work research ethics and Butler's (2003) code for social work and social work research.

The chapter then discussed ethical issues as they occurred during the research cycle. We concluded that, although research ethical codes are very important, ethical research codes only provide a framework and there is still a need for the 'morally active social work researcher'.

Suggested Reading

Banks, S. (2006) *Ethics and Values in Social Work*, 3rd edn. Basingstoke: Palgrave Macmillan.
A classic and well-written guide to the major ethical issues and dilemmas facing social workers.

Butler, I. (2002) 'A code of ethics for social work and social care research', *British Journal of Social Work*, 32 (2): 239–48.
Identifies the code and reasoning behind a separate code of ethics for social work and social care. Now also included as a section in the BASW Code of Ethics.

Hugman, R. (2010) 'Social work research and ethics', in I. Shaw, K. Briar-Lawson, J. Orme and R. Ruckdeschel (eds), *The Sage Handbook of Social Work Research*, *The Ethics of Social Research*. London: Sage, pp. 149–63.
A well-written and challenging chapter on the ethical issues involved in social work research.

Oliver, P. (2003) *The Student's Guide to Research Ethics*. Maidenhead: Open University Press.
A good introductory text on key ethical issues for social science students.

5   Research and Anti-Oppressive Practice

Introduction

This chapter will examine what is meant by anti-oppressive practice and why the concept is so important within social work, and establish how it impacts on research and research methodology. Anti-oppressive practice is a contested arena within which students and social workers often struggle to obtain an understanding without either feeling guilty or denying the potential for oppressive and discriminating behaviour.

Dominelli (1993), a key figure in anti-oppressive practice in the UK, has described anti-oppressive practice as:

> A form of social work practice which addresses social divisions and structural inequalities in the work that is done with 'clients' (users) or workers. Anti-oppressive practice aims to provide more appropriate and sensitive services by responding to people's needs regardless of their social status. Anti-oppressive practice embodies a person-centred philosophy, an egalitarian value system concerned with reducing the deleterious effects of structural inequalities upon people's lives; a methodology focusing on both process and outcomes; and a way of structuring relationships between individuals that aims to empower users by reducing the negative effects of hierarchy in their immediate interaction and the work they do together. (Dominelli, 1998: 24)

Dominelli's definition identifies anti-oppressive practice as pervasive impacting on all aspects of social work practice. It has an impact at the level of the social worker and the service user, between employer and social worker, between social worker and social worker and critically comments on the culture of the agency, their contacts and the social context in which they operate. The role of the anti-oppressive social worker is to highlight, challenge and eradicate social injustice. It can thus be argued that anti-oppressive practice is linked to a longstanding tradition of humanism and social work's long-established alignment with the experience of the underdog.

Discrimination refers to the identification of individuals and groups with identifiable characteristics and behaving less favourably towards this individual or group, than those with favoured characteristics. Anti-discriminatory practice is thus linked to anti-oppressive practice as it challenges workers to behave equitably. Anti-oppressive practice, on the other hand, is more pro-active in that it is not only about treating individuals or groups equitably, it is also about conflict and change in relation to the power imbalance between 'superior' and 'inferior' individuals or groups. Anti-oppressive practice, unlike anti-discriminatory practice, aims to bring about an equalising shift in the power relations between individuals and groups. Although this distinction between anti-oppressive and anti-discriminatory practice is conceptually distinct, in practice the two terms are often used as interchangeable.

One of the key sites for anti-oppressive and anti-discriminatory practice for UK social workers has been the issue of racism. Anti-racist practice has an important history in connection with the training and development of qualified social workers. In the late 1980s, the UK saw the racialised nationalism of Thatcherism defending 'British values' from 'the enemy within' and a promotion of possessive individualism resulting in a xenophobic nationalism (Husband, 1995). Against this background, the then social work awarding body, the Central Council for the Education and Training of Social Workers (CCETSW), official policy statement on anti-racism maintained that the:

> CCETSW believes that racism is endemic in the values, attitudes and structures of British society, including those of social services and social work education. CCETSW recognises that the effects of racism on black people are incompatible with the values of social work and therefore seeks to combat racist practices in all its responsibilities. (CCETSW, 1988 quoted in Husband, 1995: 90)

This policy statement fed into the famous CCETSW Paper 30. Paper 30 codified the Council's system for the approval of the then new Diploma in Social Work (Dip SW) including, as part of the knowledge and skills against which students would be assessed, a student's ability to recognise, understand and confront racism within a multicultural society (CCETSW, 1989, 1991b).

More recently, the GSCC Code of Practice (GSCC, 2002) requires social care employers to 'put in place and implement written policies and procedures to deal with dangerous, discriminatory or exploitative behaviour and practice' (GSCC, 2002: No. 4). As part of the Code of practice employees are expected to engage in:

> 1.5 Promoting equal opportunities for service users and carers and
>
> 1.6 Respecting diversity and different cultures and values
>
> and to act in such a way as to not:
>
> 5.5 Discriminate unlawfully or unjustifiably against service users, carers or colleagues.

5.6 Condone any unlawful or unjustifiable discrimination by service users, carers or colleagues.

(GSCC, 2002)

The Quality Assurance Agency for Higher Education (QAA) benchmark statements for social work degrees also highlights this issue of combating discrimination:

4.5 Social work is a moral activity that requires practitioners to make and implement difficult decisions about human situations that involve the potential for benefit or harm. Honours degree programmes in social work therefore involve the study, application of and critical reflection upon ethical principles and dilemmas. As reflected by the four care councils' codes of practice, this involves showing respect for persons, honouring the diverse and distinctive organisations and communities that make up contemporary society, promoting social justice and combating processes that lead to discrimination, marginalisation and social exclusion. (QAA, 2008: 4.6)

This is further reinforced and reflected by the Social Work reform Board (SWRB, 2010a, 2010b), which identified two professional capabilities of particular note:

DIVERSITY – Recognise diversity and apply anti-discriminatory and anti-oppressive principles in practice

Social workers understand that diversity characterises and shapes human experience and is critical to the formation of identity. Diversity is multidimensional and includes race, disability, class, economic status, age, sexuality, gender and transgender, faith and belief. Social workers appreciate that, as a consequence of difference, a person's life experience may include oppression, marginalisation and alienation as well as privilege, power and acclaim, and are able to challenge appropriately.

RIGHTS, JUSTICE AND ECONOMIC WELLBEING – Advance human rights and promote social justice and economic wellbeing

Social workers recognise the fundamental principles of human rights and equality, and that these are protected in national and international law, conventions and policies. They ensure these principles underpin their practice. Social workers understand the importance of using and contributing to case law and applying these rights in their own practice. They understand the effects of oppression, discrimination and poverty.

In order to begin to understand the importance of an anti-oppressive social work research stance, it is first necessary to consider some of the arenas of anti-oppressive practice. Anti-oppressive practice seeks to help the practising social worker synthesise structural critiques with ethical value bases (Horner, 2003). Anti-oppressive practice focuses on challenging and addressing institutionalised discrimination representing the interests of powerful groups within society. Under the Equality Act 2010, nine equality strands of protected characteristics are identified: race, sex, sexual orientation, disability, gender reassignment, religion and belief, just had a baby or being pregnant, being married or in a civil partnership and age. Primarily, it is an impossible task to produce an exhaustive list that would be acceptable to everyone as discrimination is also dependent upon time and context.

Researchers have also written of the impact of colonialism (Tuhiwai Smith, 1999; D'Cruz and Jones, 2004), the white Irish in Britain (Garrett, 2000, 2003), and about those who live in rural as opposed to urban areas (Pugh, 2003). The production of lists can be dangerous as:

- Lists risk reinforcing stereotypical characteristics that may be transferred to all members of these groups.
- Groupings can suggest that different groups experience separate barriers to discrimination and oppression and risks the continuation of historic segregation faced by some groups, e.g. separate services for people with different impairments.
- Lists of groups and types of people also suggest that different groups of people are competing for recognition.
- Labels and groupings can promote a simplistic 'pigeonholing' view of individual people, neglecting the point that we all have a number of identifying characteristics and life experiences that shape us as individuals.

The discourse of anti-oppressive practice (Dalrymple and Burke, 1995; Thompson, 1997; Dominelli, 1998) endeavours to engage with notions of diversity and difference and we will examine these in relation to race and gender as exemplars of the nature of the debates and insights of anti-oppressive practice.

Race and Anti-Oppressive Practice

Anti-oppressive approaches have their roots in the late 1980s and 1990s in response to a growing concern about ethnic conflict in many Western societies. This included the inner city riots in the UK, which have largely been ascribed to the alienation of young black people. Similar concerns have been raised about the levels of crime and riots involving black people in the USA, over Eastern European refugees in Germany and Italy, and a similar unease over refugees from North Africa in France. Many countries face ethnic and cultural conflicts, including the position of indigenous peoples – such as the Aborigines in Australia, the Maoris in New Zealand, the Native Americans in the USA and Canada, the Inuit in Canada and the gypsies or Romany people in Southern Europe.

Race is 'merely' a social construct that is used as a means of classifying people, to discriminate between people and to exercise control over people on the basis of colour (Everitt et al., 1992). To talk of race as 'merely' a social construct is to signify that race is not real. There is nothing we can point to and say, that is 'race'.

There are as many genetic differences between people who share physical attributes as there are between groups divided by race. Race may not exist in any scientifically meaningful sense but this is to neglect that many people act as if it is a fixed objective category.

The conceptual notion of race is intrinsically connected to the idea of racism. Lorde (1984) describes this as:

> The belief in the inherent superiority of one race over all others and thereby the right to dominance. (Lorde, 1984: 115)

In the United Kingdom, racism is about the construction of social relationships on the basis of an assumed inferiority of non-Anglo-Saxon ethnic minority groups. Racism is neither natural nor inevitable and the social construction of race and the development of racism are concrete historical processes (Harvey, 1990). This politicisation of human biology into white supremacist terms has enabled those at the top of the hierarchy to construct social relations and impose their power on others. It has also provided a highly visible and simple means to classify people as superior – white and inferior non-white. Social relationships organised on white supremacist terms lead to racism becoming internalised and to this being seen as normal. Concentrating on the biological aspects of racism neglects the importance of social relationships whose practices facilitate the oppression of those with visible racial and ethnic characteristics including skin colour, hair type, language and cultural traditions. The politicisation of such characteristics indicate that racism is a social construct whose economic, political and ideological processes represent the means by which the 'superior' group organises hegemony over the 'inferior' group.

Dominelli (1997) identifies a model of racism that includes personal, cultural and institutional elements of such processes and ideologies. Individual racism can be defined as those attitudes and behaviours that indicate a pejorative judgement of racial groups. Unjustified individual racist attitudes lacking institutional support are defined as racial prejudice. Institutional racism consists of the customary routines that ration resources and power by excluding racially 'inferior' groups. In doing so, institutional racism pathologies these excluded groups for their lack of success within the system whilst blaming them for their predicament. Thus the interaction of individual behaviour and institutional norms form the dynamic for institutional racism. Cultural racism is centred on values, beliefs and ideas endorsing the superiority of the white culture. As such, cultural racism supports and reinforces both individual and institutional racism. Solomos (2003) notes, there has also been a shift from biological superiority to cultural superiority.

Reflexive Questions

At this point you might want to consider why should social work researchers be concerned with race and racism? What do you see as the implications, if any, for social work if race and racism are not addressed?

Your answer may have included the overrepresentation of black children in the child care system. Barn (1993) highlighted the significance of race and racism on decisions made by social workers on the care careers of black children. This is a complex issue and as Boushel (2000) comments in discussing the relevance of race for children's social welfare:

> It is now clear, for example, that a specific group of Black children – very young mixed parentage children – may be particularly likely to receive state care, especially if living in white areas (Bebington and Miles, 1989; Charles et al., 1992; Boushel, 1996). In multiracial areas, African–Caribbean children looked after by the state seem more likely to return home speedily when fostered by local African–Caribbean families (Barn, 1993). More recently Gibbons et al. (1995) found 'Black and Asian' children 'are overrepresented among referrals for physical injury compared to whites … and underrepresented among referrals for sexual abuse', whilst Farmer and Owen (1995) found particularly high numbers of inconclusive child protection investigations in Black and South Asian families, especially where language problems increased official uncertainty. (Boushel, 2000: 73)

Indigenous Perspectives

One other aspect of the development of anti-racist practice has been the growing emergence of indigenous perspectives. Colonisation by Western countries following conflicts or wars has resulted in the conquered people's lives, practices and communities becoming transformed into objects of knowledge for the superior colonisers. This has reinforced dominant worldviews as normal whilst marginalising alternatives. From such a perspective discussions about race, class, gender, disability and so on all have their location within the Western world and its models of knowledge production, classification and criteria of evaluation. D'Cruz and Jones (2004: 52) quote: Tuhiwai Smith (1999: 80), who claimed that coloniser's research practices could best be summed up as: 'they came, they saw, they named they claimed'. Family group conferences have now become a 'normal' aspect of social work practice developed from the experience of Maoris in New Zealand, whilst Mumford and Saunders (2011) have written about how Maori cultural worldviews are helping inform mainstream social work practice.

Immigration, Refugees and Asylum Seekers

Following the impact of global change, poverty, wars in central Africa, the social transformation in Eastern Europe and UK membership of the European Union, the plight of refugees and asylum seekers have become the subject of a moral panic in the UK. In the 1990s asylum seekers held essentially the same rights as any other citizen. However, this position has increasingly become undermined with the Asylum Act 1993, Immigration and Asylum Act 1996 and the Labour White Paper of 1998, *Fairer, Faster, Firmer*, which all sought to minimise the attraction of the UK to 'economic migrants' (which has become a term of abuse) and removed access to social benefits and ensured that cash benefits were as small as possible (Ratcliffe, 2004). In recent years, the UK government has introduced a Points Based System (PBS). The PBS classes potential immigrants into five tiers, ranging from Tier 1 for highly skilled workers, to Tiers 3–5 for low-skilled workers, students and temporary workers. The overall purpose of this policy, as Theresa May the Home Secretary has claimed, is to limit net immigration from 'hundreds of thousands to the tens of thousands'.

Currently, the top 10 countries for migrants registering to work in the UK in 2009/10 are (in order): India, Poland, Republic of Lithuania, Republic of Latvia, Pakistan, Bangladesh, Romania, France, Nigeria and Nepal (IPPR, 2010). Of those living in the UK, 11.3 per cent were not born in the country.

Asylum seekers are also dispersed across the country into properties that may be a long way from family, friends or those from their country of origin. As such, asylum seekers are often forced into a state of poverty that would not be acceptable for any other citizen in the United Kingdom. It is thus of little surprise that Humphries claims:

> That immigration controls are inherently racist, and no account of 'acting in anti-discriminatory ways' will remedy that basic truth. I also hold that the extreme example of social work's relationship to immigration controls typifies its relationship to social policy generally, in that on the whole it adopts a role of subservience in implementing policies that have exposed the most vulnerable UK populations. (Humphries, 2004: 95)

Although this section has tended to focus on issues of race, the reader should be aware that just as 'black' is a problematic term so is 'white', to the point that Garrett (2000, 2003) claims that the racism experienced by the white Irish has been overlooked in the United Kingdom and that the mortality rate of Irish males is the only rate that is higher in the United Kingdom than it is in the country of origin. Race is only one aspect of anti-oppressive practice and simultaneously we are also male or female; or white; disabled or non-disabled; heterosexual, gay/lesbian/bisexual or transgendered; upper, middle or working class and so on. We all have more than one defining identity characteristic. Some of these attributes will imply privilege and power whilst others may render us oppressed. What about the 'structural position of a white, working class, homeless male with that of a black barrister' (Macey and Moxon, 1996: 303). As McDonald and Coleman (1999) suggest, hierarchies tend to be unworkable in practice and need to be understood as component parts of an oppressive system.

Associated with this criticism is the lack of attention given to the social division with which social work is most closely associated, that of becoming a service user and the receipt of social work or social care support. In particular, Wilson and Beresford (2000) highlight the failure of social work to address the oppression minority group members experience as service users. In doing so, they highlight five concerns about the current operation of anti-oppressive practice as it relates to service users. In particular they argue that it:

- Appropriates users' knowledges.
- Uses and reinforces inherently oppressive knowledge about service users, for example, a biomedical model of madness and distress.
- Reinforces constructions of 'clients' as passive and low status by controlling ideas of 'anti-oppressive practice' and knowledge of 'oppression'.
- Mirrors and masks traditional professional power.
- Provides continued legitimation for controlling and problematic social work practice. (Wilson and Beresford, 2000: 569–70)

For Wilson and Beresford (2000), social work – far from being part of the answer – is part of the problem.

Healy (2005) also refers to the conflictual nature of anti-oppressive practice, citing Thompson's (1997: 159) assertion that the prefix 'anti-' is very significant as it symbolises the fight against powerful forces. She is concerned that such a view polarises postures into 'them' and 'us' positions, neglecting the reality of social work that is often practised at the margins and in the grey areas of society where negotiation and compromise are essential.

Healey (2005) also raises concerns about the appropriateness of anti-oppressive approaches in relation to 'high-risk' situations. If practitioners favour structural analysis and neglect individual psychological and personal factors, then they may leave children vulnerable to the risk of child abusers or women to the risk of domestic violence. It is also argued that this approach underplays how power can be used by social workers to support and protect vulnerable people. What may be experienced as oppressive by an abuser, may be viewed as a lifeline by those being abused.

Cultural Competence in Social Work

Laird (2008) criticises social work training for being too focused on the power relations between white social workers and black service users and for paying insufficient attention to social work as an encounter between people of differing cultural backgrounds. This has resulted in women of Afro-Caribbean and Asian heritage failing to obtain help in domestic violence situations as social workers relied on notions of 'cultural privacy' and respect and were unwilling to challenge community leaders or feared being labelled a 'racist'. As Bhatti-Sinclair (2011) reminds us, 'black' as a political statement can cover people from Asian, South American, Afro-Caribbean, Far Eastern, Middle Eastern, African heritage, whilst the Asian countries can be further split into Indian, Pakistani, Bangladeshi, Vietnamese and Chinese people, who could be further split into racial, cultural or geographical groupings and so on.

Cultural competence is a contested and 'murky' concept that refers to those not only from the non-majority ethnic culture but also to other forms of identity markers, including disability, gender, sexual orientation, age and so on (Harrison and Turner, 2011). Cultural competence is an integrated and mandated aspect of social work training in the USA, where the National Association of Social Workers (NASW) (2001: 11) has identified cultural competence as:

> The process by which individuals and systems respond respectfully and effectively to people of all cultural, languages, classes, races, ethnic backgrounds, religions, and other diversity factors in a manner that recognizes, affirms and values the worth of individuals, families and communities and protects and preserves the dignity of each.

Within this document NASW also distinguishes a number of standards to support cultural competency, including ethics and values, cross-cultural skills, empowerment and advocacy. Laird (2008: 39–40) also makes the point that:

> It is not possible to be an anti-racist without knowledge of another's cultural values and norms. Such a position neither necessitates essentialising other cultures nor demands the abandonment of challenging racism. Indeed recognising the cultural differences between self and others while endeavouring to accept the norms of other people.

Whilst Laird is focused on race, anti-racist could be replaced by anti-ageist, anti-disablist, and so on, reflecting the other common identity markers. Cultural competence is an ongoing process that requires social workers to be able to stand outside their own cultural heritage and to be able to meet service users and carers within the perspective of their own cultural context. In doing this, the worker needs to avoid essentialising or making assumptions or stereotyping a particular culture, positively or negatively.

Sue's (2001) 'Multi-dimensional model of cultural competence' is based on the universal, group and individual levels and recognises the need not only to be able to acknowledge differences between the service user and the practitioner, but also to appreciate the differences between service users from the same cultural background. In this three-level model, he argues that *all humans are alike* – we have the same physiological make up, we all use symbols and share similar life experiences. At the next level down, *all individuals are, in some respects, like some other individuals* – whereby each of us is born into a set of beliefs and values that is mediated by membership of a range of different reference groups that may be based on gender, age, ethnicity, religion, sexual orientation and so on. Third, at the individual level, *all individuals are in some respects like no other individual* – we each have our own genetic endowment and social upbringing with our own unique set of experiences that makes us an individual and different from anyone else (Sue, 2001, in Laird, 2008: 42–3). It is thus imperative that for the culturally competent social worker to maintain an open dialogue between people from different cultural backgrounds that each service user or carer emerges as a unique individual in their own right.

Anti-Oppressive Research

At this stage of the chapter, you are invited to reflect upon your position in relation to oppression and write down some of the key messages that you have learnt. Having done this, you now need to consider how these messages help to inform the need for an anti-oppressive research approach.

On reflecting upon your position you may have identified some of the things below:

- Oppression exists.
- Am I part of the problem or the solution?
- Am I racist?
- Anti-oppressive practice is contentious and difficult.
- Anti-oppressive practice makes me feel uncomfortable.
- Anti-oppressive practice exists at a number of different levels.
- Anti-oppressive practice is embedded in social work values, but is more difficult to see in practice.
- Anti-oppressive practice confronts me with issues of power and discrimination.
- Potentially, if not actually, I am both an oppressor and oppressed.
- Anti-oppressive practice is about challenge – to oneself, one's agency and society generally.
- Concepts like 'race' are mere social constructs that have major life-influencing implications for us all.
- Anti-oppressive practice is about empowerment.

Your list may be much longer than the list identified above, although hopefully it has included some of the comments above. As already noted, anti-oppressive practice – as with research – is driven by moral and ethical value codes that explicitly challenge sources of privilege or power that are based on unjustifiable differences. Butler's (2002) code of research ethics adopted by the British Association of Social Workers states that:

> Social work and social care researchers must not tolerate any form of discrimination based on age, gender, class, ethnicity, national origin, religion, sexual orientation, disability, health, marital, domestic or parental status and must seek to ensure that their work excludes any unacknowledged bias. (Butler, 2002: 245)

Within the code there are references to 'working together' with 'disempowered groups' in ways that 'aim to promote social justice' (Butler, 2002: 245). As identified in Chapter 4, neither social work nor social work research are ethically neutral and both aim to empower whilst promoting the welfare of service users and ensuring access to social and economic capital on equal terms with other citizens. For example, some communities are still underrepresented in research, such as Chinese communities and newly arrived populations. No single approach will meet the needs of all groups. The circumstances of Chinese elders may differ from that of Afro-Caribbean elders or Anglo-Saxon elders. Also, as with older people generally, each person's circumstances will be unique. It is also possible that within such categorisations other forms of discrimination, like being disabled, may be marginalised or underrepresented. It should also be remembered that whether black and minority ethnic people are born in the United Kingdom or arrived from elsewhere, may significantly impact on their personal experiences, which may not be reflected in research (Hanley, 2005). In contrast, some communities are over-researched. Butt and O'Neill (2005) found that this was the case in a study of black and older people from ethnic minority communities. They claimed that researchers had often asked the same questions and produced the same findings that were evident 15 years ago. In particular, they did not want research for its own sake, but wanted action that would bring about change.

In adopting an anti-oppressive research approach, it could be argued that the researcher is abandoning the notion of objectivity. As Barn (1994) comments:

> Are we abandoning the notion of objectivity if we espouse the principles of anti-discriminatory research? Are we allowing our prejudices, our biases, our pre-conceived notions to come in the way of 'proper academic research'? If we begin to answer these questions, we need to address the whole notion of objective research. Furthermore, if we accept that there is a dialectical relationship between theory and ethnography, objectivity as a concept of purity begins to hold little meaning. (Barn, 1994: 37)

This then raises another issue as to how we are to assess research and in particular research concerning anti-discriminatory research. Hammersley (1995) has highlighted the controversial research of Foster (1990) who studied a multiethnic, inner-city school that was formally committed to anti-racist education and found that there was little evidence of racism amongst teachers or of school practices that indirectly disadvantaged black students. This was irrespective of whether you examined how the students were treated in the classroom or how they were allocated to ability groups. These conclusions challenged the perceived wisdom of the day and resulted in a predominantly negative response. Foster (1991, 1992) provided a robust response to his critics concerning the challenges over his methodological and epistemological assumptions. In particular, Foster's research challenged his critics' assumptive worldviews that took for granted that racism was endemic and institutionalised within society and therefore he could not possibly have found a situation where this was not so. In other words, he challenged a core assumption of the 'anti-racists', who were than placed in an incommensurate position. By definition, Foster's research must have been flawed as its results did not fit into their paradigmatic worldview (see Chapter 3 for a fuller discussion on Kuhn and paradigms). To accept that Foster's research was not flawed would mean that their core assumptions on racism and its ubiquitousness would need to be reconsidered. In order to deal with such a situation, Hammersley (1995) suggests that where there are disagreements about research there needs to be attempts to resolve these on the basis of judgements about the plausibility and credibility of the evidence. This process would then enable the identification of the acceptance of one of the two original positions, or more likely the development of a third. In order to promote the opportunities for an agreement to be reached, Hammersley (1995: 76) proposes the adoption of the following five norms:

- The overriding concern of researchers is the truth of claims, not their political implications or practical consequences.
- Arguments are not judged on the basis of the personal and/or social characteristics of the person advancing them, but solely in terms of their plausibility and credibility.
- Researchers are willing to change their views if arguments from the common ground suggest that those views are false.
- Where agreement does not result, all parties must recognise that there remains some reasonable doubt about the validity of their own positions.
- The research community is open to participation by anyone able and willing to operate on the basis of the first four rules; though their contributions will be judged wanting if they lack sufficient knowledge of the field and/or of relevant methodology. In particular there must be no restriction of participation on the grounds of religious or political attitudes.

Hammersley has tried to identify a structure based on the assumption that researchers are reasonable people committed to the development of knowledge. Topics like anti-discriminatory research put these assumptions to the test, challenging both the researcher and the practitioner who uses the generated knowledge in their practice.

Feminist Research Practice

Given the gendered nature of social work and the overrepresentation of women in social work as practitioners, students and service users, it is also worthwhile examining some of the issues involved in feminist approaches to social work and social work research.

> The majority of qualified workers in social work in the UK are women. The majority of those undertaking qualifying training in the UK are women. Why do you think that this might be so? What, if any, do you think are the implications of this for social work practice and research? Should we be seeking to bring more men into social work?

Reflexive Questions

Feminist perspectives have played an important role in the development of social work practice. However, it should not be assumed that there is one feminist position or approach. Harvey writes that:

> There are a number of different feminist views about the nature and mechanisms for the oppression of women. A lot of prefixes have been added in various combinations to feminism: socialist, Marxist, bourgeois, radical, positivist, idealist. Unfortunately, these labels have all not been used to mean the same thing, nor are they mutually exclusive. More profoundly, the theoretical positions embodied in different perspectives are not necessarily distinct. (Harvey, 1990: 106)

It is thus quite difficult to tie down the feminist perspective and instead we identify feminist approaches. Payne (2005) identifies five different feminist perspectives:

- *Liberal feminism:* seeks equality between men and women, particularly in the workplace, caring and family responsibilities. For the liberal feminist the answer to inequality lies in promoting equal opportunities by legislation, challenging and changing social conventions and modifying the socialisation process so that children do not accept gender inequalities.
- *Radical feminism:* highlights patriarchy, roughly translated as male dominance. This view values and celebrates the differences between men and women and seeks to promote separate women's structures within existing organisations.

- *Socialist or Marxist feminist:* women's oppression is viewed as part of structural inequality within a class-based social system. Women's role is conceptualised as reproducing the workforce for capitalism, childcare and domestic tasks. Oppressive relations need to be studied alongside other forms of oppression and class-based structures so that diverse interests can be met appropriately.
- *Black feminism:* this came about as a reaction to white feminists who saw the omni-relevance of gender for all women. This view was challenged by black women who experienced racism as their primary defining characteristic. Black feminists also claimed a heightened awareness of oppression as opposed to white feminists due to their experience of racism. Black feminists look towards connections with other socially oppressed groups to campaign for social justice.
- *Postmodern feminism:* this view identifies the complexities of social relations identifying how discourses help to shape social assumptions about the role and expectations of women. In particular this view adopts the postmodern concern to question categories and to examine social relations in terms of surveillance and discipline in relation to families and social workers. (Payne, 2005: 253)

Each of the above approaches is open to challenge. Liberal feminism can be criticised for ignoring the differences in interests between men and women and promoting equal opportunities. Equal opportunities may not be realised if other aspects of inequality prevent women from grasping the opportunities provided. Radical feminism, with its focus on gender differences and the common experience of women, is criticised for ignoring the diversity between different groups of women. The black feminist position can be criticised for its view that black women have a more complete view of social reality precisely because of their disadvantaged position. Such a view neglects the position of women who may be disabled or lesbian who may claim a similar primacy of position, leading to a potential contested hierarchy of oppressions. Socialist feminism is open to criticism by radical feminism for its failure to explain patriarchy in terms of class and economic oppression. Postmodern feminism can be criticised as it sees gender as a social construction as opposed to a sexual identity.

Each of the differing approaches to feminist scholarship can be seen to contribute to an increased understanding of gender or gender relations. Patriarchy is a key issue for understanding feminist theorising. Roughly translated, it means male dominance. Within feminist approaches patriarchy is fully assumed, identified as negative and in need of being changed. This also includes social research methods that are sometimes described as being 'malestream' and reflecting a 'masculine' view of the world. Feminists, on the other hand, seek to emphasise personal experience in that the 'scientific method', and in particular positivism, neglects the researcher's embeddedness in the sociopolitical world and neglects the importance given to gender relations in structuring this knowledge. At root, the 'male paradigm' denies the relevance of the personal. The personal is not a constituent of knowledge. Feminists reject this view and affirm the validity of direct experience. For feminists, knowledge comes from rediscovering links between the personal and political, affirming women's ways and experiences of knowing and building collective insights through consciousness-raising by forming groups to share experiences and providing mutual support.

Feminist social research approaches use a specific subset of methods and/or select a particular set of topics with the aim of challenging methodologies developed by men and of improving the position of women (Payne and Payne, 2004). In the past research has studied men, not women. Most of this has tended to focus on the public sphere, for example work or crime; the private sphere was overlooked or not considered worthy of research time. This meant that women became invisible as they were often unrepresented and restricted to the private sphere of family and children. Worse, often social scientists wrote as if what applied to men was not only masculine but also 'universal', the use of 'people' often meant 'men'. Feminists highlighted these shortcomings and sought to understand the daily lives and experiences of women. In particular, feminists argued that this required a very different approach to research and this helped promote the development of approaches like ethnomethodology, autoethnography and narratives. These approaches promoted a view that saw the need to relate to other women as 'subjects' not 'objects' moving towards a more collaborative, non-hierarchical and inclusive practice (Oakley, 1981). In seeking to capture women's experiences, feminist research argued that feminist accounts should also include 'feelings, other interests and even unconscious beliefs' (Payne and Payne, 2004: 91).

Feminist research has rightly raised the issues of women's lives and the private sphere to the level of worthwhile research. It has helped us to understand issues, such as teenage pregnancy that has traditionally been seen as stopping teenage girls under 18 from becoming pregnant, with little regard to the male's role in the process. Feminist research reminds social workers of the position of many of the women whom they seek to work with either as women, parents or carers. It also offers lessons for male social workers and social researchers in how to address and work with women's perspectives and the importance of gender for structuring social knowledge. In particular, it offers a timely challenge to patriarchy and a more holistic view of social issues. However, in giving greater priority to women's issues, it is in danger of mirroring the mistakes of previous research by neglecting the role and needs of men. It is very helpful to understand the experience of women who suffer domestic violence. However, we do these women an injustice if we do not also seek to understand why some men behave in this way and also seek to identify interventions that can both protect victims and address the abuser's violent behaviour.

Given the gender bias in social work, it is not surprising that feminist approaches have appeared attractive both in practice and in research. However, Orme (2003) sounds a note of caution: women suffering oppression cannot always be given priority, or even believed. In issues of safeguarding children, the child's needs are paramount even if there is a conflict between their needs and their mother's. This is irrespective of whether it will result in the further oppression of the mother. In research terms, feminist approaches have helped to develop qualitative methodologies emphasising dialogue, mutuality and egalitarian relationships between researchers and those being researched. Feminist research and research practices have aided the development of anti-oppressive research and have helped to ensure that the daily life of women is not forgotten. In particular, feminist research has helped to problematise gender and gender relations, ensuring that these issues are legitimate areas of concern. Central to both the discussions on race and gender has been the importance of empowerment to which we turn to next.

Empowerment

As mentioned above, anti-oppressive research (and practice) seeks to build partnerships with service users and oppressed communities to promote empowerment, but what is empowerment? Empowerment is a contentious term that has become fashionable within health and social care. However, it has been open to criticism over its contradictions (Humphries, 1996) and has been described as an abused and devalued term by Croft and Beresford (1989). Empowerment:

> has been taken to mean challenging service user's exclusion and disempowerment. Two aspects to empowerment are regularly identified: personal and political empowerment. Personal empowerment is concerned with strengthening the individual's position, through capacity and confidence building skills, and assertiveness training, to be able to gain more power. Political empowerment is concerned with seeking to make broader change that will increase objective power (political, cultural, social and economic) available to people. A particular appeal of the idea of empowerment is the way that it can unite these two concerns: individual and social transformation. (Beresford in Hanley, 2005: 15)

It is also worth noting that service users claim that people can only empower themselves, neither researchers nor social workers are in a position to do this for them.

Anti-Oppressive Research Practice

The Research Sponsor

A researcher concerned with researching in an anti-oppressive way will pay attention to who funds the research. Just as a public health researcher is unlikely to accept a commission from a tobacco company, so is it also likely that those researchers adopting an anti-oppressive research practice will only wish to secure funding from organisations that accept an anti-oppressive research orientation, wish to address anti-oppressive issues or at least are open to this possibility. This may restrict funding sources but is also likely to avoid undue future conflict.

The Research Question

In adopting an anti-oppressive research approach, the first challenge for the researcher is to consider their research question. Is it a question that seeks to empower or one that will further discriminate or oppress particular groups. This is not easy, and as can be seen in the example above, privileging the position of children and empowering them may as a result disempower their parents.

Researchers in the future might wish to consider whether they should begin with what black and minority ethnic communities may see as a priority. So, instead of focusing on what people's experiences are of service provision, they may wish to begin with what the research subjects consider to be important. If we do not do this, we run the risk of only identifying those priorities that are important to the researcher and research sponsor and run the risk of further oppressing research subjects. In a similar vein, it is not enough to search for clues as to why black people are more likely to be diagnosed with schizophrenia without asking what are the social processes that contribute to a disproportionate number of black people being diagnosed as schizophrenic. Or, in focusing on domestic violence to stop blaming the victim and begin asking: not, why do battered women stay, but what are the factors and conditions that make battering possible or even acceptable. A common feature of anti-oppressive research practice is to challenge common conceptions, for example children in residential care are all too often focused on as 'a problem' without any acceptance or consideration of their strengths or the social relations that led to them becoming looked after.

Practice Example

Barn 1994 outlined the methodological conflicts and constraints that she experienced when she attempted to undertake an anti-discriminatory research study into the processes involved in the admission of children into care in two local authorities. Barn, a black researcher, attempted to consolidate issues of class and socioeconomic disadvantage alongside issues of race, ethnicity, culture and religion into the research framework. From the outset she experienced problems with the research, where after nine months of negotiation she had failed to gain access to one of the

(Continued)

Reflexive Questions ⌇

(Continued)

local authorities who felt that her research design was too ambitious and that social workers felt their practice was being put under scrutiny, and queried the motives of higher management for agreeing to such a study. Social workers also felt that it would be inappropriate to interview service users and added that if they were to be interviewed the social workers should retain a veto as to who was seen. This raised issues as to when modifications and adaptations in real world research become manipulation by powerful interest groups. In the end this authority withdrew from the study. Another two authorities were approached, but they also refused access. The research thus progressed in only one authority, Wenfold.

In interviews, Barn faced the problem of whether respondents were telling the truth or not. She also considered the issue of whether she could obtain an accurate picture of white social workers' perceptions, especially as they might fear expressing politically incorrect sentiments. In response to black and white parents she felt that the issue was less bound by race as they did not have to fear giving an 'inappropriate answer'. Age, and the question of whether she had children, seemed to be more important than race and gender. The social workers also controlled access to the children and this created difficulties as the social workers felt that it was their job to protect the children. She also felt that social workers would be obstructive in cases where they did not have a good relationship with the child to ensure that the service user did not have an opportunity to express their view. However, Barn also comments that not everyone saw her as an outsider and that she was often mistaken as an employee and needed to assert her autonomy as a researcher.

From Barn's research it is clear how powerful agencies can shape and transform the nature of the research design to the point of denying access. In trying to act in an anti-discriminatory way, a researcher not only needs to address the issues that every researcher faces but also to maintain their commitment to an anti-discriminatory research practice and tread 'the path with much caution, diplomacy and tact' (Barn, 1994).

Barn's example demonstrates some of the difficulties of engaging with an anti-discriminatory research. Those with power are unlikely to wish their power to be threatened or questioned and as such will operate in a way that modifies the research to limit its impact or undermine its operation. Barn's research also reminds us that although as social workers we are all likely to agree that social work should address inequalities and promote social justice, it becomes a more difficult question when it is us and our practice that are under scrutiny – however laudable the aims of the research.

In considering anti-oppressive research, the researcher needs to take account of a number of practical issues, including ensuring any venues are culturally sensitive and accessible. Interpretation and translation services may be required if the research respondents' first language is not English. It is important to discuss the research with the interpreter before it takes place and to avoid using family members for this activity. Whilst it may be convenient to use a family member, the nature of the research may be sensitive to the respondent and they may not want their business known to other family members. Also, a family interpreter may reinterpret the respondent's responses as to what they believe to be acceptable. This need for interpreters can in turn increase the costs of research. This position is further exacerbated, as Hanley (2005) has noted, funding to involve black and ethnic minority communities in research is often under-resourced.

Anti-Oppressive Research Methodology

Anti-oppressive research is more than the need to avoid sexist, ageist, disablist, racist, homophobic and other types of discriminatory language in the use of questionnaires, interviews and writing of reports. Anti-oppressive research also implies the need to treat the research subjects as people and not as objects. As discussed before, there is a need for social work researchers to develop and practice cultural competency whereby they are able to stand outside their own culture and meet research respondents within the perspective of their own cultural context and avoid making assumptions or stereotyping of a particular culture. This may require a collaborative, participatory or emancipatory research approach. Everitt et al. (1992) identify three reasons as to why collaborative research may be beneficial both to the researched and the researcher alike. By giving credibility to the views of those less powerful, the researcher will gain access to the experiences of being discriminated or oppressed and of the behaviours and perspectives of those who oppress. Second, by having due regard for people in the research process, research subjects will become less suspicious of research and engage more honestly. It is also possible that by having one's views and experiences validated by research it will be experienced as empowering, thus increasing the research subject's willingness to share. Third, those with the experiences that the researcher wishes to explore are more likely to be aware of what questions matter and how answers should be interpreted.

Lincoln and Denzin (1998), identifying the crisis of representation of the research subject argue:

> Who is the other? Can we ever hope to speak authentically of the experience of the Other, or an Other? And if not, how do we build a social science that includes the other? The short answer to these questions is that we move to including the Other in the larger research processes that we have developed. (Lincoln and Denzin, 1998: 411)

In anti-oppressive research, this will imply not only working in ways that knowingly do not harm the research respondent, but also seeking to engage them effectively in the process. Heron (1996) identifies this requirement as the demand for a participative paradigm of social research including both epistemic and political concerns. The epistemic suggests an epistemology that asserts the participative relation between the knower and the known, sometimes referred to as the Other, and where the Other is also a knower, between knower and knower (Other). Knower and the known are not separate in this relationship, with the degree of participation being partial and open to change. Methodologically, such an approach commends the validation of research outcomes through the:

> congruence of practical, conceptual, imaginal and empathic forms of knowing among co-operative knowers, and the cultivation of skills that deepen these forms. (Heron, 1996: 11)

Politically, this view values human development as intrinsically worthwhile and achievable through participative decision-making.

Clifford (1994) summarises what he sees as the key features of an anti-oppressive research. An anti-oppressive research strategy would be:

- Anti-reductionist and historically specific: placing any explanation within a historically specific context and avoiding explanations based on biology, psychology and economics.
- Materialist: relating any explanation to the divisions of material wealth and power in society.
- Combining the personal and political.
- Thoroughly analysing 'difference': placing individual and groups within all the social divisions.
- Internationalist: being aware of the wider contexts which affects us all either indirectly or directly.
- Reflexive: the researcher or observer is accountable for the methods used and the knowledge claimed which does not exist outside the framework at some value-free point, but is part of the social action and thus part of the research. (Clifford, 1994: 104)

Research Dissemination

An anti-oppressive research approach would also consider the nature of the dissemination process. This would take into account how the research would be disseminated to those who were party to its production. Issues like the use of plain English, trade journals, translated versions into the subject's first language, videos, podcasts, vodcasts, DVDs and presentations all need to be assessed in order to build an effective and accessible dissemination strategy.

Ideally this strategy should be identified at the start of the process, appropriately funded and checked out with the research subjects as the research progresses. On top of this the researcher needs also to ensure, as far as is possible, that what they publish will not result in future or present harm to the research subjects.

The anti-oppressive researcher also needs to consider how they will manage the publication and dissemination of their research, particularly if this is critical of current practice or in opposition to a sponsor's views. As already mentioned in Chapter 4, gaining commissioner agreement to publication can be a very difficult and trying process, particularly where the results can be seen as disadvantageous, reputational or an embarrassment to the research commissioner.

Summary

This chapter has sought to identify the importance of anti-oppressive practice to social work, particularly using the exemplar of race and showing how this can be translated into research. The chapter began by noting that anti-oppressive practice is a historically contentious arena and although usually associated with class, race, gender, disability and sexual orientation, it is not limited to these defining characteristics and may include ageism, colonialism, urbanism and other defining characteristics by which one group becomes identified and oppressed by another. The challenge here is not to develop a longer list than anyone else but to be able to see how such social constructs act as defining or identity characteristics, which are often left unseen and unchallenged, and how these impact on services and (potential) service users.

Anti-oppressive practice in the context of research needs to be considered critically. As this chapter has shown, individuals are not uni-dimensional, people may be white, female, disabled and so on, and some of whose cross-cutting characteristics will necessarily interact with each other. Concepts like 'blackness' and 'whiteness' have been shown to be problematical and potentially restrictive. We should thus avoid seeking to establish a hierarchy of oppression or a mathematical additionality of oppressions as some of these characteristics will impact differently in different circumstances.

Anti-oppressive research implies challenge at the personal, cultural and institutional levels. Anti-oppressive research is not only about the research question and outcomes, but, importantly, about how the research is undertaken. Anti-oppressive practice is a key concept for both social work practice and research; it covers contested terrain and is associated with challenge and rebalancing social relations.

Suggested Reading

Daltymple, J. and Burke, B. (2006) *Anti-Oppressive Practice: Social Care and the Law*, 3rd edn. Buckingham: Open University Press.
Although this book focuses largely on using the law it has become a classic, highlighting the principles of anti-oppressive practice and the empowerment of service users throughout.

Healy, K. (2005) *Social Work Theories in Context: Creating Frameworks for Practice*. Basingstoke: Palgrave Macmillan.
A thought-provoking book that includes a considered critique on anti-oppressive practice.

Laird, S.E. (2008) *Anti-Oppressive Social Work: A Guide for Developing Cultural Competence*. London: Sage.
A critical book providing a sound rationale for developing a greater awareness of and need for social workers (and researchers) to become culturally competent.

Truman, C.E., Mertens, D.M. and Humphries, B. (eds) (2000) *Research and Inequality*. London: UCL Press.
A collection of papers focusing on research and the challenges involved in researching oppressed groups in a non-oppressive way.

6 Evidence-Based Practice

Introduction

This chapter will identify how research has sought to influence practice. In particular the chapter will examine the importance of the growth of 'evidence-based practice' and how it has spread from the field of medicine to many other areas of human endeavour, including social work. The chapter will consider how 'evidence-based practice' has been differently interpreted within medicine and the fields of social work and probation. The chapter also provides a critique of evidence-based practice and the different ways that it can be used to support practice and policy.

> What do you think 'evidence-based practice' means? Can you write down your definition? Can you think of any research evidence that you have used to inform your practice? Where did you get your research from and how did you know that the research was credible?

Reflexive Questions

Evidence-Based Practice

Evidence-based practice has been one of the success stories of the 1990s. When I began writing this chapter for the first edition in 2006 of this book, I put 'evidence-based practice' into Google and it identified 3,490,000 references; in March 2011 this had expanded to 11,700,000. Sheldon et al. (2005) remind us that evidence-based practice (EBP) is not a new phenomenon in social work and points to the work of the Joseph Rowntree and Mary Richmond, along with the President of the American National Association of Social Workers who in 1931 stated:

> I appeal to you, measure, evaluate, estimate, appraise your results in some form, in any terms that rest on anything beyond faith, assertion and the 'illustrative case'. Let us do this for ourselves before some less knowledgeable and less gentle body takes us by the shoulders and pushes us into the street. (Cabot, 1931:6, quoted in Sheldon et al., 2005:12)

In recent years EBP has rapidly become a global phenomenon, with practice manuals, methodological networks, research centres, journals, newsletters, tool-kits, software packages, websites and email discussion groups (Tinder, 2000a). EBP has also been trumpeted in various government publications, including, for example, the Department of Health (1998b, 1999a). Grady (2010: 400–1) in the *Journal of Evidence-Based Social Work* claimed that:

> There is growing consensus that if schools of social work are to remain competitive and relevant in the field of mental health then their courses of study must steep students in the principles of evidence-based practice …effective teaching of EBP principles will launch a new generation of social workers who are committed to practicing within an EBP framework. Such commitment to an EBP will not only strengthen practice at the individual- and agency-level but also will increase the social work profession's competency in EBP.

EBP has spread from an approach championed by medicine to cover most health-related fields, including dentistry, public health, pathology, nursing and physiotherapy and to more distant fields, including management, education, probation and social work. EBP would appear to promise clear and simple answers to difficult and messy problems and offer certainty in an otherwise uncertain world. This book's concern is with social work, but we cannot begin to understand EBP without first returning to medicine.

Supporters of evidence-based medicine claim that it was developed in order to bridge the gap between research and practice. In medicine this gap is potentially, quite literally, life-threatening. For example, Antman et al. (1992) demonstrated that the majority of contemporary textbooks recommended treatments for myocardial infection that were of proven worthlessness.

Sackett et al. (1977: 71) are generally accepted as the starting point for evidence-based medicine with the quoted definition:

> the conscientious, explicit and judicious use of current best evidence in making decisions about the care of individual patients, based on skills which allow the doctor to evaluate both personal experience and external evidence in a systematic and objective way.

'Conscientious', 'explicit' and 'judicious' are all terms open to challenge and interpretation. 'Conscientiousness' refers to being diligent and taking great care and at another level to acting in response to one's conscience. We would all probably agree that professionals like doctors and social workers should act diligently and in accordance with their conscience, so long as their conscience is reflective of our own ethical system. For example, do we wish a doctor to allow a terminally ill patient to die with dignity even if this may mean shortening their lifespan? Questions like this are more difficult to answer and are likely to be dependent upon our own ethical and moral code. 'Explicit' refers to something being precisely and clearly stated whilst 'judicious' implies proceeding from good judgement. Evidence in social work has not achieved the position whereby everything can be precisely or clearly stated, nor in working with people is it ever likely to be a question of mathematical or causal certainty. Working with people still requires a passion for humanity, a belief in human potential and a willingness and commitment to go beyond normal expectations. It is a truism to say that we want professionals to act with good judgement, but who is to decide what 'good judgement' is and what is good enough 'evidence' to base that judgement on. Inherent in the medical version of EBP is the notion that the doctor knows best.

The Cochrane Collaboration, an international not-for-profit organisation, has supported and promoted the development of evidence-based healthcare through providing up-to-date information about the effectiveness of healthcare interventions. The Cochrane Collaboration produces and makes available systematic reviews of the effectiveness of health and social care interventions. These reviews are based on the hierarchy of evidence stated below, with the most credible and trustworthy at the top and the least credible at the bottom.

1. Several systematic reviews of randomised control trials or meta-analyses.
2. Systematic reviews of randomised controlled trials.
3. Randomised control trials.
4. Quasi-experimental trials.
5. Case control and cohort studies.
6. Expert consensus.
7. Individual opinion.

(Becker and Bryman, 2004: 57)

The Cochrane Collaboration's hierarchy of knowledge can thus be seen to favour quantitative research at the expense of qualitative. Alongside the Cochrane Collaboration is the Campbell Collaboration, which was founded in 2000 to help make well-informed decisions about effectiveness in the social, behavioural and educational arenas (www.campbellcollaboration.org.uk).

Macdonald (2003) has written a helpful SCIE report on systematic reviews for improving social work. In this she identifies the following four key features of systematic reviews:

- Systematic reviews are reviews that have been conducted in ways that minimise the chances of system bias and error.
- Systematic reviews are characterised by explicitness and transparency. Protocols are an essential feature of a systematic review.
- The best systematic reviews are produced by teams comprising users, practitioners and researchers.
- Systematic reviews do not remove the need for judgements. (MacDonald, 2003: 3)

MacDonald and Popay (2010) observe that unsystematic reviews can mislead as relying on experts can result in such experts overweighting their research in comparison to those without a national or international reputation. The explicitness and transparency of systematic reviews as reflected in their protocol allows others to assess the internal and external validity of the studies under examination and their recommendations for practice.

Evidence-Based Probation

Within the social welfare field, EBP in the UK has been most enthusiastically embraced by the probation service. Probation officers work with offenders in the community and prisons whilst also being an integral part of Youth Offending Teams. In the 1970s, probation, and work with offenders, was best summed up by the phrase 'nothing works'. The 'nothing works' era in British probation is usually symbolised by the IMPACT study (Folkard et al., 1976). This famous study allocated probation officers at random to 'standard' or 'intensive' caseloads to investigate whether the results would be better when probation officers had more time to work with their clients. The overall result was that those who received the 'intensive' probation, the experimental group, were slightly more likely to reoffend than those who only received the normal probation programme. This study suggested that getting more probation officer input made things slightly worse than having less probation officer input. However, it should be noted that no advice was given as to what 'intensive' meant and there is no means of comparing what actually happened with the two groups.

This rather depressing message of 'nothing works' slowly began to be challenged. By the 1990s, the probation service began to rediscover its faith in its own methods as positive results were found in learning-theory-based methods of practical work with offenders. This later led to what Raynor (2003) described as:

Recent history's most spectacular example of wholesale conversion to evidence-based practice can be found in the National Probation service of England and Wales. (Raynor, 2003: 334)

To back up this assertion, Raynor notes that the first What Works conference was held in 1991; the launch of the Effective Practice Initiative in 1995, along with the publication of McGuire's edited collection of What Works conference papers (McGuire, 1995) and the *Underdown Report* on effective supervision (Underdown, 1998). These were then followed up by the launch of What Works pathfinder projects and the Joint Accreditation Panel in 1999. The promotion of 'what works' engendered an optimism that appropriately implemented accredited interventions would lead to a reduction in reoffending and a subsequent reduction in the prison population.

Merrington and Stanley (2000, 2004) reviewed the evidence on the effectiveness of 'what works' interventions in probation. Most of the studies included in the evaluation were based on cognitive behavioural principles. In assessing the impact of the research, they noted that the results were often less than those suggested by the research. This disparity is potentially explainable by both the complexity in the intervention and its evaluation. Programmes are difficult to evaluate and compare and as yet there is no clear 'winner' among the range of available interventions. They do not suggest that evidence-based probation is finished but argue for more targeted research to help identify which programmes are the most promising and which are not.

Underdown (1998) and Chapman and Hough (1998) also point out that the introduction of accredited programmes is not sufficient in itself to address offending behaviour; this still required the exercise of good case management skills. This additional factor creates problems in deciding upon effectiveness, as good case management will ensure that the offender is admitted to the right programme when they are receptive whilst supporting and reinforcing their learning during and after the programme. All of this creates difficulties in attributing cause and effect as the research has yet to distinguish between outcomes in response to good case management and those due to offender motivation (Merrington and Stanley, 2004).

Overall, Raynor (2003) accepts that this revolution within the probation service has not been without its critics. He accepts that EBP has yet to accommodate sufficiently issues of diversity – tending to focus on majority as opposed to minority groups – and has not been well served by its managerial arrangements. He does note though that it is not dependent on psychologists or cognitive behavioural approaches and that a return to some golden bygone age of 'nostalgic illusion' would be a mistake. Instead, he argues that:

> the way forward for probation services is more likely to be found by broadening and extending the evidence-based approach than by abandoning it. If the National Probation Service wants to pursue the reforming mission shared by most of its staff by providing alternatives to more punitive and less constructive sentences, it is not enough to show that an ever-increasing prison population is not cost-effective. It is also necessary to *demonstrate* (not simply to claim) that community penalties can provide greater tangible public benefit more reparation to the community, greater opportunities for offenders to change their behaviour, and in the long run a reduction in offending. (Raynor, 2003: 342, italics in original)

Evidence-Based Social Work

The development of EBP has been somewhat more contentious in social work. This may be because probation is a much more focused service whose primary role is to reduce offending, whilst social work has a much wider service user base and broader and often contested societal remit. This is not to say that EBP has not made inroads into social work practice:

> When professionals intervene in people's lives they should do so on the basis of the best available evidence regarding the likely consequences of their actions. Put simply, they should be as confident as possible that what they do will (1) bring about the changes sought, and (2) will do so without adverse consequences. (MacDonald, 2008: 435)

MacDonald one of the major proponents of evidence-based social care practice reminds us that as social workers it is not enough just to be well intentioned and well resourced. We can do more harm than good even when we are convinced that we are doing good. As social workers we have to be aware of the outcomes of our interventions. Social work interventions are not neutral: they can either improve or worsen a situation, or possibly even worse, have no impact at all. All too often as social workers we do not have the evidence to know whether our intervention has improved or exacerbated a family.

EBP rightly reminds us of the importance of outcomes. Too often, it is argued, social work has become overly preoccupied with processes at the expense of the task. However, it should be remembered that the best, and most enduring, outcomes will be achieved through the most effective processes. Ascertaining cause and effect is neither simple nor straightforward.

'What Works?'

EBP has rightly focused social workers on outcomes and resulted in a plethora of publications about 'what works', for example on early years (MacDonald and Roberts, 1995), child protection (MacDonald and Winkley, 1999), or leaving care (Stein, 1997). All of these publications identify that generally successful interventions are characterised by being well-organised, structured, focused, time limited and contractual. The production of such research-based practice suggests that interventions can be replicated and social workers, the delivery system, can be trained to deliver these interventions whilst maintaining programme integrity. The most extreme case of this view was experienced by the author at a conference for chief executives to mark the introduction of Youth Offending Teams. At this conference a chief executive offered his vision of the future for youth justice workers.

In this future youth offending team, workers would only be allowed to intervene using previously accredited evidence-based programmes. Having assessed an offender, the worker would then match the nature of the offence and the offender's behaviour to an accredited programme and then implement the intervention. The programme – as it had previously been accredited – would work and if it did not, he would be asking the worker what they had done wrong! This extreme managerialist approach, however, does capture one of the key criticisms of the EBP debate in that it is associated with prescriptive management at the cost of professional autonomy.

EBP contains an inherently positive feel. It challenges bureaucratic logic – the logic that proclaims that things are alright as they have always been done this way, and politics – which promotes the art of the possible rather than the logical (Nutley and Webb, 2000). In fact, it would appear almost heretical for a research book to be critical about EBP. However, I would like to raise some questions about the current overly medically colonised version of EBP. To begin with, I would like to give the reader a health warning: no evidence of no effectiveness is not the same thing as evidence of no effectiveness. Social workers should not necessarily stop doing something just because there is no evidence that it is effective. For example, we should not stop treating service users or colleagues with respect, even if there is no evidence to suggest that doing so will produce a better outcome. Similarly, not everything that is valuable is measurable and not everything that is measured is of value.

EBP and the Nature of Social Work

The first point to be made here is that social work is not medicine. Social work is not able to control the environment in which practitioners work, nor is there a prescribed level of intervention doses that will cure social work problems. The evaluation of social interventions presents problems not encountered in other, more clinical settings. Social work's service users are not passive recipients of social work practice. Each service user will have their own unique history and understandings, their own unique trajectory of personal and interpersonal problems many of which may not lend themselves easily to monitoring or evaluation. These difficulties and issues are constructed in social interaction with family, friends, work colleagues, acquaintances and the like that remain outside the control of the social worker. Service users are quite likely to have their own view of what is 'wrong' and what needs to happen to put it 'right'. Problems are rarely uni-dimensional or mono-causal, but rather multidimensional and multi-causal impacting on theirs and others lives. Social work is not merely a technical activity, but also a moral, social and political one where we need to learn to live and work with uncertainty, paradox and change.

The extreme form of the above argument suggests that social work represents an art form. EBP challenges this view suggesting that practice should be scientific and objective. This model represents social work as a rational scientific exercise. The rational actor model assumes that social workers will act on the available evidence in a 'clinical' way regarding social workers as 'information processors' operating within a closed model of decision-making (Webb, 2001). Orme and Shemmings (2010) make the point that scientific in this context excludes both professional and service user knowledge and refers to the primacy of the scientist or manager in deciding on the nature of accepted practice. The position taken by this author is that social work is both an art and a science, inextricably entwined in the personal and political. In fact it is the very complexity of social work that demands that social workers engage their hearts and their minds to develop a creative and accountable practice that is research-minded and uses the best knowledge available. If social workers are to avoid the danger of pathologising individuals whose problems are largely the result of wider social factors, and at the same time avoid being rendered impotent by the range of competing theories and explanations, then they need the skills to be able to read and assess competing alternative knowledge sources.

Critique of the Scientific Basis of Evidence-Based Practice

Trinder (2000b) and Webb (2001) both argue that EBP is predicated on a particular model of science as positivistic and behaviourist. RCTs, the 'gold standard' of this model (see Chapter 3 for a fuller discussion on RCTs), allows researchers to postulate causal connections, giving them an edge over other forms of social research. Random controlled trials potentially allow us to control for bias arising from extraneous variables and through randomisation they provide a high degree of high internal validity. However, there are difficulties in considering RCTs for social work. MacDonald (1999), a keen supporter of RCT's and evidence-based practice, acknowledges that for ethical reasons it is not always acceptable randomly to allocate service users, the desirability of large samples are not always practical and the high costs of RCTs make them less attractive to social work researchers. Potentially of greater concern to social work is their lack of explanatory power, given that there is often a loose relationship between our understandings of a social problem, for example domestic violence, and our responses to it.

To illustrate this point, if we were to measure the effectiveness of women's support groups to reduce the re-occurrence of domestic violence, how would we know whether they have been effective or not? If the reported number of incidents of domestic abuse had decreased, can we say that this was because of the new model of domestic violence management, the charisma of the support group leader, the companionship of the other women, an increase in self-confidence and self-esteem, support of a family member or friend, a new job, a new partner or even changes to the violent partner, how are we to know what was most important and generalisable in creating a change? This is also assuming that the women are reporting their positions honestly and not just wanting to make the workers and researchers feel better about their efforts. The study would not be able to tell us what forms of support group work with which victims of domestic violence, or why and under what conditions they work.

This limited explanatory ability leads to a limited purchase on being able to match intervention to service user. The ability to match effective interventions with service users is of critical importance to a practically oriented profession like social work, which demands that its practitioners engage with service users in order to address their problems and issues. On top of this, there is also a classic aggregate net-effect problem (Trinder, 2000b), whereby the positive effects of an intervention for some are cancelled out by the negative effects for others. Overall this results in a mean score, which is neither positively, nor negatively, associated with an intervention that works (or does not). RCTs can identify which interventions are more broadly effective than others, or even make a comparison with where there has been no intervention at all; however, they are limited in their ability to provide practitioners with a clear toolkit of effective interventions.

The EBP cookbook of RCTs, meta analysis, experimental and quasi-experimental designs are all located within an often unacknowledged value system and philosophical version of what counts as knowledge and how that knowledge can be known:

> Evidence-based practice proposes a particular version of rational inference on the part of decision makers. It assumes there exist relatable criteria of inferential evidence based on objectively verdical or optimal modes of information processing. In other words it creates a picture of social workers engaged in an *epistemic process* of sorting and prioritising information and using this to optimise practice to its best effect. (Webb, 2001: 63, italics in original)

EBP assumes that social workers, as rational agents, will be able to draw out the logical consequences of EBP findings. In this they will be able to apply logical principles about the likelihood of actions achieving desired ends that are informed by a behavioural probability calculus. This ignores the context in which social work decisions are often made. Social work decisions are often dependent on decisions outside a rational framework. Social work decisions may be governed by legal statute, agency imperatives, the politics of interagency relationships, professional experience or managerially led initiatives. Social workers are not free agents; they operate within a limited and circumscribed rationality, and EBP's failure to acknowledge this position seriously weakens its usefulness and appropriateness for social work.

Lack of Social Work Evidence of Effectiveness

Within evidence-based practice there is an assumption that we have sufficient robust knowledge on which to base practice. Social work has yet to reach this point. MacDonald et al. (1992) examined 95 research studies, many of which were American, from over fifty journals, which attempted to measure social work effectiveness through the use of experimental, quasi-experimental, pre-experimental, and client-opinion studies. The experimental studies included randomly allocated equivalent-group designs that provided, potentially, the most persuasive evidence of effectiveness. However, such an approach is difficult – both ethically and practically – to achieve in social work. There are major ethical issues in, for example, elder abuse if you decide not to intervene in a group of cases for the sole purpose of measuring the effectiveness of some new intervention or treatment. Quasi-experimental designs regularly have no random allocation and no pre-intervention of matching of intervention and non-intervention groups. Client-opinion studies seek the views of service users of the effectiveness of the services that they receive and whilst this is a potential indicator of effectiveness, it is only one indicator and needs corroboration from other evidential sources. Overall, these studies covered some 18 client groups and sixteen different methods of intervention. Of these studies it would be assumed that the majority would cover high-profile areas of social work, but this was not the case as only thirteen attempted to evaluate child protection work. This dearth of empirical evidence in child protection was also mirrored in other key aspects of social work practice, including work with older people and in mental health. In another review of child protection work, Oates and Bross (1995) identified a range of inclusion criteria containing a sample size of at least six subjects and have a method of comparison where at least 15 per cent of participants in the sample were known to have been physically abused. Over a ten-year period the authors were only able to uncover 25 papers that met the selection criteria, whilst none of these were concerned with routine child protection social work provision.

Trinder (2000b) notes that even in the United States, where empirical research work is at its most advanced, the outcomes of experimental and quasi-experimental work has achieved little. Muluccio's (1998) research into child welfare outcomes in the United States came to the conclusion that findings across a wide range of studies were inconclusive whilst many studies were bedevilled by methodological problems, including issues of inadequate control, underspecified interventions and outcome variables. In response to this, Parker (1998) has proposed a hierarchy for social work knowledge, defining knowledge as tentative, indicative or conclusive. 'Tentative knowledge' is where the evidence suggests that we should pause and take stock. 'Indicative' suggests that we should proceed with caution and 'conclusive' represents the highest level of scientific reliability and validity. For Parker, the bulk of social work's knowledge base remains within the indicative range, with only a small amount being conclusive.

This makes it particularly difficult for social work slavishly to pursue an EBP approach when the evidence is currently insufficiently developed to support practice. There is also a debate to be had as to whether social work can, or ever will, reach such a point. This is not to say that we should not pay due cognisance to what research evidence is available, but it does mean that we are not currently, or may never be, in the position to be totally guided by research evidence. For the evidence-based researcher, this represents a call to arms in that if we would only provide the resources then they would be able to develop the evidence base to answer practitioner questions. This perspective purely sees evidence-based research as a technical exercise in solving problems. One of the difficulties of EBP has been its colonisation by the positivist's rational scientific view that inhibits and constrains its potential to answer researcher and practitioner questions alike. As Trinder (2000c: 236) comments:

> Evidence-based practice tends to fit solutions to problems into its own world view, providing more and better information further refinement of methodological criteria or incorporating consumer perspectives into an evidence-based practice framework. The result is that there are major outstanding issues that the rational scientific model is ill equipped to handle, and would appear unlikely to resolve.

From Trinder's perspective, evidence-based practice is thus too limited a viewpoint in which to place all our faith for research to support practice.

Evidence-Based Practice and the Pragmatists

Trinder (2000b) also makes the interesting observation that EBP in social work has not only been promoted by the 'what works' camp but also by those wishing for research to have a much greater impact on practice, whom she describes as pragmatists (note that this is not the same use of pragmatists as we discussed in relation to mixed methods). These two camps are currently claiming EBP or a variant of it, including evidence-informed research or research informed practice. For the pragmatist, evidence-based practice primarily means practice informed by research. Research in this instance is not restricted to RCTs but also includes qualitative approaches, practice wisdom and service user views. Included amongst these pragmatists are Research in Practice (RiP and RiPfA), Making Research Count (MRC) and the SCIE with its governmental mandate to promote effective social care research.

RiP is a funded partnership between the Dartington Hall Trust, the Association of Directors of Children's Services, the University of Sheffield, local authorities and private and voluntary social care organisations. RiP originally described its aim as promoting 'evidence-based practice and policy in child welfare services' (Trinder, 2000b: 147), but the strapline has since been changed to 'supporting evidence-informed practice with children and families' (www.rip.org.uk). This shift from evidence-based to evidence-informed is highly significant and symbolises a distancing from the pure medical evidence-based model to a more inclusive research-based model. Evidence-informed practice can be summed by the equation:

$$EIP = PK+SU+RE$$

EIP = Evidence-informed practice
PK = Practitioner knowledge
SU = Service user knowledge
RE = Research evidence

RiP maintains an 'evidence bank' that contains a range of research information derived from a diversity of methodologies that has been assessed as useful for practitioners. Uniquely, RiP and RiPfA also target councillors and senior managers in their mission to disseminate research findings in addition to practitioners and frontline managers. RiP has been traditionally associated with child and family social work but following a merger with the Centre for Evidence-Based Social Services (CEBSS) launched an adult's organisation, Research in Practice for Adults (RiPfA).

MRC is a different type of initiative, describing itself as a national programme with local presence. MRC is currently centred on ten universities, each with a lead social work professor. Each university base has a number of paying partners drawn from local authorities, independent social care and health agencies. There are some agencies that are members of both RiP and MRC. Similarly to RiP, MRC is concerned with improving the dissemination and implementation of research findings, along with influencing the shape of evidence-based practice (www.kcl. ac.uk/schools/sspp/interdisciplinary/scwru/mrc/about.html accessed 20 March 2011).

SCIE, has already been identified in Chapter 1, and is an independent company and charity partly funded by the government with the express intention of developing and promoting best practice through empirical research, whether this is based on a quantitative or qualitative perspective. SCIE also seeks to include the service user and carer perspective in their work, incorporating both a rigid methodological approach and a participatory approach to knowledge development (Orme and Shemmings, 2010). SCIE provides a wide range of free reports, knowledge reviews, research briefings, position papers, practice guides and resource guides and the UK's most extensive social care database, social care online (www.scie-socialcareonline.org.uk accessed 7 March 2005).

All three of these organisations, along with organisations such as the Joseph Rowntree Foundation (www.jrf.org.uk), what works for children? (www.whatworksforchildren.org.uk), and the Mental Health Foundation (www.mental-health.org.uk) are committed to the dissemination of research, although the evidence on social worker's willingness to read the social work literature is less encouraging:

> the shorter and less obviously informed by research the piece, the more likely it is to be read by social workers. *Community Care* is regularly read by nearly half (47%) of professionals but only a fifth (19%) frequently turn to specialist books and fewer still (15%) use national guidelines often. The most depressing finding was that 29% never read a specialist book and a fifth were willing to say they never open the guidance which effectively brings to life the Children Act 1989. (Bullock et al., 1998: 67)

Although the above research focused on children and family teams, it is hard to imagine that the situation with adult teams is any different. In my own experience of social work *Community Care* has always been very popular, but what this high readership rate does not tell us is whether the workers read *Community Care* for its articles or just for the job adverts. Nor does it take into account that for many workers this is a free publication delivered to social work offices. In response to this concern about the dissemination of research, both RiP and MRC have developed experimental projects to identify more effective and creative ways of providing research evidence for social workers.

Clearly, organisations like RiP, RiPfA, MRC and SCIE are committed to ensuring that research makes an impact on practice. There is a compelling argument that social work practice should be informed by research in order to ensure the optimisation of effective outcomes. However, as we have already seen, social work is not identical to the biological basis of medicine, nor does it have a sufficiently sized evidence base and importantly, nor would RCTs necessarily provide the answers to social work questions.

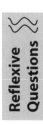

At this point you may wish to consider the question that even if there was clear research evidence would you, or your social work colleagues implement research findings that seemed to contradict what you believed to be the case? This is a question we will return to later.

For the pragmatist there is an acceptance that if research can be helpful to practice it is useful, irrespective of the research paradigm or method that produced it.

Evidence-Based Practice and the Future

It would be all too easy to suggest that evidence-based practice has become a managerialist political slogan and has no place within social work. To support such a view would be to undermine the potential contribution that evidence-based practice offers social work to become a more research-informed practice. Evidence-based practice has rightly focused on outcomes, stressed the need for reducing bias in research, promoted internal validity of research and sought to encourage service user perspectives. Importantly, the whole debate around evidence-based research has raised fundamental questions as to what should constitute evidence and as to how research should inform practice:

> It is important that all evidence be treated with caution. The methodological rigour of evidence-based practice conveys a sense of certainty and authority. As we have seen, however, absolute authority is rarely to be found. There are major areas where evidence is lacking, questions about the extent to which evidence can be trusted (meta-analysis), questions about the applicability of evidence in real-life cases and concerns about the narrowness of evidence and narrowness of outcomes. In some areas certainty is more founded, whilst in other areas, beyond the biological, the search for certainty poses considerable danger in inherently complex and uncertain worlds. (Trinder, 2000c: 237)

EBP has also brought welcome attention to the part played by research in informing practice, although it has on occasions suggested simplistic solutions to complex problems. Initiatives like RiP, RiPfA and MRC are to be welcomed, finding favour with government and social work agencies alike in order to ensure that research evidence makes an impact on practice.

EBP, though, has tended to deal with the complexity of the human condition and the political processes of research as if they were technical problems to be eliminated and overcome, suggesting greater certainty than the model deserves or can deliver on. As we have seen the model – and its dependency on RCTs – does not transpose well to social work. This is not to say that RCTs are inappropriate in social work, but that there are limited opportunities to develop RCTs and that the knowledge that they generate is not necessarily the most useful to social workers nor should we necessarily privilege this method of generating knowledge above all others. The definition of evidence needs to be expanded to go beyond RCTs and the claims of EBP need to be reduced to mirror their ability to deliver and inform social work practice.

MacDonald and Popay (2010) have sought to distance themselves from the more 'clinical' expositions of EBP by acknowledging and emphasising the need to incorporate the subjective understandings that service users and carers have of their experience. In particular they highlight the need for acceptability, accessibility and relevance/appropriateness of research. Acceptability indicates the need to develop and evaluate interventions that people want or find acceptable. They use the example of physical disability, highlighting the point that people with disabilities want interventions based on a social model of disability as opposed to the medical model that they view as reinforcing inequality and discrimination. Accessibility denotes that as well as being relevant, interventions should be available to those who wish to access them, and the eligibility criteria in research proposals should, where possible, be inclusive. They identify appropriateness as important:

> In order to improve social work intervention we must find out what matters to people and ensure that service development and evaluation does not just stem from the interests of policy makers and researchers. (MacDonald and Popay, 2010: 268)

This resonates with the rationale for service user involvement in research (see Chapter 8) and challenges the traditional models of EBP with its emphasis on the 'objective researcher'. Having said this, MacDonald and Popay (2010: 272) then go on to reassert the primacy of RCTs with conditions:

> RCTs provide the most secure basis for establishing causal links between outcomes and interventions: and for that reason alone they should occupy a more important place in social work outcome research than hitherto. This is not to say that they are the *only* method relevant to providing evidence of the effects of social work. Their very strength in establishing causation means they are weak in other respects. (Italics in original)

This attempt to broaden the scope of EBP brings it closer to evidence-informed research and research-based practice and potentially begins to open up a more useful dialogue where we can begin to consider which methods in which circumstances are best able to provide the best evidence and knowledge claims to support social work practice – including RCTs, other research methods, professional expertise and, importantly, service user and carer perspectives. Research can help to inform practice but it is not a panacea, it does not stop the social worker from having to make judgements and it is also not pretence as research can help social workers to be aware of which interventions or which issues need to be considered in which context. EBP is seductive and suggestive, especially to managers, in that it can be used explicitly to direct social work practice and it is probably more accurate in social work to talk of the more multidimensional approach of research-informed practice.

Summary

EBP continues to be an important aspect of global health and social care policies. This chapter has sought to define EBP and identify how it has been developed in probation and healthcare and then transposed onto social work and social care. This transposition has been seen to be wanting when we examined the nature of social work and the narrowness of the definition of evidence. This narrow definition results in an unhelpful hierarchy of knowledge, whereby RCTs are seen as the gold standard and stand at the top of the pyramid. If the healthcare criterion of evidence were accepted, it would result in a quantitative social work evidence-base neglecting or in denigrating the value of qualitative research. The chapter has also highlighted how social work 'pragmatists' have embraced this interest in evidence for practice to raise the profile of research and to promote the potential of research as a means of informing practice. For social work there needs to be a widening of the definition of evidence and at the same time a more realistic claim made for the possibilities of EBP as one of the key determinants informing practice, and not merely the only one.

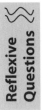

Reflexive Questions

Having read this chapter, what do you think should be considered as evidence in social work practice?
How can we know whether this evidence is credible and trustworthy?
What sources of evidence do you look for to inform your practice?
What level of evidence would be needed for you to change a tried and trusted practice?
Is it feasible or desirable to have evidence-based social work?

Suggested Reading

MacDonald, G. and Popay, J. (2010) 'Evidence and practice: The knowledge challlenge for social work', in I. Shaw, K. Briar-Lawson, J. Orme and R. Ruckdeschel (eds), *The Sage Handbook of Social Work Research*. London: Sage, pp. 264–80.
This excellent chapter provides a clear exposition and rationale for EBP with an attempt to be inclusive to other approaches whilst seeking to champion a more outcomes-based social work practice.

Trinder, L. and Reynolds, S. (eds), 2000 *Evidence-Based Practice: A Critical Appraisal.* Oxford: Blackwell Science.
This is an edited collection of articles looking at evidence-based practice in a range of subject disciplines and suggests that the further you get away from the controlled medical ward, the more difficult it is to achieve the ideal model of evidence-based practice.

7   Getting Research into Practice

Introduction

The title of this chapter comes from an initiative in the early 1980s when I was a child care team leader in practice. Along with a colleague, who was similarly favourably disposed towards research we decided to establish 'GRIP' Getting Research into Practice (not to be mistaken with RiP that appeared a number of years later). Having recruited some like-minded colleagues we organised a conference, which was a great success, and then set up a programme of research seminars for staff in the local authority. These were initially well attended but as time progressed support and energy dwindled with the initiative dying out. Although we tried to resurrect it at a later date this was never successfully achieved. At the stage of the death of the initiative I wondered why my colleagues could not see that research would provide us with the answers to many of our questions and help us to become more effective practitioners and able to deliver a higher quality service.

On a similar theme, it needs to be remembered that even the best research does not necessarily change anything. At times a small study can have effects beyond what could have seemed possible at the outset. It is not possible at the proposal stage to predict accurately the influence that any research may have, although it is possible to try and create a receptive culture for research messages.

This chapter seeks to identify why research has not enthused practitioners and why it has not had the impact on practice that researchers would have liked. As part of this discussion we will examine the proclivities of researchers and practitioners/managers, barriers and drivers for research and the nature of research influence through practitioner researchers, inspection regimes and whole organisation initiatives. The chapter will also consider the publicising of research and identifying some of the current initiatives promoting dissemination.

Before we discuss the barriers to research informing practice, you should consider whether you agree with one of the two following positions: that research has impacted sufficiently on your practice or that it has not. Can you think of an example when you have used research to inform your practice? What reasons did you give for your answer? I would now like you to think about and write down what you see as the barriers to research informing practice.

Barriers to Research Informing Practice

It is always illuminating to ask social workers why they do not use research more often in their practice. Below is a list of some of the answers. No one has yet suggested that they have maximised the contribution that research can make to their practice, although they are not always clear about what has been missing. The barriers from a practitioner's view include:

- I'm too busy.
- Relevant research is not easily found.
- 'Lies, damn lies and statistics.'
- If you are caught reading research someone will assume that you do not have sufficient work to do and give you another case.
- I don't know where to look.
- You can find research to prove anything.
- We don't have access to the Internet/electronic journals.
- Research doesn't address the problems I face in my day-to-day work.
- When you find research it is not easily readable.
- Research complicates matters when all I want to know is what to do next.
- I don't know how to interpret and assess research.

You may have identified some of the above or other possible reasons, but I am sure that you will agree that there are many reasons that are given as to why social workers do not use research more effectively. It should be noted that this chapter does not set out to blame social workers, or for that matter researchers for this set of affairs. Instead, this chapter seeks to understand the range of factors, including organisational and researcher-oriented factors, which militate against a more effective use of research. In many ways this chapter seeks to find a way forward in which research can become 'useful' (for practitioners) and have 'greater impact' (for both researchers and service users). This resonates with our earlier discussions about quality in social work research needing to achieve the twin standards of practical relevance and academic rigour.

Social Worker Issues

'Too Busy'

From the above set of barriers a number of key issues emerge from the perspective of the social work practitioner. Sheldon and Chilvers (2000) have highlighted being 'too busy' or 'pressure of work' as the key obstacle for research-informed practice. From 1341 responses (58.7 per cent of the total distributed), pressure of work was the highest recorded obstacle to developing an evidence-based practice approach (mentioned by 98.3 per cent of respondents). This result (98 per cent) was repeated in a follow-up study in 2002 (Sheldon et al., 2005). The result is not surprising given the acknowledged national staffing shortage at the time, which is likely to be repeated with the implementation of the austerity measures across public services.

It is also worth reflecting on whether even if there were a full complement of social work staff, issues of being 'too busy' and 'work pressures' would still be given as key reasons for not using research. Without a change in the social work culture it is highly likely that this will continue to be the case. For many workers, research continues to be viewed as a luxury or an add-on, rather than embedded in the way that social workers think and work. This view suggests that research will only be considered when there is space and will always be vulnerable as not being a 'real' part of the job.

Inadequate Valuing of Research

The importance of research is also reflected in the comment whereby if someone is seen as having time to read a book or journal then they are not making good use of their time. Associated with this view is the accusatory presumption that such individuals must also have sufficient space to take on extra work. Thus to be seen reading a journal or book implies that you have insufficient 'real' work to do. The perspective represented here is one where research is not seen as a legitimate social work task to undertake in the office. It is also a comment on a view of a social work office as a busy, bustling place where people do not have sufficient time to engage in anything that is not specifically 'work' related. Such a view, although understandable, is potentially very dangerous as it neglects the need to update knowledge continually and to reflect critically on its application to practice.

Between 1998 and 2002, Sheldon and his colleagues indicated that 48 per cent and 46 per cent, respectively, of respondents indicated that they had read literature pertinent to their work in the week prior to the survey, with the number increasing from 45 per cent to 62 per cent of this occurring at home. In both surveys the most popular publication read was *Community Care*. *Community Care* is a trade magazine that is often read from back to front as the back contains the jobs pages and allows social workers to compare their salaries with colleagues in neighbouring authorities. *Community Care* is free to many staff and also contains social work news, opinions and short research pieces, but most importantly it is a prime source of adverts for social care posts.

Research Complicates the World

Research complicates matters is, of course, a valid comment in that research and social work have two differing objectives. Research tends to complicate issues by making them more complex to reflect reality whilst practitioners and policy-makers are more concerned with simplifying things so that action becomes possible (Booth, 1988). There is a genuine tension here, social workers have to act upon the world, whereas researchers help us to understand the world and identify potential interventions. In reality the two operations are linked, but in practice the social worker will not thank the researcher who points out the negative impact of government policies whilst they are faced with a single-parent family living in poverty. Both perspectives are required as the changing of government policies may in the longer term reduce poverty but does not address the immediate, the here-and-now needs of single parents living in poverty.

In a similar vein it can be argued that researchers are more concerned with emphasising dispassionate precision, whilst social workers are embroiled in a world of feelings and messiness. It could be said that researchers are more concerned with the word and social workers with the deed. Researchers become attached to the 'why' question, whilst social workers are more concerned with the 'how' question. It also often seems to be the case that no matter how good the research, it does not match the needs of the practitioner.

One other aspect of this criticism comes from the claim that researchers are more concerned with the development of concepts, whilst practitioners and managers are more concerned with their use. Gopineth and Hoffman (1995) also noted that researchers are able to draw conceptual boundaries around their studies as opposed to the practitioner and manager whose world tends to be less clearly defined, and often messier.

Research is not Valid

There are a few statements that we can consider under this heading that 'Research is not valid', including: 'Lies, damn lies and statistics' and 'You can find research to prove anything'. These two statements suggest that it is impossible to find distinctive answers from research as it can be used to prove anything. We have noted, on more than one occasion, that research is a contested arena, but that this does not mean that anything goes. There is also an increasing body of knowledge within social work research about 'what works', where and with whom. Coupled to this there is also a growing need for a critical research literacy to be able to distinguish between research that should and should not inform practice.

Research Literacy

This section covers the comments concerning the readability of research and the lack of awareness of how to interpret research. The first question identifies a commonly expressed view concerning the accessibility of research evidence. Traditionally research was contained in long research reports or peer-reviewed journals, written for researchers by researchers. It is thus not surprising that practising social workers found research difficult to access, read, evaluate and identify key practice messages.

Many researchers will now also produce research reports that include an executive summary highlighting key messages, thus giving busy practitioners ready access to the results and recommendations. Also, there has been an information revolution with the ability to access research through the Internet, with more and more journals being available online accompanied by a growth in electronic books and databases, allowing practitioners and researchers to undertake quickly computer-based interrogations of journals, books and research reports at the touch of a button. Although, as one response above suggested, not all social workers have access to electronic journals as many local authorities will not pay for these.

This leads us onto the second aspect of the barrier that highlights the difficulty that even if you have the skills to identify and download research articles, how will you know if the information is valid and reliable? Of course, for peer-reviewed articles these will, as their name suggests, be peer reviewed, although this does not guarantee that they will be of the highest quality. As the name suggests, the peer-review process is based on the belief that peer reviewing by two other unidentified academics will quality assure the contents of the article. The reviewers will examine the article's methodology, its ethical approval and content, its readability, contribution to knowledge and whether it is an appropriate article for that journal. The reviewers are also likely to make suggestions about how the article can be improved. There are, however, limitations to the peer-review process as the peer reviewers may have established perspectives or paradigmatic views that may act as a barrier to publishing new or alternative perspectives. This may lead to what is known as 'publisher bias'. The peer review process is not infallible as shown by the case of the infamous MMR paper published in *The Lancet* that suggested that the MMR vaccine was not safe: the paper was later withdrawn by the journal (Murch et al., 2004).

One other aspect of journals is worth noting: that more and more social work journals are seeking to gain, or increase, their impact factor. The higher the impact factor, the more prestigious the journal. Journals apply to Thompson Scientific to be assessed for an impact factor and Thompson Scientific then makes a judgement on the quality or 'citability' of the articles in the journal. Within social work, American journals tend to have the highest impact figures.

However, while this measure carries no guarantee about any individual article it does suggest that, on balance, the journals with higher impact figures are more likely to contain more articles of quality.

The case for books is even less clear as books are published with the intention of making money and not of spreading academic knowledge. If a book can disseminate academic knowledge as well as make a profit then it is a bonus, whilst if it is good science but sells poorly then it will be seen to be a failure. Just because something is published in a book or in a journal does not necessarily make it correct. In order to address this issue of published research the next two sections concern undertaking literature reviews and critically appraising social work research.

Undertaking a Literature Review

There has never been so much published knowledge available for students, social workers and researchers and it is therefore important for research-informed social workers to be able to undertake online database searches using keyword searches, but also be able to search library catalogues, official websites and online repositories of articles/research reports, which many universities have now developed.

Jesson et al. (2011: 10) identify the purpose of a literature review in as follows:

> Where you show that you are both aware of and can interpret what is already known and where eventually you will be able to point out the contradictions and gaps in existing knowledge.

Jesson et al. (2011) identify two major types of literature review, the traditional or normative review and the systematic review. Aveyard (2010: 18) states categorically that: 'There is no place for a narrative review in health and social care'. Aveyard conceptualises the traditional or normative review as having unfocused research questions, lacking a research strategy, with no clear appraisal method and not being repeatable. Jesson et al. (2011) are less damning, claiming that the traditional review is the style most available to undergraduate and postgraduate students, that it is often critical and reflective, providing insights that may be overlooked by the quality assurance steps in a systematic review model. Such a review often features authors whom the writer believes have an important contribution to make to the research question under investigation and seek to develop a logical argument in a systematic way to tell their story and identify why their research is important. A critical review should also access knowledge from all journal sources and not just high-impact journals. Whilst the impact factor may be a general mark of quality, it does not mean that quality papers are not published in other journals with a lower, or even no, impact factor.

Jesson et al. (2011) also contest Aveyard's description that the research question is unfocused and in fact emphasise the importance of defining the research question as essential to the literature reviewing process, irrespective of its type. Systematic reviews in comparison, in Aveyard's (2010: 19) view, contain a well-focused research question, a search strategy with comprehensive and explicit methods, rigorous appraisal, a review method that is repeatable and is 'not for the faint-hearted'. It could also be added that it is usually beyond the scope and finances of most student researchers and is most often undertaken by research teams. However, the appeal of such an approach is in its claim to an objective, transparent, technical process that can be repeated to verify its results. Whilst this fits easily into an evidence-based approach (see Chapter 6), it does not necessarily sit as well with qualitative research approaches.

A traditional literature review may contain peer-reviewed articles, books, professional journals, newspapers, PhD theses, government publications, voluntary or private sector publications, think tanks and Internet publications. A systematic review is likely to be more focused on peer-reviewed articles, the strengths and weaknesses of which have already been discussed earlier in this chapter. As many students and early career researchers have not developed sufficient understanding of the research topic under consideration, they are unlikely to be able to undertake a systematic review. It is thus worth considering adapting the traditional, or narrative review, with its critical and reflective properties matched alongside a focused research question and explicit research strategy to maximise the benefits of a defensible and valid reviewing of the literature.

Critical Appraisal of Social Work Research

As previously noted, for the research-minded social worker, even after identifying relevant literature it is often difficult to choose which research best meets their needs in deciding how to intervene (or not to intervene) in a particular situation. As the benchmark statement for social work qualifying degrees claims, the research-minded social worker must also be able to appraise critically social research and the evidence for social work (QAA, 2008: 5.1.4). Critical appraisal refers to the process whereby the reader looks for the strengths and weaknesses in a research study. To be able to do this, the research-minded social worker has to be 'research literate' and able to differentiate between those studies that they should spend more time on and those that they should not. Just because something is published it does not mean that it is worthy of the social worker's most precious resource, their time.

In seeking to appraise critically an article it is worth asking some questions of each stage or section of the research article. This will help to structure your understanding of the subject and help to identify its strengths and weaknesses whilst breaking the whole into a set of achievable tasks.

Shepperd (2004) provides a useful starting point when he splits up the process of a journal article into problem formulation, literature review, main body of data and conclusion. However, Newman et al. (2005) have developed a more systematised approach to help practitioners appraise quality: decide whether the study is sufficiently trustworthy to justify implementing its results and to consider how relevant the research is to practice. They have developed specialist questionnaires for different types of research study. This book is only going to consider their quasi-experimental (Appendix A) and qualitative research tools (Appendix B). Each tool usefully begins with 'screening' questions, which if answered in the negative the reader is strongly advised not continue to work through the rest of the questions nor apply the research to their practice. If the reader can answer 'yes' to most of the questions then it is likely that the research is of a high quality and that the reader would want to apply the research to their practice or service user decision-making. Conversely, if the answer is 'no' to most of the questions then it should probably not be used to inform practice or decision-making.

> Find an article in a subject area that you are interested in, using either a quasi-experimental research methodology or a qualitative approach, and apply the appropriate questionnaire. Regular applications of these questionnaires will speed up the process and help you to ascertain which articles are deserving of your time and effort and which are not.
>
> **Reflexive Questions**

Both of these appraisal systems have been developed for social work research and provide systematic ways of appraising research material. It should be noted, however, that an increasing number of research studies use both quantitative and qualitative research methodologies. In these cases social workers could use the appropriate critical appraisal tool for those parts of the research process that are quantitative and qualitative, bringing the research answers together at the end. What these tools do not do is remove the requirement for the social worker, or researcher, to engage their critical faculties and exercise their judgement. Critical appraisal tools are not 'black boxes' or 'technical fixes' but structured and standardised ways of making judgements as to the validity and usefulness of a research study.

Reflexive Questions

Researcher Issues

You might like to repeat the first task of this chapter from the perspective of a researcher. What do you consider to be their barriers to research implementation?

In completing the exercise this time you may have considered some of the issues listed below:

- Researchers do not have the same level of job security.
- Differences in time scales.
- Social workers don't read.
- Social workers aren't interested in research.
- Social work does not have a research culture.
- Researchers are driven by the Research Excellence Framework.
- Researchers want sponsors to have the full copy of their experience and work.
- Researchers don't understand the politics or realities of practice.

Some of the ideas that you had may be the reverse of those listed by practitioners, whereby researchers may bemoan the lack of research literacy or willingness of workers to accept complexities, ambiguities and contradictions. However, you may be beginning also to consider alternative explanations embedded in the contexts in which social work researchers operate.

Differing Expectations of Research Outcomes

The researcher and practitioner are likely to have different expectations of the research outcomes. Researchers, understandably favour a substantial report that does justice to all their hard work. Social work practitioners, on the other hand, prefer an executive summary highlighting key issues but most importantly providing straightforward 'realistic' and 'real world' practical solutions to their particular problems and issues. The published word is still the standard for judging academic excellence in research. This is also likely to sustain the position that researchers continue to write for research audiences deliberately avoiding non-academic outlets. If this continues to be the case social work researchers will be missing an opportunity to influence practice and will be failing to connect with other audiences, restricting the growth and potential impact of their research.

Researchers are Politically Naïve

Researchers, managers and practitioners occupy different positions in the political process of the research. It is sometimes claimed that researchers fail to understand the political culture of an organisation and in so doing are unable to understand fully how an organisation operates. Certainly, I have experienced this from both sides of the debate.

> **Practice Example**
>
> As a manager I can still remember a meeting with a researcher who had undertaken research into the implementation of a new policy in our organisation, but whose report the director wished to change. Prior to the meeting with the researcher, the senior management team met together and 'critically' assessed the report looking for points that we could 'demand' to be changed with a view to then being able to get the recommendation that the Director did not like changed. When the researcher appeared, they were warmly welcomed and made to feel comfortable before the full might of the senior management team was brought to bear on them. A couple of years later I met the same researcher, now an established professor in a different context and she advised me that she felt that she had been 'beaten up' by the senior management team. She felt that this had been done totally unfairly as her report, she felt, reflected very positively on the organisation, not negatively as presented at the meeting.
>
> From the other side, as a researcher, I have been summoned to a meeting with local authority senior managers where the first item on the agenda was 'what did the director need to know before they met with their business manager?' In this case the politics of the organisation were such that they did not want certain aspects of a particular policy change being described in the way that the frontline workers wanted it presented, but instead wanted to present a management perspective on the same policy. Such situations are very difficult as in this case there were two irreconcilable views about the need for change, drivers for change and potential benefits – with the workers blaming the management and the management pointing to agency policies and external events. In this type of situation the researcher can easily get caught up in the politics of the organisation and in so doing offend one group or the other, resulting in either the report being left to gather dust on a bookshelf or the workers feeling that they have been sold out! Gladly, following some hard bargaining by both sides, the report was accepted.

Managers, especially senior ones, spend a lot of their time handling relationships with colleagues, the public and the media seeking to gain and maintain influence. As such, they are attuned to the nuances and importance of information and how it may be used and abused. It should also be remembered that researchers need to gain access to organisations in order to obtain their data and in this respect managers can be particularly powerful gatekeepers, opening or closing doors.

In these types of situations researchers need to be able to draw on their value base, interpersonal and political skills to steer a path through such a 'politically' conflictual situation. Certainly, awareness of the political dynamics of the organisation being researched can help the researcher, but it can also compromise the research if the researcher then seeks to appease the powerful interests within the organisation at the expense of the data being considered. Researchers are not necessarily politically naive but they do need to be aware that it is the sponsor who has the final say on whether any changes result from the research or not. These political dynamics become particularly challenging when the sponsor is a government department and is unhappy with the results and conclusions being drawn from the data that they may perceive as being critical of them or the government's policy.

Researcher Employment

Coupled with the last point are the differing employment positions of the researcher and those researched in relation to the research. The two are often working to different timescales. This is not simply because managers and practitioners work to short and demanding timescales whilst good research may take years to complete, write up and publicise. Research contracts will only cover a particular time frame, and once the research is completed the researcher needs to move on to another research project whilst organisational managers and practitioners are likely to remain in their post dealing (or not dealing) with the results of the research.

Differing Worlds of Researchers and Social Workers

It is clear from what has been said that the interplay between the worlds of the social worker and the researcher can, at best, be viewed as problematic. The two worlds suggest a number of incompatibilities in terms of: time and timescales; accessibility of research; differing views of the value of research; differing expectations about the product; and awareness of organisational politics. This can become a defeatist position as it suggests that the received models' view of the researcher and social worker are of occupational groups inhabiting incommensurate worlds. Such a view neglects the point that both social work and research are essentially mediated activities. Neither activity exists in isolation and both are influenced by internal rationales and values and external factors, which serve to mediate and influence the relationship between research and social work. Research impacts on practice, for example the work of Parker (1966) on the likelihood of placement breakdown and the age of foster carers' own children has influenced generations of social workers practitioners. On the other hand, practice influences research, not only because researchers want to study the issues of the day, but also because at least some of these issues – for example, interprofessional working – reappear as among the priorities of funding bodies.

Organisational Issues

Culture

In this chapter we have explored some of the barriers to social workers being able to utilise research and barriers to researchers being able to have their messages heard. Within this process a number of problems have been suggested as social work issues but are in many ways responses to organisational imperatives. The taken-for-granted assumptions within an organisation, the structures within which social workers undertake their task mediate and play a part in promoting or hindering the development of a research culture. The way that organisations use, support, talk about, commission or not commission research provides subtle messages to staff about the importance given to research and its findings. The very culture of an organisation can promote or inhibit the use of research. Schein has usefully defined an organisational culture as:

> The pattern of basic assumptions that a given group has invented, discovered or developed in learning to cope with its problems of external adaptation and internal integration, that worked well enough to be considered valid and, therefore, to be taught to new members as the correct way to perceive, think and feel in relation to those problems. (Schein, 1984: 3)

This classic definition helps us to understand the pervasiveness of culture and how it becomes transmitted to new members 'as the way things are done around here'. Culture acts as a filter, allowing some ideas into the organisation and filtering others out. In relation to research it is possible to see how culture, often from the top down, but not necessarily so, can promote the development of a research-informed culture or act to prevent research becoming part of the organisation's 'way of doing things around here'.

Managerialism

This has been discussed much more fully in Chapter 1 and readers may wish to revisit this chapter. In terms of social care organisations, their performance on key indicators has increasingly become a major driving force for change.

Performance indicators can represent both a push towards a more creative practice or a re-entrenchment of safe practice. The previous UK Labour government had an indicator for placement stability for children whereby local authorities were measured on the percentage of looked after children who experienced more than three changes of placements in a year. This indicator rightly encouraged social workers, and their managers, to find the right placement first time round, but it may also stop young people from moving on to more appropriate placements if it was going to impact negatively on the authority's performance indicator. An over-concern with performance indicators will lead to a functionalist practice orientation that will inhibit creativity and learning. What works will become defined as what achieves good outcomes in the performance assessment framework. Agencies report that the principle of measuring performance is right, but that the 'how' of both content and delivery are more open to question. This is particularly the case for performance indicators as Law and Janzon (2005) report that the jury remains out on whether or not their introduction has resulted in better services. It would be a naive director who ignored the performance framework. Social workers, and their managers, need continually to adopt and maintain a critical attitude towards the indicators or best practice or they will become the servant of performance indicators rather than dealing with the complexity and messiness of being human and focusing on working with service users on their difficulties and problems.

Resources

Most social care organisations will have libraries, access to the Internet and policy documents that are all potential research resources. It is only in recent times that basic grade social workers in many of these organisations have had access to the Internet. Sheldon et al. (2005) noted that in their 2002 survey, only 58 per cent of respondents had access to the Internet and a quarter had no access to library facilities. How widely available such opportunities are within an organisation provides subtle messages as to how that organisation encourages or discourages research.

Staff Development

How organisations manage and promote their staff development and training opportunities is also important. If social care organisations only provide training in those matters that are directly related to practice, for example the implementation of a single assessment framework for older people or core assessments for children's workers, then they are in danger of becoming

increasingly instrumental and rule bound in their practice. Besides the necessary training on policies and procedures, staff development opportunities
and training events should also include the possibility of learning about
wider social care issues informed by the latest research. This might include
attendance at workshops run by RiP, RiPfA or MRC or similar organisations.
Social workers are expected to demonstrate their continued professional
development to re-register with their care council and organisations have an
opportunity here to promote activities to support the development of
research mindedness. The organisation may also sponsor staff on Post
Qualifying courses or higher degrees. All these activities, including any support that is offered in terms of time or finance will help to develop the
research orientation of the organisation's culture and the place of research as
a legitimate activity within the organisation.

Developing a Research-Minded Culture

Walter et al. (2004), in seeking to improve the use of knowledge within social
work, identified a typology of three different arenas for promoting research-
informed practice. This model consisted of: the research-based practitioner
model; the embedded research model; and the organisational excellence model.
These models are explored in greater detail below, alongside the ideas of the
practitioner researcher and the learning organisation.

Research-Based Practitioner

The research-based practitioner model is founded on four key premises:

- It is the role and responsibility of the individual practitioner to keep abreast of
  research and ensure that it is used to inform day-to-day practice.
- The use of research is a linear process, accessing, appraising and applying
  research.
- Practitioners have high levels of professional autonomy to change practice-
  based on research.
- Professional education and training are important in enabling research use.
  (Walter et al., 2004: 25)

This model focuses on the day-to-day experience of the individual practitioner
as to how they operationalise research in order to help inform their practice. In
this model of the research-based practitioner, it is the individual practitioner's
responsibility to ensure that they are conversant with contemporary research and
that they will implement research findings to inform their day-to-day practice.

Inherent in this model is a linear view of research, whereby research findings are accessed and appraised by practitioners who then apply the results to the problem in hand. This model, besides being linear, is uni-directional as the practitioner is seen as the recipient of knowledge and plays no part in the research process or in identifying what research should be undertaken.

Walter et al. (2004) also report that, although there has been a wide range of initiatives and activities to support access to research for social care staff, 'they had found no studies that had formally evaluated the success of such initiatives' (p. 28). The notion of the research-based practitioner is currently an act of faith awaiting evidence to identify whether it works, and if so, what conditions can best support its development.

The next section develops the idea of the research-based practitioner further and seeks to examine the potential of practitioner researchers.

The Practitioner Researcher: Contributing to Both Worlds

The practitioner researcher is a special case of the research-based practitioner. The CWDC funded between 60 and 70 practitioner research projects per year between 2006 and 2010, whilst Shaw and Lundt (2011) report on an initiative in Scotland between a national social work agency and a university partner. A practitioner researcher is a social worker that, either in their spare time or as part of their current employment, undertakes research that is small scale and is carried out by the professionals who deliver these self-same services. This research is likely to have local relevance and focus on resolving a 'practice puzzle' and usually comes with a commitment from the practitioner researcher to change and improve practice (Shaw and Lunt, 2011).

Employer-led support for practitioner research may involve providing time, research resources, access to files or people that might be done for a fixed period or as part of a permanent post. Practitioner research also highlights the tension within social services whereby the employer is likely to have to agree to the relevance of the research question and may act in a range of roles, including those of 'benign observer', 'critical friend' or 'controller'.

In the 'benign observer' role the employer allows the researcher to undertake their research with little interest or interference in the subject chosen, the methods deployed the analysis of the data and any recommendations that flowed from the results. The authority discharges its minimum responsibilities via research governance in response to the Department of Health's Research and Governance framework discussed earlier. This type of organisational practitioner research model is representative of employers who have la laissez-faire attitude towards research and do not value the potential benefits that it may bring.

In the 'critical friend' role, the employing organisation takes a more proactive role. Here, the employer seeks to promote the research but also wants to ensure its validity and relevance so that its results will be based on valid and credible data. In this scenario, the employing organisation goes beyond its minimum duties and seeks to maximise the interests of its staff group and will also wish to support projects that align themselves with the organisation's strategic plan and potentially impact on the way that the organisation or its workers operate.

The 'controller employer' is the type of employer who does not only dictate the research topic, the methodology to be applied and how the results will be disseminated (if at all). In this type of organisation the practitioner researcher becomes 'a tool' of the management. Management oversees the research to ensure that the analysis and results will reflect their view on the issue under investigation and that any recommendations will be those that they want.

On first examination the organisation as 'critical friend' seems to be the most desirable of the three typologies, but is not necessarily the most appropriate in all cases. If the area under study is of limited importance to the organisation and is being supervised by a reputable researcher, the organisation may decide that their investment of time will provide minimal benefits. Thus the first two types may be appropriate at different times for the practitioner researchers whilst the third type is much more problematic. In these circumstances, it is a mute question whether the practitioner researcher would be better advised not to undertake the research at all, given the likely interference that they will encounter from management.

Limitations of the Practitioner Researcher

As we discussed earlier, social workers already have some of the key skills required of a researcher in terms of interviewing and analytical skills. As a member of the organisation that they are researching a politically aware practitioner researcher is more likely to be able to identify who they need to gain approval from, who would make an effective ally and who is likely to be cynical or disruptive. These are issues that often cause difficulties and take professional researchers a long time to discover. On the other hand, practitioner researchers may have a particular difficulty because of being known to their organisation. This can either make access easier or more problematic; colleagues may behave badly if they do not value the worker. Practitioner researchers also have the difficulty that some of their colleagues may find it problematic to see them outside their role as a colleague and seek to restrict the opportunities for their colleague to behave as a researcher.

Shaw (2004) raises more critical concerns about the role of the practitioner researcher and their limited ability to influence agency and wider social work practice. In particular he highlights issues to do with the research being agency owned, employer led, a solitary activity, non-collaborative, non-collective, insider research and bounded in terms of both profession and discipline. In a later article, Shaw and Lundt (2011: 15) note that notions like 'insider' and 'outsider' research are problematic and that it would be better to consider practitioners as researchers inhabiting an 'uncomfortable but creative marginalisation marked by an identity that is neither research nor practice'. Shaw and Lundt identify two other perspectives, one of which views practitioner research as a small-scale academic research project for aspiring academics and lastly practitioner research as a form of social work practice.

The Embedded Research Model

The embedded research model is based on the view that:

- Research use is achieved by embedding research in the systems and processes of social care, such as standards, policies, procedures and tools.
- Responsibility for ensuring research use lies with policy makers and service delivery managers.
- The use of research is both a linear and instrumental process: research is translated directly into practice change.
- Funding performance management and regulatory regimes are used to encourage the use of research-based guidance and tools. (Walter et al., 2004: 26)

In this model, practitioners are not expected actively to seek out research evidence. Research enters practice via the infrastructures of regulatory frameworks, inspections, policies, procedures and practice tools. In the practitioner-researcher model the key link was between research and practice; in this model it is between research and policy. This model does not assume practitioner autonomy and in fact may seek to restrict it in order to meet the embedded research-based performance management indicators.

This model does have a major advantage over the practitioner model as the difficulties experienced by practitioners in accessing research whilst managing workloads are overcome as this task falls to policy-makers. This model does assume, though, that practitioners do not wish to engage their powers of critique and appraisal and are willing to do what their organisation asks them to do without question. This model does not require practitioners to own the research that they use, only to apply it. This creates the danger that the embedded research model is open to becoming another example of management control.

Having examined the practitioner-based model and the embedded research model we now move onto the organisational excellence model.

The Organisational Excellence Model

The organisational excellence model is based on:

- The key to successful use rests with social care delivery organisations: their leadership, management and organisation.
- Research use is supported by developing an organisational culture that is 'research minded'.
- There is local adaptation of research findings and ongoing learning within organisations.
- Partnerships with local universities and intermediary organisations are used to facilitate both the creation of use of research knowledge. (Walter et al., 2004: 26)

Within this model the responsibility for developing a research-informed practice does not lie with the individual practitioner or policy-maker, but with the organisation and in particular its leadership and management. This model recognises that individual social workers are constrained and empowered by the structure and culture of the organisations in which they work. In particular this model places organisational learning to the fore. Research knowledge becomes integrated into organisational knowledge and the view of research becomes cyclical rather than linear. Within the model there is a focus on local learning that is often collaborative between researchers and practitioners whereby practitioner knowledge becomes integrated with research knowledge. Practitioners test out research knowledge finding out what works and what does not, informing researchers so that they can consider their findings in relation to the practice experience and further sensitise their research to this new information. This creates an iterative and dynamic example of the research supporting practice and practice supporting research. However, the role of service users in this model is unclear and although there is space to develop this within the model users there is no mandate to do so.

This organisational excellence model also points towards the current interest in learning organisations, which is explored below.

The Growth of the Learning Organisation

In recent years there has been an increasing interest in the notion of a learning organisation, first in the private sector, and more recently in the public sector.

Reflexive Questions

Think about any team or organisation that you have been a member of. Would you have described it as a learning organisation? What do you consider are the essential components of a learning organisation? Do you think that such an organisation is more likely to exist in the statutory, voluntary or private sector? Why?

Background to the Learning Organisation

The notion of a learning organisation appears intuitively attractive, who would want to work in a non-learning organisation? Besides being inherently attractive, what does it mean? The concept of the learning organisation appears to have developed from two distinct strands. The first of these is concerned with the nature of organisations and their imperative for environmental adaptability to survive. The second strand developed out of the increasing awareness of the limitations of traditional staff development wherein individuals would be developed but this did not necessarily translate into organisational impact or better-quality services. This represents an ongoing struggle for the compatibility between personal growth and organised human relationships. The learning organisation has been informed by the work of both Schon (1971) and Bateson (1972). Schon brought the term 'learning system' into the mainstream of organisational thought and Bateson is recognised for his work on types of learning that was later developed by Argyris and Schon (1978), who suggested that most organisational learning was single loop (error-detection and correction) and that only rare glimpses of double-loop learning could be found. Double-loop learning results in changes to operating assumptions, norms and values. There is also a third type of learning called deutero-learning, which is concerned with learning to learn and occurs when organisational members engage in reflecting and enquiring into previous episodes of organisational learning or failure to learn. In doing so they discover what has facilitated or inhibited learning and are thus able to invent new strategies whilst evaluating and generalising what they have produced. This begins to point towards the characteristics of the learning organisation that cannot be brought about by training individuals, it can only happen as a result of learning at the organisational level.

> A learning company is an organization that facilitates the learning of all its members and continually transforms itself. (Pedler et al., 1991: 1)

This concept serves as a statement of a managerial goal that an organisation can be redesigned so that it is capable of adapting, changing, developing and transforming itself. The learning organisation does not only deliver services, for action is not enough. Action in the learning organisation seeks to resolve the immediate problem but, just as importantly, it also seeks to learn from the process. Action then becomes not merely the search for the 'right answer' but a service provision as experiment. Service provision becomes reframed as a form of action research intended to improve effectiveness and performance-evaluating practice and learning from both success and failure. Ideas like 'partnership', 'integrated services' and 'single assessment' become experiments rather than solutions and we begin to learn from them rather than being swept along with the latest fad.

Baldwin (2004) also notes that a value base of promoting participation and democracy is essential to supporting the development of the learning organisation. To avoid becoming no more than a slogan, the learning organisation is produced out of social relations, including those that characterise inequality including relations based on gender, class, disability, 'race', sexuality and so on (Gould, 2004). Participation within a learning organisation does not stop with the employees of an organisation but includes all the stakeholders as all are seen to benefit from the increased learning potential. In social work these stakeholders would not only include other social care organisations that commission or deliver services, but also all those who can contribute to meeting the needs of the organisation's service users. Stakeholders would also include service users and potential service users. Service users would be valued for their experiences of the impact and appropriateness of social work practice and would be systematically involved in the development and evaluation of the services provided and for potential new services.

In the conclusions to an edited book on learning organisations, Baldwin (2004) comments that there is no evidence of fully functioning learning organisations within the social care sector, but there are glimpses appearing in some organisations.

Barratt and Hodson (2006) as part of RiP have identified five key foundations to create an infrastructure for a more research-informed practice organisation that goes some way towards becoming a learning organisation. These key foundations are:

- Giving a strategic lead: need for a senior manager to spearhead the initiative.
- Setting expectations: what evidence should be used where, how and by whom.
- Encouraging learning from research: promoting a learning organisation.
- Improving access to research: making it easy for staff to access high-quality relevant research.
- Supporting local research: encouraging staff to generate their own evidence during the course of their own practice.

To support these foundations they have developed a practical guide and a series of tools to enable social service teams to audit their practice and identify strategies for promoting greater use of research including:

- Developing a vision of evidence-informed practice and communicating it.
- Establishing a steering group with a clear action plan.
- Including the importance of research-informed practice in the recruitment and selection processes, induction, supervision and progression criteria.
- Winning the hearts and minds of first-line managers.
- Developing a learning culture.
- Supporting staff to keep themselves up to date.
- Developing local research libraries, access to Internet and research updates.
- Enabling service self-evaluation.

In a similar vein SCIE (2004) has also developed a self-assessment resource pack for developing learning organisations. The previous UK Labour government adopted the notion of a learning organisation as an aspirational goal within its modernisation agenda (DH, 1998b, 2001b, 2001c). However, this self-same governmental interest in the learning organisation represents a contradiction as Baldwin (2004) views it as a major threat to its realisation. He notes that managerialism and the learning organisation represent mutually distinct ways of conceptualising organisations in terms of how they should be structured, who should work in them and how employees should be treated. In particular he is concerned that the learning organisation as constructed through social relationships is in danger of being proceduralised and structured so that:

> It is almost as if this discourse has taken the words of the learning organization development and subverted them in a tokenistic fashion that enables the speaker to sound as if that is the goal while never having to walk down the road towards the destination. (Baldwin, 2004: 164)

Gould (2004) notes that the learning organisation, by definition, if it is seeking to learn continuously from and influence its changing environment, must itself always be in the process of change.

On initial examination, the promotion of a learning organisation suggests a supportive environment for the research-minded practitioner. However, the promotion of this concept by the government may militate against its development or represent a form of colonisation. Workers and students need to be concerned that the promotion of the learning organisation does not lead to the development of the more bureaucratised and routinised 'evidence-based practices' (see Chapter 6), restricting creativity whilst promoting instrumental views of the social work task ignoring the milieu, values and contradictions in which social workers are asked to perform.

Improving the Use of Research for Practice

We have examined different ways that research might be introduced to practice via two practitioner models, a model of embedded research and two organisational models. None of these models has all the answers. The practitioner models focus on individual responsibility and autonomy of practitioners to impact on their individual caseloads or service area. The embedded model with its emphasis on policy requires the worker to be the instrument of implementing policy and procedures within regulatory frameworks over which they have little influence. The organisational models emphasise the importance of organisational learning and highlight the point that individual learning is not enough. The learning company also emphasises the importance of participation and how stakeholders can contribute to a dynamic model of research, policy and practice.

In their analysis, Walter et al. (2004) argued for a whole systems approach as the best way forward for social work. This approach acknowledges that each of the models are limited but that together they begin to impact on all the different aspects of the social care system. Whilst there is considerable value in such a suggestion, there are significant tensions between the models: the practitioner model's emphasis on individual autonomy and responsibility is at odds with the embedded research models instrumental view. This instrumental view is in conflict with the excellence and learning organisational models that emphasises collaborative and participative learning and a joint iterative research learning process that is opposed to the non-reflective linear-policy research process in the embedded model. Whilst conceptually it is clear that there are tensions between the different models, this is not to say that organisations are incapable of holding the tensions and contradictory aspects of each of the models in their own service delivery systems.

The emphasis on regulation and accountability will ensure that the embedded model is part of all social care organisations. In the areas where there is choice, the research-based practitioner and practitioner researcher can coexist within the organisational excellence and learning organisation formats as long as the individual learning does not get stuck at the level of the individual and processes are established to share this knowledge. It is also true that different problems will require different research approaches and what may be relevant for one problem will not be relevant for another or at different points of the same research cycle. What is needed, though, is some research evidence to identify under what circumstances and for what problems these models can be combined effectively.

Summary

This chapter has sought to begin to identify issues concerned with why research has failed to make the impact on practice that researchers would desire. We focused on three major areas of concern linked to social workers, researchers and organisations. In relation to social workers we highlighted problems concerning social workers being 'too busy', not valuing research, research complicating matters and a lack of research literacy amongst social workers. These problems were then further considered when the researcher perspective was highlighted noting the differing expectations for research outcomes of researchers and social workers, political naivety of researchers, the employment position of researchers and the differing worlds of social worker and researcher. The analysis then moved on to how organisations learn in terms of their organisational cultures, drivers and training and how staff development can promote or inhibit a research-minded practice.

Following this we then looked at ways of getting research into practice and bridging the associated tensions. In particular we identified the importance of practitioner models, the embedded research model and organisational models. The strengths and weaknesses of all three models were identified.

It was then suggested that all three approaches can together help to promote a holistic research-informed practice but that we cannot totally ignore the tensions between the different models. Lastly, it was also noted that we do not have any robust evidence that these approaches will work; and more research needs to be focused on promoting research in practice.

Suggested Reading

Barratt, M. and Hodson, R. (2006) *Firm Foundations: A Practical Guide to Organisational Support for the Use of Research Evidence.* Dartington: Research in Practice.
Provides a rationale and practical exercises and support materials to develop a research-informed practice.

Gould, N. and Baldwin, M. (eds) (2004) *Social Work, Critical Reflection and the Learning Organization.* Aldershot: Ashgate.
This is a useful book for those wanting to begin to understand the nature of learning organisations and their potential applicability to social work.

Jesson, J.K. with Matheson, L. and Lacey, F.M. (2010) *Doing Your Literature Review: Traditional and Systematic Techniques.* London: Sage.
Provides practical guidance on both traditional and systematic reviews, whilst championing the benefits of traditional reviews that have inappropriately come into disrepute in other texts.

Walter, I., Nutley, S., Percy-Smith, J., McNeish, D. and Frost, S. (2004) *Knowledge Review 7: Improving the Use of Research in Social Care Practice.* London: SCIE.
A comprehensive review of the evidence of research being used to inform practice. This publication is available free from SCIE.

8 Service Users and Research

Introduction

In this chapter we explore the involvement of service users in improving social work practice and in particular we focus on the increasing participation of service users in social work research. Before discussing how to involve service users in research, we ask why should service users be involved in research? Having done this we discuss the methodological, ethical and practical issues and how these may be addressed. This chapter also seeks to contribute to the debate about the benefits, costs and limitations of involving service users in research. In what aspects of the research process can service users be involved and what are the knowledge claims you can make from involving service users in the research process?

Before going on much further, I would like you to consider what you understand by the term service user?

Reflexive Questions

The term service user is used in this text to refer to those who are at the receiving end of service provision provided by social workers and social care workers. Statutory agencies, voluntary bodies or private agencies may provide these services either voluntarily or non-voluntarily. This is not to imply a dualism between those who receive and those who supply social services. Most of us, whether social worker or social researcher, will use social services either directly or indirectly. For example, we may have mental health needs or a child with a disability, or indirectly through the provision of residential or domiciliary care for a relative. We should also remember that the spoken word is more than its dictionary definition and it is thus important to problematise the notion of a service user, as such a label forces onto the recipient of a service an inferior status. Shaping Our Lives, a national service user network, have questioned the use of the term 'service user':

The term 'service user' can be used to restrict your identity as if all you are is a passive recipient of health and welfare services. That is to say, a service-user can be seen as someone who has things 'done to them' or who quietly accepts and receives a service. This makes it seem that the most important thing about you is that you use or have used services. It ignores all the other things you do and which make up you as a person. (Shaping Our Lives Network, 2009)

The idea of a service user, as a homogenised entity, is to reduce all those who use services to be viewed through the prism of one aspect of their lives. This denies the multiple identities we all have: a service user may also be a school governor, a magistrate, a parent or even a social worker. The term 'service user' identifies a person by their dependency on a service rather than any other aspect of their lives.

It is also questionable – with the government's current promotion of personalisation (HM Government, 2007; Gardner 2011) and, in particular, the development of individual budgets where budget holders commission their own support – whether it is appropriate to call such budget holders service users.

The Growth of the Service User Movement in Social Work

Social work has a proud tradition of seeking service user views that goes back to the seminal *The Client Speaks* (Mayer and Timms, 1970). Mayer and Timms systematically recorded the views of 'social work clients', the term we used to use when indicating a service user, identifying what they felt about social workers what they saw as helpful and what they did not.

Reflexive Questions

If you are (have been or were to be) a social work service user, what qualities would you want from your social worker?

In 1996, the National Institute for Social Work reported on a study on standards for working with service users and carers commissioned by the Department of Health. This report began by stating that:

It is easy to summarise what people who use services and carers value in their contacts with social service workers: they value courtesy and respect, being treated as equals, as individuals, and as people who make their own decisions: they value workers who are experienced, well informed and reliable, able to explain things clearly and without condescension, and who 'really listen': and they value workers who are able to act effectively and make practical things happen. (Harding and Beresford, 1996: 1)

In other words, service users and carers respected those workers who respected them, workers who were experienced, able to listen and able to make things happen.

The push for a service user mandate comes from both the consumerist (Beresford, 2005) or from the 'top down' (Ferguson, 2008) tradition of the 1990s and the democratic or 'bottom up' approach of developing participation in order to improve the quality and effectiveness of services.

Ferguson (2008) helpfully sums up the difference between the two models in four key respects:

> Its origins ('bottom up', emerging out of collective movements rather than 'top down') its aims (social change and social justice, rather than simply involvement in services), ideology (a social, rather than an individual or biomedical model of health and disability) and its methods (often involving collective action, rather than 'partnership') with its service providers. (Ferguson, 2008: 70)

From Ferguson's analysis, the 'bottom-up' approach is more critical and radical than the 'top-down' approach. The 'bottom-up' approach contains an inherent challenge to the status quo, seeking to promote social change and social justice. It is also clear that the top-down or managerialist approach has held sway in recent years and, either consciously or unconsciously, has been used to strengthen the status quo.

In recent years service user involvement has become embedded in organisational requirements, policy and legislation for social work. The involvement of service users and carers has been a central theme in the modernisation agenda of New Labour, which put service users at the heart of social care (DH, 1998b, 2000a) and the National Health Service (DH, 2000b). This growing movement has expanded into all aspects of social work. Service users and carers are represented on the General Social Care Council (GSCC) (Hasler, 2003) and are likely to be similarly represented in proposed joint health and social care regulatory body. They are involved in the planning and delivery of social work education at both pre- and post-qualifying levels (Citizens as Trainers et al., 2004; and Molyneux and Irvine, 2004). Whilst there is a long history of service user involvement in the policy development and practice in social work, there is a much shorter history in terms of social work research. In the next section we go on to identify the benefits and frequently advanced arguments about why service users are not routinely involved in social work research.

The Benefits of Service Users Involvement in Research

This section could also have been titled, 'Why bother about service user involvement in research?'

Reflexive Questions

Before we begin to explore the nature and some of the claims made for involving service users in research, you might want to write down what you perceive, to be the benefits, if any, of involving service users in research?

You might want to compare your list with that of Involve whose remit is to promote public involvement in NHS, public health and social care research. Involve have identified the following reasons for service user involvement in research (Hanley et al., 2004: 2–4):

- *People who use services will be able to offer a different perspective:* this point reminds us that although we may be an expert in the matter under research it does not mean we know everything. Without the service user perspective it could be argued that any picture of service effectiveness would be incomplete. Knowledge about service users is incomplete if it does not include the knowledge that service users have of themselves.
- *People who use services can help to ensure that the issues that are identified and prioritised are important to them:* service users or carers can identify research topics or priorities that would not necessarily be identified by researchers.
- *Public involvement can help to ensure that money and resources aren't wasted on research that has little or no relevance:* as previously noted social work is an applied discipline and it is important for social work research to address the needs of service users, but also to identify interventions that service users are willing to use and are effective. It would be of little benefit to identify a wonderful new intervention if it was not needed or that nobody was willing to use it.
- *People who use services can help to ensure that research doesn't just measure outcomes that are identified and considered important by professionals:* it cannot be assumed that researchers can identify all the outcomes that are important to service users. After all, service users are ultimately the end users of research and understandably are important stakeholders in assessing the effectiveness of the research.
- *People who use services can help with the recruitment of their peers for research projects:* service users may understandably be suspicious of the motives of researchers and as such be unwilling to become involved in the research. Working with a voluntary organization or self-help group can often assist with recruitment of researchers especially with hard to reach groups who by definition are less likely to be willing to come forward.
- *People who use services can help access other people who are often marginalised, such as people from black and minority ethnic communities:* this is the other side of the last point. Being able to work with a marginalised service user as a researcher is likely to provide greater opportunities to be able to identify other potential service user respondents from the same community of interest.
- *People who use services can help to disseminate the results of research and work to ensure that changes are implemented:* service users are often keen that the results of the research are effectively disseminated. This may take a number of

forms in that many voluntary organizations and user-controlled organizations have their own websites, newsletters and or magazines that will publicise research summaries. It also possible that service users can help present research results at conferences. If prepared properly, service users can be a very powerful voice for publicising the key messages from the research.

- *Involvement in research can help empower service users:* involvement in research can help to raise self-esteem, develop new skills, promote well-being and help improve employment prospects.
- *The involvement of the public is becoming an increasing political priority and requirement of research funding bids:* pragmatically researchers if they wish to have their bids accepted by many research councils and commissioners they have to demonstrate how service users will be meaningfully involved in the research.

Whilst Director General of Research and Development at the Department of Health Professor Dame Sally Davies stated in the forward to an Involve publication that:

> I have always taken the view that public involvement in research should be the rule not the exception. It is fundamental to ensure high quality research that brings real benefits for patients, the public and the NHS. (Staley, 2009: 4)

Earl Howe (2010) a government minister in the foreword to the annual National Institute of Healthcare Research (NIHR) stated that:

> The Government is … committed to collaboration between those doing research and those who gain from research in all sectors of the economy.

It would thus appear that there is genuine support for the involvement of service users in research and given this support it is interesting to ask why researchers do not involve service users more.

The Reasons Given Why Researchers Do not Involve Service Users

Looking at the above it is difficult to see why researchers do not involve service users, but this is evidently the case and we need to look at their reasons in more detail to see why this is so.

Before we discuss the reasons given by researchers, you should write down at least three reasons why you believe researchers would not want to involve service users in the research process. Do you think that these reasons are justified or not?

Reflexive Questions

Lack of 'Representativeness'

This concern is regularly raised in the literature about service user involvement in policy, practice or research. This concern asks how we can ensure that those service users included in the research are typical of all other service users. It is patently unreasonable to assume that one or two people can be representative of all people who use similar services. As we have already identified the term, service users does not signify a homogenous group and there is no agreed meaning of 'representativeness' just as there is no 'one' service user voice (Molyneux and Irvine, 2004). The Association of Directors of Social Services (Jones, 1995) drew up practice guidance indicating that service users and carers contribute perspectives based on their experience not on their representativeness. Involve also highlights the importance of the service user perspective as opposed to trying to ensure some mechanistic representativeness:

> In essence it is not reasonable to expect one or two people to be representative of all people who use similar services. But then it is not reasonable to expect one doctor to be representative of all doctors either. It might be helpful to reframe this in terms of thinking about seeking **perspectives** rather than representativeness. If you want a range of perspectives, involve a range of people. (Hanley et al., 2004: 5, bold in original)

Service users, especially if they are recruited from democratically constituted groups, may be representative or even typical users but their legitimacy arises from their personal experience. This personal experience is likely to be similar to others using similar services in similar circumstances. Equally, researchers are not a homogenous group; you just have to read their differing views in the academic journals or in earlier parts of this book to note this. Researchers have diverse views and experiences; they have no greater claim to representativeness than do service users.

'The Usual Suspects'

A special case of representativeness is the issue of the 'usual suspects'. This view suggests that it is always the same people who get asked to represent service user views. Attached to the non-representativeness of this approach is often an assumed bias or cynicism that organisations, or researchers, are hand-picking those people who are most likely to agree with them or represent the 'acceptable' face of that service user group. At the extreme this may just be another form of tokenism or manipulation, where there is an illusion of participation but no real change in the locus of power or even the willingness to consider change.

However, this is to miss the point. In requesting service user participation in, for example, a research advisory group, you will want to ensure that you involve those people who are able and willing to participate in meetings. They will also need to be able to present their views to a variety of individuals with a range of professional expertise, including researchers and research sponsors. These representatives may not be 'typical' but they will be able to offer insights from their perspective and may help to develop a snowballing effect, where other service users hear of the research opportunities and express their interest in joining the research team. Service users may need support in developing their confidence and skills in presenting their arguments in such settings and chairs of such groups need to be inclusive in the way that they structure and run their meetings.

'The Research Can't Be Objective if Service Users Are Involved'

The statement that 'The research can't be objective if service users are involved' presupposes that researchers are objective and neutral – but this is not the case, researchers like service users will want to become involved in research that excites and interests them. People who use services, including researchers, can be supported to avoid becoming overly emotionally attached and biased towards a research study.

It is possible that the research may become personally upsetting for service users and consideration needs to be given to their personal support. This is an important aspect of the ethical considerations in relation to a research project (see Chapter 4). Such support should obviously be considered when researching sensitive subjects, for example the impact of child sexual abuse or compulsory mental health admissions to hospital, but may also be required for less sensitive subjects. All human beings are different and involvement in the research process may awaken, or trigger, a previous unhappy experience or incident.

'It'll Be too Expensive and Time-Consuming'

Involving service users and carers will cost more money and take more time (Kirby, 2004; McLaughlin, 2005). To involve service users or carers effectively is not resource neutral. If service users or carers are to be used as co-researchers they will need to be trained for this role. The TRUE project (Lockey et al., 2004) found that service user research training was essential and led to actual involvement in research and a desire to be involved in more research. The initial costs in terms of time and resources did result in research involvement and ensured that the investment was not wasted. The training also had enormous value for the participants' personal development, self-esteem and self-confidence. The benefits of service user participation are more often identified in terms of personal development than organisational change (Carr, 2004) and this is one of the key challenges for such research to demonstrate positive outcomes as well as empowering processes. Researchers and research sponsors need to include these extra costs within bids. To avoid doing this is to undermine the quality and potential usefulness of the research output.

'Service Users Will have Unrealistic Expectations of Research and its Implementation'

The argument that, 'Service users will have unrealistic expectations of research and its implementation' suggests that service users will underestimate the amount of time and effort required whilst at the same time overestimating the impact that the research will have on changing services. This is not necessarily a problem if researchers, service users and research sponsors can be clear from the outset about the amount of time that the research project will take, who will be involved, the nature of the research outputs and the potential for these to be put into practice. What is important here is that researchers and research sponsors should not promise anything that is not within their gift to deliver.

So far this chapter has identified the mandate for service user involvement in research. In so doing we have identified what can be seen as the major advantages of such an approach and some of the reasons given by researchers or research sponsors for not including service user involvement in the process. Hopefully, this has included the reasons you have identified as well. If this is not the case, you may wish to consider how your reasons for not involving service users could be addressed. The chapter will now consider the philosophical underpinning of service user involvement in research and look at different levels of service user involvement, including service user led research.

The Philosophical Underpinning of Service User Research

When considering service user research it is important to look into the assumptions behind involving service users in the research process. Building on the work of Christensen and Prout (2002) with young people, it is possible to suggest a typology of four different models. These four models view service users as objects, subjects, social actors or active participants in the research process. The first of these perspectives perceives service users as objects to be acted on, measured and researched. This is the traditional quantitative model of research whereby the research is carried out by a researcher who would determine a baseline, undertake their **experiment** and then measure the changes to the situation, attributing any changes to the nature of the intervention.

The second viewpoint perceives the service user as subject and in so doing brings them into the forefront to the research process. This represents a much more service user centred approach, but potentially has the shortcoming of being tempered by researcher views as to the ability or maturity of the service user. This could be particularly important when considering the position of children and young people, people with a mental illness, people with learning disabilities or those suffering from dementia. Clark (2004) has shown that it is possible to begin with notions of competency when researching the experience of children under five and the importance of viewing young children as 'beings not becomings' (Qvortrup et al., 1994: 2 quoted in Clark, 2004: 142). Such a view can be translated to other marginalised groups who are viewed as not being fully competent.

The third approach views service users as social actors who have the ability to act on, change and be changed by, the world that they live in. In this perspective service users are seen as autonomous individuals, with agency and, critically, not part of another system whether this be the family, work or school.

The fourth perspective is a special case of the last approach whereby service users are seen as active participants in the research process (Christensen and Prout, 2002). In this perspective service users are not seen merely as social actors but as co-researchers collaborating and participating in the research process to co-produce new knowledge. This begs two important questions, one concerns the level of involvement of service users and the other as to which, if not all, parts of the research process service users can become involved in. The next section deals with the first of these two questions.

Levels of Service User Involvement in Social Research

There is a critical difference between going through the empty ritual of service user participation in research and service users having sufficient power to impact on the outcome of the research. Arnstein (1971) has famously identified a ladder of citizen participation, which also transfers to service user research. This ladder has eight rungs: manipulation, therapy, informing, consultation, placation, partnership, delegated power and citizen control. The first two of these rungs, manipulation and therapy, are identified as non-participation whilst the next four rungs are seen as mere tokenism with only partnership, delegated power and citizen control viewed as citizen power. A simpler approach by Hanley et al. (2004) identifies three points on the same continuum: consultation, collaboration and service user control. Hanley et al.'s continuum is explored next.

In contrast to Arnstein, Hanley et al. (2004) present a positive view of participation and ignore the possibility that service user involvement in research may be illusory or non-participatory. For example, consider the position of a service user who agrees to be a member of a research steering group. This would appear to be offering a degree of service user involvement, but if the steering group is always held at times when the service user cannot attend; no thought is given to venue or the need for alternative caring arrangements; if the language of the steering group is so specialist or jargonistic that it is exclusive and excluding, it would be totally inappropriate to suggest that this was real participation. In reality this would appear to be non-participation dressed up in the guise of service user involvement. For this reason and for the fact that most research council and many research commissioners require researchers to identify how service users have been involved in the research, Hanley's model should consist of a fourth point, that of tokenism. This would mean that the new continuum would consist of tokenism, consultation, collaboration and service user control.

Consultation

Consultation is integral to modern UK society where we have the notion of the 'listening bank' and satisfaction surveys for everything from the purchase of holidays, to toasters and cars. However, asking people about their satisfaction with services is notoriously unreliable. Compliance, unequal power relationships between those asking the questions and those answering them and a lack of understanding of alternative possibilities will all potentially act to influence those being questioned towards a positive response, unless the appraisal instruments are quite sophisticated (Gutek, 1978).

Hanley et al. (2004: 8) suggest that:

> When you consult people who use services about research, you ask them for their views to inform your decision-making. For example, you might hold one-off meetings with people who use services to ask them for their views on a research proposal. You will not necessarily adopt those people's views, but you may be influenced by them.

One of the major difficulties with consulting people is that when asking their opinion, there is no guarantee for them that you will act on their views, although they may influence you. One of consultation's greatest strengths is its imprecise definition that generates what McLaughlin et al. (2004) describe as 'useful ambiguity' allowing consultation to mean different things to different people.

Practical Example

A local authority and a primary care trust want to know whether **D/deaf** and hard of hearing service users are satisfied with the quality of services on offer. Together they arrange a meeting for Wednesday at 3pm at a local Deaf club. At the meeting only three people turn up and the research officer assumes that people must be happy with the services, otherwise more people would have turned up.

Looking at the above example do you believe that the research officer was correct in their evaluation of the situation? If not, what issues might they need to address to improve the situation? How would you have done it?

I hope that you would have first considered that D/deaf and hard of hearing people are not a homogenous group; D/deaf people do not all necessarily go where hard of hearing people go and young D/deaf people do not necessarily attend adult Deaf people's haunts. The choice of venue may at first appear sympathetic to D/deaf people but this is not necessarily the case, it may not be where the majority of D/deaf people go, never mind those who are hard of hearing. The researcher should have first found out more about their target group in order to identify where they congregate so as to maximise access. They could have talked to some members of the D/deaf and hard of hearing community to identify where such places are and which is the best day(s) and time(s) to arrange a meeting. They could also have worked with this small group of service users to examine how best to present the issues in a format and language that is accessible and understandable to the service user group. They will need to consider such issues as transport and caring responsibilities. This all needs doing prior to considering issues such as interpreters and communication requirements. Also, and most importantly, as McLaughlin et al. (2004) demonstrate, you may need to address what consultation means to certain groups, for example D/deaf people who are not used to being consulted and therefore do not know what is expected of them in such a situation.

Reflexive Questions

Consultation is the lowest level of service user involvement as identified by Hanley et al. (2004). Consultation can be seen to be a simple process, which if you have never involved service users in research before can be a 'safe' place to start. This is particularly the case as consultation does not commit those consulting to act on any particular suggestion. The locus of power resides firmly with those undertaking the consultation, not those being consulted. Many people who use services find it frustrating to be asked their opinion without any commitment from those asking to act on that opinion. It is unsurprising that those communities who are regularly subject to consultations complain of 'consultationitus' or 'consultation overload'. Beresford and Croft (1993) claim that there are compelling reasons why certain powerless groups are regularly asked their views on issues without any tangible outcomes to the process. 'Consultation fatigue' can result in ill health for those individuals or organisations that are regularly targeted without clear outcomes. One other disadvantage of consultation is that you may miss out on service user's ideas as the responses are constrained by the researcher's agenda. In such situations consultation can become a pseudonym for social control and non-participation.

Collaboration

Collaboration occupies the middle ground between consultation and service user control. Collaboration implies a degree of ongoing service user involvement. For example, this might include service users: being active members of the research steering committee; collaborating on the research design; undertaking data collection; acting as researchers in analysing and interpreting data; contributing to the writing of the report: and undertaking an active part in the publication and promotion of the results. Collaboration can mean any or all of these things. Collaboration exists in the grey area between consultation and service user control; as such it represents a broad spectrum of participation. It is also important to remember that one person's assessment of a situation as collaborative may not be shared with those who are being collaborated with.

Collaboration increases the likelihood that any outcome measures or assessment criteria will be relevant to the research participants. Again, collaboration provides for the possibility that those service users in the project will help access other service users. As such, the collaborators can act as informal research sponsors helping with the recruitment and informed consent of potential research subjects. This can be particularly important with groups who are seldom heard. Moreover, once the data has been collected service users can help with the contextualisation, interpretation and understanding of the data and ultimately with the co-production of new knowledge. Collaborative research projects are more likely to result in service users feeling greater ownership of the results and being more likely both to publicise the results and to take on board any changes required as a result of the research findings.

On the debit side, collaboration can be costly in terms of time and resources without any guarantee of a better outcome. Collaboration is likely to demand extra resources for service user time, service user travel costs and other expenses.

On top of these costs additional resources may be required, for example in the training of service users, producing plain English versions of research papers and providing for the support and development needs of the service users.

Collaboration, unlike consultation, requires a different mindset from the lead researcher. The researcher must be willing to share ownership of the project and be actively seen to take into account other people's suggestions and to behave in a collegial way. For some professional researchers it may be very difficult to accept shared power. Such an approach also demands that researchers may require an expanded skill set to include facilitation and negotiation skills.

User Control

User-controlled research is still in its infancy and remains a contested arena. Broadly speaking, user-controlled research is located at the opposite end of our continuum and suggests that power resides not with the researcher but with the service users. It is the service users who decide on the research question, the data collection techniques, data analysis and conclusions to be drawn for practice.

In a review of service user controlled research, Turner and Beresford (2005: vi) identified four key aims of service user-controlled research:

- The empowerment of service users and the improvement of their lives (through both the process and the purpose of research).
- Being part of a broader process of making social and political change.
- More equal relations of research production (where the people who carry out the research and are the subject of the research relate to each other on much more equal terms).
- Being based on social models of understanding and interpretation (like the social model of disability).

They also identified another important issue in which there was no agreement. The service users consulted by Turner and Beresford could not agree as to whether user-controlled research meant that the research had to be undertaken by service users or whether researchers can be commissioned by service users to undertake the research under their control. It is thus clear that there is still much work to do in clarifying the contested parameters of service user-controlled research.

The 'disability movement' has been instrumental in the development of this type of research. The 'movement' views traditional research as furthering the careers of able-bodied researchers at the expense of disabled people that led to Finklestein (1985) famously making the statement of 'no participation without representation' (quoted in Barnes and Mercer, 1997: 6). Research was viewed as 'ripping' off disabled participants, by simply using them to obtain information without any involvement in the construction of the research agenda or what was seen as legitimate to research.

The roots of this critique of social research on disability can be traced back to at least the 1960s and the case of the disabled residents in Le Court, Cheshire Home (Barnes and Mercer, 1997). The disabled residents asked expert researchers from the Tavistock Institute to support their struggle to gain greater control over their everyday lives. This was a three-year funded research study that quickly alienated the residents. The 'unbiased social scientists' followed their own agenda and their report rejected the resident's complaints and recommended a reworking of traditional practices, even though they categorised institutional life as a 'living death' (Miller and Gwynne, 1972). The residents felt betrayed by the report and labelled the academic researchers 'parasites' (Hunt, 1981). Several of the disabled people in the Le Court protest later helped form the Union of Physically Impaired Against Segregation (UPIAS) in 1975. UPIAS became central to the development of the social model of disability critiquing experts and professionals who claimed to speak on behalf of disabled people, but who in UPIAS's opinion only pursued their own interests:

> We as a Union are not interested in descriptions of how awful it is to be disabled. What we are interested in is the ways of changing our conditions of life, and thus overcoming the disabilities which are imposed on top of our physical impairments by the way this society is organised to exclude us. (UPIAS, 1976)

Similar to consultation and collaboration, user control is both a point on a continuum and a range of potential options orbiting this point. For example, it is unclear whether user control refers only to the research process and whether it also includes identifying research funding and writing the research bid. Generally, it is academic researchers who write research bids. It is only recently that a few research commissioners have identified funding to allow service users to become involved in the writing of research bids.

The advantage of user-controlled research is that it is more likely to address questions that are pertinent to service users. It is also possible that it will focus on issues that are not considered by researchers and can often reveal evidence that would otherwise be missed. As service users or their organisation(s) own the research, there will be a higher commitment to making an impact on policy and practice. Being involved in a user-controlled research project can be an empowering experience for those whose previous experience has been concerned with being the research objects of others. Hearing the voices, concerns and recommendations of service users is also likely to impact on professionals who are concerned with improving the quality of service provision.

User-controlled research is not without its disadvantages. User-controlled research requires researchers to hand over power and the control of a project to those who use services. Some researchers, research sponsors and research funders may find this difficult or unacceptable. The research itself may not be viewed as independent as those who have most to gain are those undertaking the research. There is, though, a difference between a rigorously implemented research design, analysis and evaluation and biased research. Bias is not a problem solely restricted to user-controlled research and the same techniques used to reduce bias in traditional research can be implemented within user-controlled research.

We have considered four different levels of service user involvement in research: tokenism, consultation, collaboration and user-controlled. All except the first of these may be appropriate in different research circumstances. Different levels of involvement will depend on the lead researcher, the research topic, the resources available, the skill levels of the service user researchers, the research method and the funding body. The involvement of service users in research is not just about having an extra person at the steering group or someone different conducting interviews. It is also about issues of democracy, social justice, quality of communication, providing opportunities for different contributions and for other contributions to be valued. Involvement is a complex and multifaceted activity wherein the same research project service users may be consulted, collaborated with or even, required to take the lead:

> The involvement of people who use services, when done well, positively affects not just **what** is done in research, but also the **way** it is done. (Hanley et al., 2004: 12, bold in original)

It should also be noted that service user research is not restricted to people with physical disabilities but can also include any service user group. In principle it should be possible to involve any service user group in research in an intellectually honest manner. The research process does rely on intellectual skills and will therefore be less open to young people, those suffering an episode of mental illness, those with learning disabilities or older people with cognitive impairment, but this does not mean that these groups do not have a contribution to make about their lives and their experiences of living those lives. Nor does it mean that they will not be able to make an effective contribution, although alternative research tools and techniques may require development. In these cases it may say more about the academic researcher's ability to communicate effectively and identify appropriate research instruments and strategies.

Having considered the different levels of service user involvement in research, this chapter now considers some of the practical issues often raised in relation to service user research, in particular we focus on meaningful involvement, rewards for service users, recruitment, training and the position of children and young people as co-researchers.

Meaningful Involvement

As noted earlier, when researchers seek to involve service users in research, this participation must be more than merely tokenistic. The meaningful involvement of service users requires careful thought and planning to ensure an effective contribution to the research. If participation is poorly implemented, it is likely to have negative consequences for the research and for service users who will be less likely to trust researchers in the future. Poorly implemented participative research not only runs the risk of having negative consequences for the research in hand, but may contaminate the field for future researchers.

Kirby (2004) identifies a range of questions to be asked about the meaningful involvement of children and young people. These questions, with minor adaptations, are just as suitable for all service users:

- Is service user involvement planned from the beginning?
- Are service users involved in deciding how they want to be involved? Is participation always voluntary?
- Will they be supported to get involved in ways that suit their needs, abilities, interests, access needs, and availability?
- Will all the information about the research be shared, so that they are able to make informed opinions and decisions?
- Will their views be genuinely listened to, and influence decisions along with the views of other stakeholders?
- Will they be treated as equals? How will you demonstrate respect for their contribution?
- How will they personally benefit from being involved?
- Will disabled members have the opportunity to contribute equally? (Kirby, 2004: 10–11)

In addition to this set of questions, thought should also be given as to how service users' contributions will be acknowledged in the research report and any future publications arising from the research. This may be as a co-author, as a member of the research team, a steering group member, interviewer or whatever. It is important that service users should be acknowledged for their contribution to the research just as any other contributor to the research would be. It is also possible that because of the nature of the study – for example, in cases of research into sexually transmitted diseases, domestic abuse or criminal behaviour – service users may not want to be acknowledged by their full name but by their first name, pseudonym or a nickname. Some service users may also see themselves as championing certain issues, and naively believe that they are aware of the consequences of 'going public'. It would appear patronising not to allow service users to 'go public' but service users should be reminded that once the research is in the public domain there is no control over how or who will use it.

Fair Return for Participation

A guiding principle of involving service users in research should be that there should be no exploitation of service users by researchers. This represents a development of beneficence and non-malevolence discussed earlier. When service users, either as respondents or as co-researchers, become involved in research they may contribute large amounts of time and energy as well as providing access to their networks, language and culture. This is time, knowledge and experience that could have been spent in pursuing a job, domestic work, education or contributing to their own or their family's survival. This time cannot be reclaimed and it is thus only fair and just that service users should be recompensed for this time and effort.

> You might like to think about how you would recompense service users who were acting as co-researchers? Are there any circumstances in which you would not consider money as an appropriate reward? Having done this, can you consider what you see as the advantages and the disadvantages to recompensing service user researchers?

Reflexive Questions

Before beginning to discuss recompense it is important to be aware that under the research governance framework (DH, 2001a), all individuals engaged in research which falls within the remit of the Department of Health require an 'honorary contract'. This is irrespective of whether the service user is paid or is a volunteer. This requirement seeks to ensure that sponsoring organisations take overall responsibility for the research, that they can meet their obligations to ensure the health and safety of all those involved in the research and cover any liability. If service users are given an 'honorarium' payment they technically become employees, albeit casual workers and health and safety and employment legislation come into force. However, the issue of paying service user researchers is a constant concern and Involve (2010) rightly challenge us to justify why members of the public should not be paid for their time and expertise to a level consistent with other members of the research team. Whilst this will depend on a variety of factors and circumstances it is patently unfair to expect people who are unpaid to sit alongside paid non-executive members of a research advisory group, or to be expected to give their time for free when others are being paid for research work as part of their day job. Similarly, if the advisory group is entirely voluntary, payment for time cannot reasonably be expected.

It can be argued that paying service user researchers will compromise the independence of their views. This argument is, however, myopic as it is not one that is made in relation to professional researchers and should not therefore apply to members of the public.

In terms of payment the first point to note is that recompense does not necessarily imply cash. The researcher may provide gift vouchers to be redeemed at a local shopping centre or the procurement of a specialist piece of equipment or membership of a local gym as potential rewards. The research may also provide financial support to a service user organisation as an alternative to giving recompense directly to the co-researcher.

A co-researcher, like any other researcher, feels valued when they are recompensed for their efforts. Recompense is also likely to increase motivation and can act as a stimulus for the completion of the less exciting research tasks. It is also likely that if service user researchers are being paid, not only will they take themselves more seriously but also professionals and other organisations will take them more seriously.

On the negative side, once service users are paid there is a change in the relationship that becomes more contractual and potentially controlling. Paying service users may also impact negatively with service users losing some or all of their state benefits, and with children and young people it may result in inappropriate pressures for them to act as employees.

In paying service user researchers there is the potential danger that some people might just join the research to be paid rather than because of any special interest in research or the research topic. Bringing money into the equation potentially identifies a new arena for dispute concerning the need to treat co-researchers with transparent fairness and equity. It is thus important that issues of recompense and expenses are covered in a written form at the beginning of the research process to avoid any misunderstandings.

However you look at it, bringing money into the equation will impact upon the research, for good or ill. What is crucial is that researchers should discuss recompense at the beginning of the research so that service users who consider being involved in research can take this into account in their decision.

The Limits of Service User Knowledge Production?

This section has argued for the inclusion of service users in the research process. However, many of the research studies in relation to service user involvement included in this chapter focus more on processes than outcomes. The process of involving service users can be beneficial to service users but it does not necessarily ensure a better research product. Questions are yet to be answered as to how far service users can be involved in all aspects of research. In particular the more advanced forms of qualitative and quantitative research are likely to go beyond what can be taught in a short research methods course for service users. It also begs the question that if service users receive research training to a level that they are able to engage with the more advanced statistical analysis or critical discourse analysis, do they become more researcher than service user? It should also be noted that not all researchers will be competent in all aspects of the research process and are often members of teams put together to cover the range of skills required to answer the research question and maybe we should be judging service user researcher skills as part of an overall team approach.

In summing up, it is just as disingenuous not to engage service users where they could benefit a research study as it is to believe that they can deliver something that they cannot. Lead researchers need to be aspirational in relation to service user researchers whilst still being grounded in what is reasonably possible.

Knowledge Claims for Service User Researchers

It is quite clear from what has been written in this chapter already that involving service users as researchers is justified in terms of making the traditional types of knowledge claims as discussed in Chapter 3. Generally, service user researchers have been more involved in qualitative types of research. This is not surprising as it can be argued that such approaches are more in sympathy with service user researchers as they seek to understand the perspectives of those involved in the research process. There is, however, no reason why service user researchers cannot be involved in quantitative research and cannot make a significant contribution in being part of a steering group or helping to design interview schedule questions or in analysing data (McLaughlin, 2009).

However, Beresford makes an argument that service user researcher knowledge claims should be seen as a special case as service users' knowledges are different from all the other participants in social work and social research in that:

> They alone are based on *direct* experience of such policy and provision from the *receiving end*, service users' knowledges grow out of their personal and collective experience of policy, practice and services. As in all identity based groupings and movements they are experientially based. (Beresford, 2000: 493)

This type of privileging claim is often described as standpoint theory whereby knowledge claims are dependent on an individual's membership of a particular social group, in this case service users. Viewed from this perspective only service users can understand other service users, claiming a privileged position for service users who are the end users of social work services and experience both the intended and unintended consequence of social policy and social work actions and are therefore in a better position than academics and social workers in knowing what needs to be done. Whilst it is right to support service users in their struggle, it is another to privilege their knowledges above all others, as Hammersley (1995: 71) points out:

> Whilst we must recognise that people in different social locations may have divergent perspectives giving them distinctive insight, it is not clear why we should believe the implausible claim that some category of people has privileged access whilst others are blinded by ideology.

Helpfully, Nolan et al. (2007:190) suggest:

> if we accept that differing types of knowledge and experience contribute to a full understanding then no one has privileged 'insider' knowledge, but everyone has differing knowledge from which everybody can learn. Herein lies the nub of the issue.

Children and Young People

This specialist section seeks to highlight some of the key issues involved when collaborating or working with young service users as co-researchers. Up to now the chapter has dealt with service users as a totality; in this section we focus on just one of the potential service user groups to act as an exemplar of this type of research. It should also be noted that children and young people might be members of more than one service user group. Children and young people may also be physically disabled, suffer from mental health problems, be asylum seekers or have a combination, or all of these identifying characteristics:

> There is no right way to involve children, just as there is no ideal technique to use in research with children. You may want to involve children in every aspect of your research, or to consult them about specific areas. (Save the Children, 2004: 42)

As this chapter has demonstrated, there is a great value in participatory research; however, there will be research topics and contexts where a more traditional approach will be more suited. Controversial topics like child sexual abuse or violence against children may not be acceptable by powerful adults or ethics committees as suitable for research by children and young people.

Some of the issues highlighted in this section are developments of those already discussed in relation to service users generally and may also be appropriate to other vulnerable groups. In particular I would like to highlight the mandate for young service users' involvement, the advantages offered by this participatory approach, the employment position of young people, informed consent and safeguarding young service users.

Mandate for Involvement

The mandate for children and young people's involvement comes from both the children's rights agenda and the government's policy statements. The United Nations Convention on the Rights of the Child (United Nations, 1989) sets out the benchmarks for the rights of children everywhere. Articles 12 and 13 are of particular note. Article 12 promotes a child's right to participate in decision-making by being informed, involved and consulted on all matters that impact upon their lives in accordance with their age and maturity. Article 13 promotes the right to information and freedom of expression through any medium of the young person's choice. As Roberts (2004) notes, this means that the research agenda in researching with service users is also a participation agenda.

A number of the government publications supporting service user involvement have already been identified in this chapter. In relation to children and young people it is also worth noting that the publication of *Listening, Hearing and Responding* (DH, 2002) includes an action plan for the involvement of children and young people and the establishment of the Children and Young People's Unit (CYPU). Government bodies under the previous Labour government like the Children and Young Person's Unit have claimed that:

> The Government wants children and young people to have more opportunities to get involved in the design and evaluation of policies and services that affect them or which they may use. (CYPU, 2001: 2)

Both the children's rights and government policy agendas have promoted the involvement of young service users.

The Advantages and Disadvantages of Young Service Users as Co-Researchers

It is one thing to argue that young service users should be more involved in the design and evaluation of services and policies, but it is another to identify what are the advantages and disadvantages of such an approach.

Think about a research topic that you feel would be of significance to children and young people, for example bullying or divorce. Now identify what you feel are the major benefits of involving peer researchers to investigate your research topic. Now think of any disadvantages or costs that you can see to involving young peer researchers in your research topic.

Reflexive Questions

There are a number of benefits claimed for involving people as co-researchers (Smith et al., 2002; Jones, 2004; Kirby, 2004; and McLaughlin, 2006) These include:

- Identifying research issues and questions overlooked by adults and researchers.
- Enhancing the range and quality of data collected.
- Speaking a common language not always accessible to adults.
- Ensuring the accessibility of research tools.
- Aiding the recruitment of peers.
- Accessing places where adults are not welcome.
- Advising on the user-friendliness to young people of any publications, web-pages or the like.
- Disseminating the research results and conclusions.

The benefits are not merely restricted to the research and both young service user researchers and adult researchers may benefit from the experience. Young service user researchers may benefit from being actively involved in research that addresses issues that affect their lives, and the involvement may improve their confidence and self-esteem whilst also improving their employability. For adult researchers, it provides them with an opportunity to understand young people's issues and concerns in greater depth, benefit from young people's energy levels and can also be great fun (McLaughlin, 2005)! Adults cannot act as a proxy child. The world is continually changing with iPads, Facebook and other social net-working opportunities, making it difficult for adults to understand the reality of children's lives. As Save the Children (2004: 13) comment, 'Adult researchers may have less insight into the daily lives of children than they think they have.' If this is the case then children and young people need to be more involved and included in research.

Just as importantly, it could be argued that organisations that promote the empowerment of children and young people in society should also reflect this commitment in the way that they commission research. To do this, by definition, would mean the promotion of service users as research sponsors as well as service users as co-researchers or peer researchers.

So far we have only looked at positives and some of the costs have already been identified, but with young people we would want to highlight difficulties in recruitment, the research is likely to take longer, cost more and there may be certain research activities that are less attractive or inappropriate for young people.

Recruiting young people as researchers can be problematical, although an existing youth group or organisation could be approached. But, if you want to work with a group of socially excluded young people they are, by definition, difficult to recruit. The very act of recruitment can become a major task and a time-intensive activity in its own right.

Researching with young service users is likely to take longer as the quality of the research is directly dependent upon the quality of the preparation. It cannot be presumed that young service users will already have the skills to contribute effectively to a research project. It is highly likely that they will need support and preparation for undertaking research, analysing and interpreting the data, writing up the research and disseminating the results. Preparation and training need to fit into the other activities in a young person's life. Lead researchers need to acknowledge that a young person's lifestyle has a different rate to that of an adult researcher's. Issues such as friends, partners, education and/or employment will potentially take precedence over the research process. It is also likely that because of these issues the research will have to be undertaken in 'bite-size chunks'. It may thus be prudent to over-recruit the number of young service user researchers you may need. This is all likely to result in the research taking much longer and as a consequence costing more and being more resource-intensive.

Young service users (as do other service users) require the research training and research materials to be engaging and interesting if they are to become committed to the research project for any length of time. Consequently, some stages of the research process may be less appealing to young people than to others. For example, some young people may find it particularly difficult to engage with the analysis or with the writing up that may appear overly technical, difficult, time-consuming and boring. This is potentially the case for those whom schooling is/was not a successful experience. This does not mean that young people cannot participate in the analysis or comment on draft reports but that it might require greater effort and the development of alternative techniques.

One other difficulty that needs to be acknowledged is that this type of research does not suit every researcher. Some researchers, possibly because of personality or life experience, may not be comfortable working with young service users. This should not be unexpected but it is often overlooked. Social workers often choose to specialise in different client groups bounded by age when working in adult teams or child and family teams, it should not be surprising then that social work researchers may do the same.

Employment of Young Service Users

The employment legislation for young people is complex, with young people considered to be of compulsory school age until the last Friday in June of the school year in which they reach their sixteenth birthday (note that this is proposed to be raised to 18 in 2013). Whilst of school age, a research sponsor will need to register the research work with the local education welfare department. Forms will need to be completed and consent sought from their parents and the school. It is possible that a school may decide not to give their consent, for example if the young person's class attendance is below average. Failure to register may invalidate an employer's insurance policy. There are also time restrictions on how long and when young people are allowed to work in both term time and school holidays. These times also vary with age, although generally children under 14 years of age are not eligible for work. This makes it difficult for young people under the age of 14 to engage in collaborative research, although treating them as volunteer researchers helps to circumvent this requirement. Other arrangements in terms of insurance, health and safety and covering expenses would still need to be addressed.

The rules for those no longer subject to compulsory schooling vary between those in the 15–17 age band and those 18+. A staggered national minimum wage rate applies to this group, with the full national minimum wage rate applying to those aged 22 or above. Some organisations pay young people an honorarium for their time and skills (from about £10 to £50 per day in addition to expenses). If under 14 years of age, this work is not counted as 'being employed' as the young person is not taxable nor likely to earn enough to start paying tax (Steele, 2003). Those young people in receipt of benefits are expected to declare any income and it is good practice for the research sponsor to remind young people of their responsibility.

Informing-for-Consent

Informed consent was discussed in Chapter 4 and is usually used to refer to those who are being asked to participate in a research study. In the case of service users, it can also be argued that the service users who are being asked to become researchers need to be able to give their informed consent to becoming researchers. The idea of being a researcher can seem very exciting to a young service user who may be unaware of the expectations of the role and what it will demand of them. It is thus imperative that young service users who wish to become researchers should be fully informed, as far as it is possible to do so, about what will be expected of them. They are then in a position to opt in, or out, with a realistic view of what is likely to happen. For example, researchers are expected to retain confidentiality and young researchers who are researching their peers need to be very clear that this also includes them and that they cannot go telling their friends about what research respondents have said. It is imperative that this informing-for-consent should be checked out at regular intervals to ensure that the co-researchers are aware of the expectations in relation to confidentiality and are provided with the opportunity to back out or be supported with any difficult issues. It is also good practice to develop a service user job description that service user researchers can retain to remind them about what they have agreed to.

Safeguarding Young Service Users

As France (2004) notes, researchers who come into contact with children and young people have a responsibility to protect them from harm, this is irrespective of whether their contact is professional or informal. This clearly raises issues concerning the limits of confidentiality. For young service user researchers, we may wish to debate what the thresholds are and what happens after these thresholds have been crossed. Young service user researchers need to know what the consequences are if they disclose something, how it will be acted on and what that process will be. Ideally this should be dealt with through discussion or the use of potential scenarios, but adult researchers need to be aware that the responsibility is theirs to inform the young people. If a young person is unable to sign up to the confidentiality protocol then they should be asked to leave the research team or to adopt an alternative role in the process that would not expose them to such sensitive material.

For young service users acting as researchers the demands of informed consent and confidentiality act both ways. Anything that they say, to adult or peer researchers, may be dealt with in this way and anything that is told to them by other young people is subject to the same standards.

In seeking to safeguard young co-researchers, they should not be asked to interview adults by themselves at unknown addresses or in closed rooms. Interviewing in pairs is advisable not only because of the safety issues but also to provide support and learning. The lead researcher also needs to know where the young co-researchers are and to provide regular supervision and debriefing. McLaughlin (2005) also found that teenage girls needed to interview in pairs when interviewing teenage boys who saw this as an opportunity for 'speed dating' and were more interested in 'chatting up' the girls than in answering the research questions. As a principled position, young co-researchers should be aware that their own safety is paramount and that this is placed above the completion of the research tasks (Save the Children, 2004).

Other practical considerations need to be borne in mind, including matters such as ensuring that travelling arrangements are appropriate for young service users. Parents, or those with parental responsibility, also need to be aware of these arrangements. Importantly, supervision or mentoring arrangements need to have been established to support the co-researchers throughout the process and any papers that they are asked to read should be sufficiently child friendly and free of jargon to make them understandable.

What can be expected of young people will vary in relation to their maturity, age and ability. Researchers need to consider these interrelating issues when deciding what they want young service users to undertake in relation to the research. Young people researching other young people will also need to consider how they can best communicate with other young people. This may require the use of a mosaic approach involving multi-method research styles, including the use of computers, pictures, smiley faces, Post-its, cameras and drawings as well as the usual interviewing styles (Langston et al., 2004).

In working with children and young people in the UK, researchers need to have a satisfactory Enhanced Criminal Records Bureau check. This should also include young people above the age of 18 who are part of the research process. This is especially important if the researchers intend having unsupervised access to young co-researchers or young service users as part of the research. This is not always necessary for other service user groups, but is desirable when working with vulnerable individuals. The police check cannot be a guarantee of acceptable behaviour and research sponsors need to consider how they can minimise the risks and ensure that adult researchers and young co-researchers behave in acceptable ways.

Conclusion

This chapter has set out to highlight a growing movement in research: that of involving service users as researchers. Social work can be proud to have been at the forefront of this movement. Whilst the chapter has been very much in favour of service user involvement in research, this support has not been uncritical. Service users as researchers should be supported when it would add value or additionality to a research proposal; it is neither always necessary nor always appropriate. Before deciding when to involve service users the research sponsor, or lead researcher, needs to examine the research question, the types of research methods to be used and the funding in the proposal. If it is deemed that such an approach would benefit from service user involvement, then the lead researcher needs to decide with the service user researchers at what level(s) this can best be achieved and whether this is to include seats on the advisory group or to have them involved in the whole research process or just parts of it. Having made the decision to involve service user researchers, funding needs to be made available to provide the appropriate training and remuneration and to cover research expenses. The lead researcher also needs to be aware that the research is likely to take longer and although the benefits may be potentially greater there is no guarantee that they will be. If you do not have the time to do this properly or the resources to fund such a programme, then it would be better not to involve service users. Service user research is not a universal solution. However, service user research will provide an often overlooked perspective of social work research – that of the service user, not as a subject of intervention, but as a co-creator of knowledge providing an oft-missed piece of the bigger puzzle.

Summary

This chapter has sought to examine the issue of service user involvement in social research. The chapter began by identifying the policy and government drivers for the promotion of service user involvement in social work practice and education. This was then developed in relation to social research with the identification of the claims made for the involvement of service users in research and an identification of some of the difficulties related to service user research. Having identified a rationale and value for service user research, issues relating to the philosophical underpinning of this and a critical appraisal of levels of service user involvement were discussed. Generally, service user involvement in research tends to be at the lower levels of involvement, whilst service user controlled research is still developing. Following this discussion, there was consideration of what the meaningful involvement of service users meant and how a fair return for participation could be ensured in order to avoid the exploitation of service user researchers. There was also an important discussion on knowledge claims, standpoint theory and the importance of ensuring the place of service user researcher perspectives of themselves within the research process.

The chapter then moved onto an examination of the possibilities, difficulties and methodological issues involved in working with young service users as co-researchers. In particular this section focused on issues concerning the employment of young people, informed consent and safeguarding young people.

Suggested Reading

Hanley, B., Bradburn, J., Barnes, M., Evans, C., Goodare, H., Kelson, M., Kent, A., Oliver, S., Thomas, S. and Wallcraft, J. (2004) *Involving the Public in NHS, Public Health, and Social Care Research: Briefing Notes for Researchers.* Eastleigh: Involve.
This is a very useful practical guide giving useful information and details on involving the public at each of the different stages of the research process.

The guide can also be downloaded at www.invo.org.uk, along with a range of other guides for researchers and members of the public who are interested in becoming involved in research as service user researchers.

McLaughlin, H. (2009) *Service User Research in Health and Social Care.* London: Sage.
This is a highly accessible book that is the first text to analyse the involvement of service users in research from the conception of a research idea to the end of the project.

Nolan, M., Hanson, E.R., Grant, G. and Keady, J. (eds) (2007) *User Participation in Health and Social Care Research: Voices, Values and Evaluation.* Maidenhead: Open University.
This is an edited book with a range of examples of service user research in practice.

9 Interdisciplinary Contributions to Social Work and Social Work Research

Introduction

Social work services don't have all of the answers. They need to work closely with other universal providers in all the sectors to find new ways to design and deliver services across the public sector. (Roe, 2006: 8)

The above quotation is one of the three key messages of the Roe Commission into the future of social work in Scotland and this chapter sets out to highlight the importance and growing contribution of interdisciplinary practice and research. Galvani (2008: 105) captures the essence of this approach when she highlights the difficulties faced by people with substance misuse problems:

Many have a number of problems that precede, coincide with and/or result from the problematic substance use. These problems commonly include experiences of child abuse, domestic violence, financial difficulties, housing problems, trouble with the police, family breakdown, loss of employment, and physical and mental health problems. No one professional can be an expert in all these things. No one agency can provide all the services that a person may need. Multi-agency working is therefore essential.

In order to deal with these complex and 'wicked' social problems there is a need for an interprofessional approach, as no single worker, or agency, has all the identified resources or skills to meet the needs of someone with substance misuse problems. There is also a belief that such work would develop a natural reciprocity, whereby the interprofessional relationship was seen to be of mutual benefit to each of the partners helping them to achieve their goals whilst reducing risk and resources (Glasby and Dickinson, 2008).

In recent years there has been a growing awareness of the interdependence of services and this has been a feature of service development worldwide including: Australia (Hugman, 2003; Rogers, 2004); America (Pew Health Professions Commission, 1995; Stone et al., 2004); and the UK (Leathard, 2003; Trevillion and Bedford, 2003). In the UK, since 1997, interprofessional, collaborative or multiagency working has moved quickly up the policy agenda where it has been supported by a raft of legislation, special initiatives and funding. This has in part been a response to identified failures of the professions to work collaboratively, which has been a consistent theme in modern child abuse deaths, ranging from that of Maria Colwell (1974) to that of Baby Peter (2007). The issue of interprofessional working reached a new zenith with the death of Victoria Climbié (2000) about whom the public inquiry identified the failures of interprofessional working as a significant contributor to her death (Laming, 2003). This has led to the situation whereby Wilson et al. (2008) claim that:

> The direction of public policy for the delivery of health and social care is therefore clear: interprofessional working is regarded as a key requirement of its delivery, a statement that holds good in relation to work with children, families and adults. (Wilson et al., 2008: 389)

Although we have described a direction of travel towards greater interprofessional practice, this has been against a backcloth of policy mandates and legal mechanisms promoting cooperation between health and social services whilst at the same time experiencing a greater fragmentation between children and adult services. This is particularly so in social care in England, with children services being the responsibility of the Department for Education and adult services the Department of Health.

It is somewhat ironic that the drive towards 'joined-up working' and 'seamless services' in England has resulted in the development of fault lines between children and adult services. These fault lines are likely to increase as we see the development of adult and children's trusts as two separate entities making it increasingly possible that we will end up discussing the intersections between adult and children services as the future sites for interprofessional practice. We know that parents with mental health difficulties may require support with their child care or that domestic violence is often associated with child safeguarding issues, and the need for workers to be able to work across the intergenerational divide is getting greater with workers specialising in one area often feeling deskilled or incompetent in the other.

The emphasis on joined-up thinking for joined-up problems can be seen in initiatives like the Crime and Disorder Act (1998) that led to the creation of the youth crime service and the establishment of the interprofessionally staffed Youth Offending Services, including social workers, police officers, educational and health representatives. At this point it is worth noting that terms like 'inter-professional', 'interdisciplinary', 'multiagency' and 'collaborative working' are notoriously difficult to define and although each term has a slightly different nuance they are often conflated. Interprofessional working in these contexts is defined by Higham (2001: 21) as:

> situations where workers belonging to one professional discipline practise beyond their own boundaries in partnership with professionals form other disciplines (Ovretveit, 1993, 1997). This kind of practice is sometimes known as multi-disciplinary practice or inter-professional practice (Leathard, 1994). (Higham, 2001: 21)

Of particular importance to us from Higham's definition are the notions of a profession and a discipline.

Before going to examine the notion of a profession, can you consider what you believe a profession to be? Can you name three professions that meet your definition? Would social work be included in your definition? Why is this so? What about the soldiers, police officers, nurses, publicans, doctors, lawyers and footballers?

Reflexive Questions

Is Social Work a Profession?

In today's society many occupational groups claim to be made up of 'profession-als', the Army invites you to come and 'join the professionals'. We talk of profes-sional footballers or of the Police whilst many people still look towards the time-honoured professions: doctors, lawyers and clerics.

Hugman (1991) notes that, traditionally, the notion of a profession has been developed from a 'traits' approach in which a set of identified characteristics were held to constitute a profession. Being a member of a profession is seen as a high status position within our society whereby, for example, the medical profes-sion has been able to claim that it is a profession by successfully organising itself to maintain a high standing in society and protect a high level of material reward. This has been based on three distinct characteristics: it has restricted entry to the profession via a strict set of criteria or qualifications; it has a professional association that monitors and controls the conduct and performance of its members; and it is generally accepted that only those whom it licences are quali-fied to practise medicine (Giddens, 2001). In so doing, the profession is able to exclude unwanted individuals whilst at the same time enhancing the reputation and market share of its own members. In contrast, occupational groups like social workers, nurses or physiotherapists have been viewed as semi-professions or bureau professions (Payne, 2000). These occupational groups are seen as aspiring professions but lacking in the autonomy of practice. The trait approach has come under criticism as it ignores that the claims for professions like medicine or the law should not just be accepted but should be opened up for questioning rather than being seen as benchmarks for others to achieve. Second, the extent to which a trait is assigned to a profession is in reality a claim to exclusion and exclusivity, which needs to be challenged as opposed to being accepted as a social fact. Third, such an approach ignores issues of power and how certain occupational groups can muster up sufficient weight and support to call themselves, and be called by others, professionals. The issue of whether an occupational group is a profession is a debate about power. It is a claim to exclusivity and power whereby an occupational group benefits from asserting itself, and getting others to view and treat it as a profession.

It could be argued that social work is now a profession in that entry to the profession is controlled through the social work degree qualification. The care councils have taken over the role of controlling and registering those who may and may not be admitted to the profession. Also, it is only those who have the appropriate qualifications and are registered who can legally call themselves social workers following the protection of the title of social worker in April 2005. On such a tri-partite definition, as suggested by Giddens (2001), social workers could justifiably claim to be members of a profession.

Others may point out that being a member of a profession has traditionally indicated a model of individual practitioner responsibility. Doctors are deemed to hold 'clinical responsibility' for patients, and lawyers are deemed to be 'individually responsible' for their own practice. Clearly social work has not reached these degrees of individual responsibility, being located primarily within statutory or voluntary bodies. It is worth noting, though, that the levels of individual responsibility within the traditional professions have also been reduced at the same time as social work's autonomy has been increased. The medical governing bodies have come under increasing scrutiny with the British Medical Association being criticised by Dame Janet Smith's public inquiry into the deaths of Dr Shipman's patients (Smith, 2004). Increasingly, lawyers are required to specialise and are employed in non-legal organisations. In all of these cases, consumer organisations, the development of complaints systems and increasing social pressures have reduced the autonomy of the traditional professions.

Our understanding of the nature of professions needs to become more nuanced. We need to consider issues like autonomy and responsibility more broadly, along with concepts of power and the ability of an occupational group to persuade other occupational groups to respond to them as a profession. There is also a sense in which all this does not really matter. It could be argued that social work should distance itself from the claims of exclusion and exclusivity and care less whether we are, or are seen as, a profession and instead focus on our duty to our service users and to ensure that we act in a professional manner.

Is Social Work a Discipline?

It is rarely asked what a discipline is or whether social work is a discipline or not. Deetz (1993), in writing about communication studies, has argued that there are at least three different approaches to the notion of an academic discipline. The first of these suggests that a discipline represents a world organised into academic units or departments. On this criterion, social work is obviously a discipline as it is represented in many universities throughout the world as a separate department or unit.

Discipline 2 reflects a world organised around topic interests. Again social work can be defined as a discipline as it is seen to be a distinct phenomenon with clear topic interests. Discipline 3 represents a world organised around competing modes of explanation. This is where social work struggles: it could be argued that there are just too many competing and contesting explanations. In this sense the future of social work as a full discipline commanding of respect and productive in research terms relies heavily upon the failures of sociology, psychology, economics and so on to deal effectively with explaining social phenomena and failing to provide clear direction for social workers and social care practitioners. To the extent that these disciplines fail to account for the nature of social work there is then a danger that social work becomes translated into more than just an underpinning for social care, but becomes reconceptualised into something that every human being undertakes in negotiating reality. This requires social work to address questions of ontology and epistemology (see Chapter 3) in order to establish its intellectual core and avoid being at the beck and call of other academic disciplines. Social work thus becomes an activity that is located in the home, the street and in public and private life. Although its activities are social, psychological and economic, it cannot be reduced to any one of these disciplines.

Importantly, it should be noted that the case for social work research is not limited to the activities of social workers, but represents the underpinning of social care – social work skills, knowledge and values that are relevant to the wider social care audience – and we must not confuse social work research with research on what social workers do.

The Discipline of Interdisciplinarity

It may seem strange to be discussing whether social work is a discipline when as we have already noted there has been a growth in interdisciplinarity and interprofessional practice, including in the number of multi-professional or multiagency teams and a general acceptance that this represents the way forward for services in the future (Morris, 2008). Somewhat incongruously, it is probably more important than ever that social work is able to articulate its uniqueness, values and core activities. To engage in multi-professional teams or interdisciplinary ventures without being clear about the unique contribution of your own professional or disciplinary background is to run the risk of being colonised by other more articulate or older professions.

There is thus a paradox, in seeking to work or research in multi-professional teams requires a strong professional identity to maximise the contribution of the individual disciplines or run the risk of the team being reduced to those who shout loudest. Conversely, too strong a professional identity is likely to lead to disruptive arguments concerning territory and boundaries. What is required are mature professionals who are clear about their own contribution and are able to value the contribution of others and who see it as a strength that others may view the same situation through a different professional lens.

Alongside this growth in interdisciplinarity, Delanty and Strydom (2003) have noticed a decline in disciplinarity. The natural, human and social sciences can no longer be so sharply separated from each other. The natural and social sciences share many similar areas of concern, including the 'environment', the 'body' and 'risk'. The rise of these new discourses has demanded a new complexity and inter-relationships. Second, there has been an increasing trend within social sciences to become more and more interdisciplinary. Research has become increasingly driven by problems (e.g. the reduction in crime), ethical political concerns (e.g. asylum seekers) and policy-directed programmes (eradicating poverty) than by single-disciplinary specific traditions. It would be premature to say that there is a crisis in disciplinarity but it would also be naive to ignore the current trend and unquestioned acceptance of interdisciplinarity.

Interdisciplinary Practice

In seeking to address individual, family, community and society's problems social workers come into contact with a wide range of professions. These professions potentially include health visitors, teachers, probation officers, police officers, psychologists, education welfare officers, GPs, nurses and paediatricians in relation to child protection; community psychiatric nurses, GPs, gerontologists, psychiatrists, nurses, occupational therapists and housing officers in relation to elder abuse. These groups may come together in a number of ways. Traditionally they have been based separately and have met together to focus on an individual problem or concern. More recently, following Section 31 of the 1999 Health Act,

NHS bodies and local authorities have been given the 'flexibility' to respond to user-focused services by joining up services or by developing new coordinated services as well as by working with other organisations. These resulted in the formation of learning disability trusts, mental health trusts and more recently to children's trusts. This has led Highman (2001: 21) to comment that social workers in the future will either practise in interdisciplinary teams or work in partnership with professionals from other occupations, much more so than with colleagues from their own profession.

Before we go on to identify the benefits of interprofessional practice you should try to identify three things that you think would be improved through interprofessional practice. What would you see as the potential problems in achieving these benefits? Would you want to work in an interprofessional team? If so why?

The benefits claimed for interdisciplinary practice teams include the factors listed below (Hudson, 2002; Leathard, 2003; Torkington et al., 2003).

- Reduces fragmentation and duplication in an increasingly complex policy and welfare context.
- Reflects the government policy agenda on 'joined-upness'.
- An integrated approach shaped around the needs of service users, not professionals.
- A single strategic approach, with a single set of aims and targets.
- More effective use of staff and resources.
- A more satisfying work environment in terms of service provision and staff support.
- Recognition that professionals can have as much in common with members of another profession as they do with their own.
- Effective interprofessional working can help to meet the collective goals of individual organisations while providing a better overall quality of service.

All of these positives are very persuasive, but Hudson (2002) has claimed that a closer reading of the literature on interprofessionality has tended towards a more pessimistic outcome. Hugman (2003) in reflecting on the experience in Australia has commented that with all the attempts to promote interprofessional developments in the Australian context, the boundaries between professions have reformed rather than been reduced:

What are the incentives for any of the health and social welfare professions to move beyond their 'tribal circles'? when the very understanding of the benefit to service users is seen as differently from within these separate perspectives (and attempts to weaken boundaries have been experienced as a collusion with the attack on professionalism per se from economic rationalism). Until that question is addressed we may expect the 'tribal' circles to remain strong and hence to risk continuing to 'go round in circles'. (Hugman, 2003: 65)

It can thus be argued that although interprofessionalism promises many benefits these benefits have been difficult to realise.

One area that has been identified as a potential driver for change are well-organised and structured programmes of education and training to support interprofessional practice. Barr et al. (2005: xvii) suggest that, just like interprofessional practice, 'interprofessional education is bedevilled by terminological inexactitude'. Carpenter and Dickinson (2008: 3) use the definition derived from the Centre for the Advancement of Interprofessional Education (CAIPE, 2002), whereby interprofessional education occurs on:

> occasions when two or more professionals learn with, from and about each other to improve collaboration and the quality of care.

Zwarenstein et al. (1999), using the guidelines for systematic reviews developed by the Cochrane Collaboration, concluded that no rigorous evidence existed on the effects of interprofessional education, although they also found no evidence of ineffectiveness. In a review of post qualifying programmes, Zwarenstein et al. (2005) found that there was a growing body of evidence showing positive effects on the delivery of care, although these effects were not evident in all settings and were particularly weak in primary care. This suggests that the field of interprofessional education is a fruitful one for more detailed, substantive and sophisticated research.

Interprofessional education is taken to its logical extreme in the UK where there are six courses offering joint nursing and social work qualifications. These joint programmes stem indirectly from the Jay Committee (1979), which was intent on replacing the medical model by a social model in working with people with learning disabilities and, following resistance to this view the then General Nursing Council and CCETSW came up with the compromise of a dual qualification (GNC and CCETSW, 1982).

Reflexive Questions

Practice Example

The University of Salford provides a BSc joint qualification in social work and learning disability nursing. The impetus for this programme came from learning disability managers who believed that neither qualification suitably prepared staff for employment with people with learning disability. What was needed was a joint qualification. The BSc programme at Salford lasts three years and is jointly validated by the GSCC and the

Nursing and Midwifery Council. Students on the programme have to reach the occupational standards of both professions and experience placements in both settings and be taught by staff from both social work and nursing.

Post hoc surveys have regularly reported that the students have enjoyed their experience of being exposed to two different cultures, learning the ability to work in multidisciplinary teams, and being helped to understand the potential contribution of each profession. On top of this the students were also able to see the importance of holistic assessments and of putting the service user at the centre of service provision. When the first students graduated in 1998, they were traditionally employed in nursing, although there has been a gradual rebalancing of this position with approximately half now taking up posts in social work or learning disability trusts. Due to the small number of students taking dual qualifications nationally and the lack of independent evaluation it is difficult to estimate the impact of dual qualification holders on practice.

The above example may be seen as either an extreme instance of interprofessional education or an instrument of 'professional engineering'. It is also interesting to speculate on other potential combinations like community psychiatric nursing, health visiting or teaching and social work. Such dual qualifications are not what are meant when we traditionally talk of interprofessional education, but they do offer an alternative way forward.

So far we have identified the policy drivers for interprofessional practice, examined the notion of a profession and a discipline and begun to tease out the claimed and potential benefits of interprofessional education and practice. This has also been tempered with some cautionary notes on the difficulties experienced seeking to try and achieve these benefits.

This book is primarily concerned with understanding social work research and the context of practice has been a necessary grounding for our discussion in relation to research. Interdisciplinary research can be understood in at least two different ways. The first of these involves researching interprofessional practice and the second of these concerns interdisciplinary research of social issues or problems. The rest of the chapter will focus on these two issues.

Researching Interprofessional Practice

As already mentioned, there has been a move towards an uncritical acceptance of interprofessional practice as the answer to dealing with the 'wicked' social problems. There are thus at least two ways of conceptualising the need for interprofessional research. The first concerns the integration of professional groups within an entity like an adult or children's trust, or where the research addresses questions in relation to particular social problems, like reducing the misuse of drugs.

Reflexive Questions

Can you identify what you would consider to be the benefits and costs of multi-professional research teams?

Multi-professional research teams may consist of a team of researchers from different disciplines where the researchers undertake all aspects of the research, only interview those from the same profession or a team whereby, for example, the health staff member may undertake the qualitative work and the social worker may take responsibility for the quantitative work. Whichever way the research team is organised, the important issue will be the need for an ongoing dialogue between the research team in order to ensure that all voices are heard and issues of competing interpretations and analysis are recognised and addressed.

For some questions, like an evaluation of the effectiveness of a children's trust including social work, education and health staff are likely to benefit from researchers from each of the different professional disciplines. Such combinations of professional backgrounds are likely to ensure that:

- The questionnaires or interview schedules are meaningful to the different professional groups.
- The research team has credibility with those being researched.
- The priorities of the different professional groups can be better identified and understood.
- The nuances between the different professional groups can be captured.
- Any report will speak with greater authority and be less open to claims of privileging one professional group at the expense of the others.

All the above assumes that the research team is a well-functioning group with mutual respect for each of its members' professional backgrounds and research skills. There is a dual requirement here. If a researcher in the team is a poor researcher this may reflect badly on their professional background and vice versa where a member of the team's professional background is less valued by the research team, which may result in their research contribution being less valued. Such teams in addressing issues like the functioning of adult or children's trusts, will also have to face the challenge of not only having the right research skills within the research team but the added dimension of the constitution of the team and the team's biases and views of the different professions. This may add an extra dimension to the quality of the research or may just as easily act as a barrier to an effective co-produced research report capturing the differing professional perspectives accurately.

This is not to claim that those who have never been a social worker, youth worker or nurse cannot research issues like this. Such a position would be inherently objectionable and open to ridicule. It is, however, to claim that if researchers also have a professional background that they can utilise in their research then this is potentially likely to make a more informed research product. Such apposition is not guaranteed and does require the research team to be able to address both differing research and professional perspectives in an open and honest way.

Interdisciplinary Research

Before going on to discuss interdisciplinary research, what would you consider as interdisciplinary research? How would interdisciplinary research be different from 'normal' research? What would you see as the benefits and weaknesses of interdisciplinary research?

Reflexive Questions

Traditional research usually implies research based within one of the major research traditions or disciplines. Obviously it is possible to consider mixed methods approaches, as has been demonstrated earlier. It is important for researchers to consider when a uni-disciplinary approach would be more appropriate than an interdisciplinary or multidisciplinary one. It may well be that it is the nature of the question that will drive the approach.

We first need to clarify our terms, accepting that in doing so we are not reflective of everyone who uses these terms who may define them slightly differently. A multidisciplinary research approach is characterised by the autonomy of the various disciplines, for example sociology or psychology, and does not lead to changes or challenges to the existing disciplinary structures. As such, multidisciplinary research approaches may help to address a complex mental health problem, but the result of this research will not necessarily impact upon any of the individual research disciplines that have helped to inform the research. Interdisciplinary research, on the other hand, suggests a research approach that is characterised by the explicit formulation of a common framework. Interdisciplinary research does not borrow its research credibility from its constituent disciplines, but creates its own common methodology and may in time become a discipline in its own right.

Within single discipline research centres there is often a statement indicating a desire and wish to work in an interdisciplinary way, which is often translated into working with other single discipline research centres. You might, for instance, have a social work, nursing and an education research centre jointly bidding for a safeguarding children's research project. Alternatively, some research centres define themselves as a children and families or gerontology research centres, containing a wide range of academic disciplines, including social work, health and education that may bid for the same project. There are also those research centres that do not use service user classifications but instead use terms like social justice or social inclusion who could also bid for the same research project. University research centre titles and the configurations of staff included within them come and go as universities try to provide an external looking face that captures the expertise of their staff whilst also keeping an eye on both the research assessment exercise and potential funders.

When we have more than one discipline contributing to a research project, there is a danger that the resulting knowledge production becomes no more than a mere accumulation of knowledge supplied from more than one discipline. This in itself is not necessarily to be derided, as a multidisciplinary approach may be justified but is something different from an interdisciplinary one.

Interdisciplinarity involves the explicit formulation of a single discipline transcending common methodology. This may mean that the form that the research takes will involve differing disciplinary researchers working on different themes but within an agreed common methodology. Gibbons et al. (1994) develop this further when they suggest that interdisciplinary research turns into transdisciplinary research when the research is based upon a common framework that is shared by the disciplines involved. The next section identifies the main claims by Gibbons et al. (1994) and their potential impact on social work.

Transdisciplinary Research

> Transdisciplinarity arises only if research is based upon a common theoretical understanding and must be accompanied by a mutual interpenetration of disciplinary epistemologies. Co-operation in this case leads to a clustering of disciplinary rooted problem-solving and creates a transdisciplinary homogenised theory or model pool. (Gibbons et al., 1994: 29)

Transdisciplinary research is characterised as the favoured form of research in Mode 2 knowledge production. Gibbons et al. (1994) define two ideal types of knowledge production, Mode 1 and Mode 2. Mode 1 is represented as being governed largely by the academic community, mono-disciplinary, homogenous and hierarchical. Mode 2, in contrast, is described as being carried out at the point of application; transdisciplinary, heterogeneous, more heterarchial and

TABLE 1   *Key characteristics of Mode 1 and Mode 2 knowledge production*

Characteristics	Mode 1	Mode 2
Context governed by	Academic community	Application
Discipline	Single	Transdisciplinary
Nature	Homogeneity	Heterogeneity
Organisational	Hierarchical	Heterarchial
Quality control	Less socially accountable and reflexive	More socially accountable and reflexive
Preferred research style	Single researcher	Collaboration of different disciplines

transient whilst it's quality control structures are described as more accountable and reflexive. These can be summarised in Table 1

Key Characteristics of Mode 1 and Mode 2 Knowledge Production

According to Gibbons et al. (1994) Mode 1 is largely governed *by* the academic community *for* the academic community. In this context Mode 1 can be identified with 'pure science' whose primary goal is the pursuit of knowledge governed by the cognitive and social norms that direct basic research. In contrast, Mode 2 is carried out at the point of application, and is intended to be useful to someone and may be considered as applied science. Earlier in the book we noted that social work is an applied activity whereby the social worker's role is not merely to observe the world but to engage with it in ways to address individual, family, community or social difficulties and problems. Social work research may, and hopefully does, produce new knowledge, but this is not the primary purpose of the research. The primary purpose of social work research is to promote and develop effective social work practice, enabling and empowering service users. Thus social work on this criterion can be seen to be a potential Mode 2 discipline. A Mode 2 discipline is organised towards a practical goal and faces the double challenge of being of a high academic quality and of practical relevance. This feature of Mode 2 is also transferable to research focused on social problems that require not only the combined and collaborative approach of different professions but also the combined and collaborative approaches of differing research traditions and disciplines.

Transdisciplinarity has four key features:

- A distinct and developing framework guiding problem-solving efforts.
- Problem solutions will contain both empirical and theoretical components.

- Dissemination of results is initially accomplished through the process of their production.
- The whole process is dynamic.

Transdisciplinarity refers to a:

> movement beyond disciplinary structures in the constitution of the intellectual agenda, in the manner in which resources are deployed, and in the ways in which research is organised, results communicated and the outcome evaluated. (Gibbons et al., 1994: 27)

In transdisciplinary contexts, the traditional boundaries between pure and applied research, theory and practice become less important as the focus is primarily on the identified problem. Preference is given to collaborative work as opposed to individual performance and excellence is judged by a sustained ability to contribute in the new, temporary and open organisation in which individuals work whilst addressing the issues and problems. Such an approach represents a shift away from fundamental truths towards modes of enquiry oriented towards contextualised and localised results.

One of the key differentiating characteristics between Mode 1 and Mode 2 is the nature of quality control or what is to count as knowledge. Those claiming to produce knowledge have to follow certain rules, but also have to be trained in the appropriate procedures and techniques. Mode 1 is governed by a system of peer review that promotes a system of professionalisation and institutionalisation channelling researchers to work on key problems for the advancement of the discipline and suggesting likely solutions. By comparison Mode 2 is less self-sealing and is likely to create more problematic claims to knowledge, as the knowledge will fall outside of the normal disciplinary structures and is therefore less likely to be accepted. Mode 2 not only has to meet the normal academic criterion of acceptance but will also address wider social questions including, 'Will this solution empower or disempower service users?' 'Is this solution ethical?' and 'Who benefits and who loses from this proposed solution?' As such the quality control in Mode 2 is multidimensional, bringing to bear a wider range of criterion that does not automatically imply an inferior standard.

Although Mode 1 and Mode 2 have been characterised here as differing paradigms they do interact with each other. Researchers trained in Mode 1 can become Mode 2 researchers. Some of the outputs from Mode 2 may re-enter Mode 1 and act as the springboards for future discovery within that discipline.

Whilst Mode 2 would appear a highly attractive model of knowledge production; however, for social work it is not without its difficulties. Gibbons et al. (1994) recognise that such a model is very difficult to achieve and warn against researchers who claim that they are behaving in transdisciplinary or interdisciplinary ways but in reality are disciplinary bound. Different disciplines are identified by their different methodologies, epistemologies and ways of understanding the world that may well be incommensurate. Sociology focuses on the group and psychology on the individual and it is not possible to aggregate psychological understandings to create sociology or to disaggregate sociological understandings to create psychology. Further difficulties are likely to be experienced in creating a common language. Academically it may only be possible to gain a range of differing perspectives on the same problem using one of the disciplines to integrate the others. This may include a series of touching points between the different disciplines. Also, if we are unable to escape the received disciplines how would it be possible to create new disciplines, or how do we explain where disciplines came from in the first place?

Multidisciplinarity, Interdisciplinarity, Transdisciplinarity and Social Work

It is apparent from the above that social work, either by choice or by external mandate, cannot ignore the importance of interprofessional approaches in practice and research. To ensure that this does not develop in an ad hoc or indiscriminate way requires the development of a robust research culture that is able to address these challenges. To achieve this we have identified three distinct models. The first of these, multidisciplinarity, is represented by a team of researchers who come from either different disciplines or professional groups to focus on the same problem. The different professions may include social workers, health personnel, psychologists and teachers when examining the issue of the educational achievement of children looked after or researchers from a social policy, psychological and sociological perspectives to examine the same phenomena. At the end of this exercise none of the individual professions or disciplines will be changed by the research, as it will be absorbed within each single profession or discipline. Whilst this represents a defensible research position and will be appropriate in many situations it is not appropriate in all. For example, if we accept that the different disciplines of social policy, sociology and psychology all have potential insights into the educational achievement of children looked after, how do we decide which discipline's perspective is the most important and most influential? Without any form of an integrating super-discipline, each of the differing disciplines will end up making claims that will be justifiable within their own disciplinary perspective, but potentially incommensurable with each other. For example, if we find that the educational difficulties of looked after children are the result of personal issues, the range of measures to address these will be different than if we discovered that the social policies and structures of health, social work and education were conflictual and undermined looked after children's education.

Interdisciplinarity represents a development of multidisciplinarity whereby the issues of disciplinary primacy become resolved through the creation of a common framework and common methodology. Thus, in the example above there would be an agreed process for establishing the different weights of the differing explanations and an agreed way of looking at how and when they individually contributed and what the outcomes were when they interacted. Thus, if it was found that there were personal issues for young people looked after and the organisation and policies of health, social services and education were undermining educational achievement, attempts would be made to find out how these different explanations impacted on each other whilst also providing explanations in their own right. Given time, the methodology for such a process could potentially herald the beginning of a new understanding on how to promote educational attainment or even a new discipline.

The third model, transdisciplinarity, represents a progression of the interdisciplinary typology, highlighting a model that focuses on application, heterogeneity and social accountability with collaborative researchers. This model is not restrained by disciplinary boundaries but moves beyond them into new forms of research processes, knowledge production and potential ways of working. In the example of educational achievement, such an approach may challenge what is meant by educational achievement and whether young people looked after share this view. A transdisciplinary approach with its emphasis on new configurations of problem solution might also contain organisational, mental health, educational and nutritional specialists as it sought to find effective ways to improve the educational experience and outcomes for looked after children. Such an approach is likely to challenge traditional gaps in terminology, approach and methodology with an emphasis on developing ways of addressing educational achievement that not only include personal, social and structural issues but also seek to combine these in a locally contextualised and applied way. It remains difficult to describe a transdisciplinary approach, but for our purposes it is probably best considered as an extension of an interdisciplinary approach.

Summary

The chapter began by discussing whether social work was a profession and whether it was a discipline. Neither answer was straightforward. The chapter then sought to identify the trend away from individual professional working and towards multiprofessional working and then to interprofessional working in order to address society's 'wicked' problems and to ensure that the service user is at the centre of the service and not the professional. If this trend continues, as seems probable, social workers are more likely to be located in interprofessional teams than in single professional groups. This trend towards interprofessionalism raises important questions for social work, including that which asks what is the nature of social work and the social work profession, the degree to which social work should be self-policing and the relationship between the state and the professions (Trevillion and Bedford, 2003).

The chapter then discussed the nature and rhetoric of interprofessional education and the benefits claimed for it. Again the evidence for such claims has yet to be robustly developed. This is against a background of an increasingly uncritical acceptance that interprofessional education is the way forward.

In seeking to promote interdisciplinary working we then looked at multidisciplinary, interdisciplinary and transdisciplinary research. Disciplinary approaches have served us well in the past but are only able to provide solutions within their own discipline and are restricted by their own methodologies and insights. Again it was noted that the new approaches promised much and may potentially deliver much in the future, but have yet to do so. This is not to decry the advances in nanotechnology or the genome project but to say that in social work research and practice, the benefits are yet to be visible.

Suggested Reading

Glasby, J. and Dickinson, H. (2008) *Partnership Working in Health and Social Care*. Bristol: Policy Press in association with Community Care.
A well-written short introduction to the key issues involved in partnership or interprofessional practice. It is one of a series of books looking at different issues in relation to partnership working.

Gibbons, M., Limoges, C., Nowotny, H., Schwartzman, S., Scott, P. and Trow, M. (1994) *The New Production of Knowledge: The Dynamics of Science and Research in Contemporary Societies*. London: Sage.
A challenging book that sets out the argument for Mode 2 and the emergence of transdisciplines in science and research.

Journal of Interprofessional Care
This journal is dedicated to researching and discussing issues in relation to interprofessional working.

10 Whither Social Work Research

Introduction

This chapter begins with a review of the previous chapters looking at the implications of what we have discussed for the development of the research-minded social worker. Following this analysis we look toward a potential future for social work and the role that research might play in that future. This discussion is based on the acceptance that the notion of social work is contested and changing, but it is this uncertainty that makes it all the more important that researchers and social workers engage in dialogue. This dialogue must begin to explore how research can help to inform practice and how practice can act as a springboard for research. Just as research requires practice to become more research minded, so practice requires research to become more practice minded. Research and practice need to become critical friends, learning and challenging each other to deliver better outcomes for service users and carers. This suggests a model of research and practice that is not linear, but iterative where research and practice are continuously critiqued, one by the other, helping each to become more specific, useful and relevant.

At the beginning of the book it was claimed that good research can be synonymous with good practice and the book has sought to show how and why this statement should become a reality. Preston-Shoot (2002) has lamented that social workers have all too often been expected to pay little attention to theory, research and the literature underpinning their profession once they have qualified. On entering employment, the practice culture of their new colleagues and supervisors takes over and often what matters most is 'moving the work' and 'taking your share' rather than working with service users to address identified needs. A team leader recently said to me that on her first day as a social worker, she found a number of cases on her desk and undertook a child protection investigation that afternoon and it did her no harm! Such views beg the question why such organisations need qualified staff. It also questions whether students should join such organisations that appear only to want those who will process work, do what they are told, will not question why and are not encouraged to contribute to the organisation's learning.

The CWDC has developed a Newly Qualified Social Worker (NQSW) programme to support the skills, competence and confidence of NQSWs in order to improve job satisfaction and promote the retention of staff. The programme ingredients included reflective supervision, training for supervisors, protected time for training and development, funds to support training and a reduced workload. The evaluation of the first year of the programme (Carpenter et al., 2010) reported that NQSWs valued reflective supervision where this occurred but often this was squeezed out by case demands and that a number of authorities had subsequently commissioned external providers to undertake the reflective supervision. Providing caseload reduction also presented significant challenges for many of the authorities where team managers often felt the pressure from the NQSWs not to allocate more work but also the pressure from management to ensure that all work was allocated. Whilst most workers and authorities were in agreement with the CWDC initiative, this was easier to agree than to deliver.

Within England the SWRB are committed to developing an assessed year in employment before providing social workers with a licence to practice. The NQSW programme presenting an indication of what the assessed and supported year in employment could look like providing a real opportunity for newly graduated social workers to become research-minded practitioners, but only if their supervisors are able to provide the time for case management and reflective supervision.

Before moving onto potential scenarios for the future of social work research it is helpful to be reminded of some of the key debates and discussions as identified in this book.

Before the key themes are reviewed you might like to put down four bullet points of what you consider to be the most important learning points or themes that you have discovered from reading this book.

Reflexive Questions

Back in Chapter 1 we identified why research was critical to the continued development and survival of social work. This was against a backdrop in which the nature of social work and, by definition social work research, is contested and changing. The book identified the agreed IAASW and IFSW (2004) working definition that emphasises the key importance of human rights and social justice as fundamental to social work and its practice. This begins to identify the research agenda for social work and the values and interests that drive social work research.

This acceptance that social work research is grounded in the 'real world' also helps us to begin to understand that the nature of social work is mediated by the nature of society. In this context social work practice is contextualised by the nature of society we inhabit in this the third millennium, the impact and the fall-out from the global banking crisis, the legal system in which it operates and also the sites where it is practised. It is in this context that this book has sought to understand and explore the importance of research for social work.

The Research Business

One clear message from this book is that social work research is rarely undertaken solely for the purpose of enhancing and developing our knowledge. Social work is a practice discipline, and it is incumbent upon those who see themselves as social work researchers to consider how their research can be translated into behaviours so as to support practice actively. This does not mean that pure research is eschewed but that it is used to promote understanding and to act as a springboard for applied research and practice. Of particular concern is the underfunding of social work research in comparison to health research and the likely impact of this disparity on the infrastructure of social work research and the modernisation of social care. The Joint University Council Social Work Education Committee (JUC SWEC, 2006) agreed a social work research strategy in 2006 whose aim is to:

- Maximise the HEI contribution to social work and social care service improvement.
- Develop a strong evidence base for social work and social care services.
- Build a workforce capable of using evidence critically and effectively.

Whilst we can all probably agree to the sentiments of the committee's aims there is still significant work to be done before they can be realised.

Research Philosophies

Having identified the business of social work research and its importance to the development of social work practice we then moved on to examine two of the major paradigms of social research, positivism and interpretavism. The underpinning philosophies, including ontological and methodological assumptions, were identified and critiqued. It was noted that positivism was linked to quantitative methods favoured in the USA and interpretavism to qualitative methods favoured in the UK and Australia. Both methods were seen to represent mutually incommensurate points of view. To believe in one is by definition to disbelieve in the other. This philosophical impasse is circumvented in practice whereby researchers often use mixed methods and the implications of this pragmatic perspective were discussed. Either the researchers are deluded or the philosophical incommensurability is only that, philosophical. A mixed methods approach does not sidestep philosophical issues, though, and researchers need to be aware that merely adopting a 'chocolate box' approach to choosing methods is not necessarily appropriate either.

Social Work Research is Ethically Driven

Chapter 4 examined the need for ethical research highlighting some of the abuses that have occurred to research subjects in the past. This chapter also sought to argue that ethical research was much more than ethical approval from a research governance and ethics committee. This was not to say that gaining such approval is not important, but that often the most difficult ethical questions only occur once the research has begun and were not envisaged in the original approval. To this end it was argued that social work researchers need to become morally active researchers throughout their research study as ethical issues appear at stages of the process.

Throughout the book the reader is reminded that to act ethically in research is not merely desirable but essential. Good intentions are not enough; the social work researcher has to be able to show that they have considered as fully as possible any likely harm that their research may present to research respondents and how these risks can be reduced. Ethics are inherently embedded in social work practice and must also be similarly embedded in social work research.

Anti-Oppressive Research

Intertwined with the importance given to the ethical nature of social work research is the need to develop anti-oppressive research practices. Social work is unequivocally committed to anti-discriminatory and anti-oppressive practice. Both concepts are often conflated. What anti-discriminatory and anti-oppressive research practice actually are is historically highly contentious. Concepts like 'blackness' and 'whiteness' have been shown to be problematic and potentially restrictive. Anti-oppressive practice in research though does contain a commitment to highlight, challenge and eradicate social injustice at whatever levels within society such oppression or discrimination should occur. For the social work researcher this represents a double challenge in that the research process itself should not be discriminatory or oppressive and that the areas of research focused upon should represent a commitment to an anti-oppressive stance. This can create difficulties in gaining access to research subjects such as which employer is likely to agree to a research project that shows themselves or their staff as oppressive or discriminatory.

Traditionally, anti-oppressive practice is associated with issues of race, gender, disability, sexuality and age. More recently issues of colonialism, urbanism and spirituality have been added to this list with an acceptance that there may yet be more areas of anti-oppressive structures that have still to be named or discovered. It also needs to be acknowledged that individuals are not uni-dimensional, but have multiple cross-cutting dimensions in that they may be a black, female, paraplegic, homosexual, older person of Maori descent living in a rural setting or any other combination of the potentially differing discriminatory identities. It is also possible that any individual will be both the subject and the perpetrator of oppression in different aspects of their lives. Social work researchers need to be aware of the danger of falling into an uncritical stance in response to anti-oppressive research and the hierarchy of oppression trap where it is claimed that one aspect of oppression is more privileged above all others. Current conflicts like those over immigration, refugees and unaccompanied asylum seekers bring these issues to a head, challenging both the social work researcher and social worker as to the nature of their role in this highly politicised arena. It is also likely that with the austerity measures currently in place in the UK and many other countries that the issue of the 'deserving' and 'undeserving poor' will come to the fore as governments reduce welfare expenditure.

Evidence-Based Practice: Today's Research Answer

Having previously examined the importance of philosophical and ethical approaches, we then moved onto the growing influence of evidence-based practice. Evidence-based practice is strongly supported by governments, as it is seen to promise effective and economical social interventions. In trying to understand evidence-based practice it was necessary to return to medicine where it first became established and has made substantive strides. Evidence-based practice was seen to be based on the conscientious, explicit and judicious use of current best evidence, all terms which are open to challenge and debate. Evidence-based practice steers clear of this debate and instead looks towards a hierarchy of research evidence with the systematic reviews of randomised control trials at the apex and expert consensus and individual opinion at the bottom. This hierarchy of evidence is heavily weighted towards behaviourist and positivistic assumptions involving quantitative methods. Whilst these assumptions may hold true in medicine (although even here there are questions being asked) they are more contentious in the social professions. Evidence-based practice presents a rational-logical approach that does not necessarily transfer well to social work. In particular, social work does not have a sufficiently developed evidence base and even if this were possible, the degree of certainty – unlike biological knowledge – poses inherent problems in an uncertain and complex world. It was also noted that social work researchers had welcomed the attention that evidence-based practice had brought to the research contribution to practice. Social work researchers have adapted this interest in research to talk about research-informed practice emphasising a distancing from the hierarchy of knowledge and the worst of the logical rational assumptions.

Getting a Grip on Research

Chapter 7 sought to identify how practice can be used to inform research and vice versa. In particular, we highlighted the barriers to research from a social worker's perspective, researcher's perspective and from an organisational perspective. From this it was clear that there were many barriers to the successful incorporation of research into practice. These barriers included social workers being 'too busy', not valuing research and research not being in an accessible form. For researchers, the barriers included issues in relation to the REF, differing expectations about research outcomes and the format in which research should be published to promote researcher careers. Organisational culture and managerialism with its focus on performance indicators can inhibit or promote research within an organisation. One way of beginning to (re)align these differing interests between social work researchers, social workers and organisations was the notion of the learning organisation. The learning organisation encourages reflective and reflexive practices whilst seeking continually to facilitate the learning of all its members and at the same time emphasise interconnectedness and connectivity. Within the learning organisation action is viewed not only as an attempt to solve a problem but also as a mini experiment to promote learning. Walter et al. (2004), in a review aimed at improving the use of research in practice also highlighted two other ways in which research can inform practice in what they termed the practitioner research model, the embedded research model and the organisational-excellence model. For Walter et al. (2004), it was not a question of whether one model was better than any other but a need for all three models to be used to promote a holistic strategy for the promotion of research to inform practice. Such a view, though, does not say anything about how these three strands can be balanced and whether too much of one will negatively impact upon the others.

Service Users: The New Research Orthodoxy

One of the major changes in recent years has been the centrality given to service users within the world of social work. As previously indicated, the modernisation agenda has stressed the importance of placing the service user at the centre of service provision that was seen to be driven both 'top down' and 'bottom up'.

In recent times there has also been an increasing interest in involving service users in research that is seen as both beneficial to service users and to the research. Service users may benefit the research by offering a different perspective, ensuring that the issues identified are important to service users; ensuring that the questions are relevant and understandable; aiding in the recruitment of potential research respondents; and promoting the dissemination of results. Nonetheless researchers remain reticent to involve service users as co-researchers, citing difficulties about resources, effort and service user representativeness.

However, if service users are to be involved in research it is necessary to consider what aspects of the research they should participate in, to what degree and what training they will require to be able to discharge this task effectively. As yet we are only in the process of exploring the limits of involvement. It is unlikely that service users will have all the skills of a researcher, which is not to say that with training and practice many of these could not be taught. However, it is open to question whether a point is reached when the service user becomes more researcher than service user. This becomes paradoxical, as it is the service user's experience that is valued and it is this experience that contributes to new understandings in social work research and practice processes. It also needs to be remembered that involving service users in research does not necessarily ensure better research or better outcomes. Service user research is no panacea but an alternative research approach with its own strengths and limitations.

Interdisciplinary Research and the Research Process

Recently we have seen the closing down of social service departments and the development of a new mosaic of social work sites of practice. In many of these sites social workers are required to be members of new teams working with other professionals to address society's 'wicked' problems. It is widely accepted that no one profession now has all the skills or capabilities to do it all by themselves. The new orthodoxy emphasises the importance of joined-up thinking, integration and joined-up working.

For social work research the nature of interdisciplinarity and interprofessionalism poses two particular challenges. The first of these is to identify the conditions under which interprofessional working achieves better outcomes for service users and to identify ways in which interdisciplinary research can become an effective research tool. The chapter also put forward the challenge that not to engage in interprofessional practice or research when it was required was as wrong as to engage in such approaches when a uni-professional approach was required. Interprofessional approaches are not always appropriate. This chapter also discussed the nature of Mode 2 knowledge production and how this appeared to be more reflective of much current social work research with its emphasis on application, transdisciplinarity, heterogeneity, heterarchical, social accountability and its emphasis on collaborating researchers from different disciplines.

Messages from Social Work Research

Research, like social work is a messy social and political activity, and as we have seen in the earlier chapters of this book it is highly contested and fraught with ideological, ethical and moral debates. As Humphries notes:

> Neither social work nor social work research is a neutral activity. Like other social practices they are both subject to external and internal forces that influence them towards being instruments of 'empowerment' or otherwise. That they are unambiguously a 'good' cannot be taken for granted. (Humphries, 2005: 279)

Social work exists in those grey areas within society where it has to grapple with the tensions inherent in providing care for those who are unable to care for themselves and to protect those who are unable to protect themselves. Social work inhabits the intersections between service users and carers balanced between social care managers and other health, voluntary and private social care sector managers. Given this uncomfortable position one beacon to help social workers steer a course through the competing demands and interests is to be able to use social work research that has been informed by the same value base as social work itself. Such a knowledge base will seek to provide practitioners with tools to practice effectively, empower, challenge oppression and engage service users as human beings.

The Future of Social Work Research

At this point it would be very easy to be pessimistic about the future of social work research and social work practice. As we have described in this book, the

UK is currently in a period of contradiction where a myriad of social work practice sites have replaced the old unified social work structures heralded by Seehbohm (1968). The very terms social care, social work and social work research are contentious and are open to debate and dispute. No longer can students graduating from qualifying courses expect to go into local authority social work posts. Students are now just as likely to find employment in the independent sector in voluntary organisations, private agencies or in one of the multitude of multi-agency teams in youth justice, learning disabilities or mental health. This is also likely to lead to social workers being employed in multi-professional as opposed to uni-professional teams. This trend is likely to continue as too are the governmental demands for managerial control over practice and budget reductions are played out in practice and performance management indicators. For the first time in the UK social work is an all-graduate workforce with a protected title and a requirement to register and reregister with the requisite care council. In England the SWRB (2010) are developing a professional capabilities framework of which knowledge and critical reflection and analysis are two of the nine building blocks. To achieve these two capabilities (and others), social work students and qualified social workers will need to be able to evaluate and use current social work research evidence. On top of all this we are likely to see the introduction of the NQSW status and an assessed and supported first year in employment with the aim to transform social workers and social work practice (SWTF, 2009).

The future is notoriously difficult to predict and the certainties of one age, for example steam engines, become outmoded in the next. One thing is for certain, though:

> Doing more of the same won't work. Increasing demand, greater complexity and rising expectations mean that the current situation is not sustainable. (Roe, 2006: 8)

The above quotation from the *Report of the 21st Century Social Work Review: Changing Lives* aptly illustrates the point that social work cannot stand still; it must be responsive to the context in which it operates and relevant to those whom it wishes to serve.

In recognition of the importance of research-informed practice, the UK government created the Social Care Institute for Excellence (SCIE) and more recently the NIHR School for Social Research (adults only) to promote the use of evidence to support practice. Local authorities and voluntary agencies have been signing up to national organisations such as the RiP, RiPfA and MRC in an acknowledgement that research is desirable and can impact upon better practice. Research has never had such a prominent place in social work. Managers and government are keen to promote evidence-based practice and the evaluation of individual practitioner performance. Practitioner research is well accepted and seen as important to both agencies and practitioners.

The future remains imperfect, our only guarantee is that change will happen. Social work, if it is to survive, has to function within and outside the context in which it is located. It has to explore the possibilities of the context for creative practice and at the same time to identify ways in which to move towards other futures that highlight the moral nature of the social work task, acknowledge and embrace the growing importance of service user and carer involvement, whilst highlighting anti-oppressive practice and interagency working. No professional group, and this is as true for social work as it is for lawyers, doctors or ministers, has an unequivocal right to survival. If social work is to survive it must engage with contemporary debates and seek to shape, as much as be shaped by, external events. In seeking to engage in this debate, this book has highlighted the importance of the contribution that research can make to the future of social work practice and how practice can contribute to social work research. The book has argued for the research-minded practitioner and the research literate workforce that it is able to contribute to the research agenda, capitalise on the insights from research and also distinguish between knowledge that is valid and credible and knowledge that is not. Social work research can potentially become a key tool for social workers in seeking to attest to the profession's professionalism and support it in its attempts to achieve a transformative practice dealing both with the issues of social control and care.

Knowledge production and research-informed practices are important, but social work research also has to strengthen its standing amongst the other disciplines within academia. One of the distinguishing features of social work research is its applied nature, but that does not mean that it should eschew basic research. Basic research helps to provide the conceptual blocks for understanding practice and developing ways in which those blocks can be used to transform practice developing new ways of working that empower service users and social workers. For social work research there is an inherent requirement to be practice oriented but also for it to be effective it must be recognised within the academic and wider society as a legitimate knowledge-producing discipline.

Researchers need a research-minded culture amongst practitioners to put their research into action but this also requires a practice-minded culture within research organisations that are committed to reaching out to practitioners and to providing knowledge and messages for practice in accessible and understandable formats. For social work or social work research to thrive, practitioners need to learn to listen to and assess the advice of researchers but also researchers need to listen to practitioners to learn about the realities and complexities of practice. This is not a one way, but an iterative entwined process, whereby practice issues become research problems and research solutions become practice tools.

It has become increasingly important for social work research to emphasise what Butler (2003: 27) has described as a 'value based, politically aware and engaged form of endeavour'. Such a stance will inevitably push social work research into conflict with other parts of society and the academic world. However, that is to be expected if social work research is to demonstrate a respect for persons, promote user self-determination, work for the interests of service users and promote social justice. For social workers to be able to act effectively in these domains they need to be able to work with all the tools at their disposal. It is one of the key arguments of this book that good social workers make use of social work research, an oft-underused tool in their toolbox.

Abbreviations Used in the Book

ARPANET   Advanced Research Projects Agency Network – US Department of Defense development of the World Wide Web

BASW   British Association of Social Workers – professional membership organisation for qualified social workers

BERA   The British Education Research Association is a membership organisation whose aim is to sustain and promote a research culture in education

BSL   British Sign Language – native language of deaf people

CAFCASS   Children and Family Court Advice and Support Services – looks after the interests of children involved in family proceedings, including adoption and divorce

CAIPE   The Centre of the Advancement of Interprofessional Education is dedicated to the promotion and development of interprofessional education (IPE) with and through its individual and corporate members, in collaboration with like minded organisations in the UK and internationally

CCETSW   Central Council for the Education and Training of Social Workers – the forerunner of the General Social Care Council

CEBSS   The Centre for Evidence Based Social Services based at Exeter University was the most concrete manifestation of the 'what works' approach in social care. Set up in 1997 its main aim was to ensure that decisions taken at all levels of Social Services were informed by good quality research

CSCI   The Commission for Social Care Inspection was a social services inspectorate until March 2009 when it combined with the

	Healthcare Commission and the Mental Health Act Commission to create the Care Quality Commission
CWDC	Children's Workforce Development Council – a part of the Department of Education supporting the development of the children's workforce, including children's social workers; to be disbanded in 2012
CYPU	The Children and Young People's Unit was a unit established by the UK government to promote children and young people's issues
DETR	Department of the Environment, Transport and the Regions
DfE	Department for Education – responsible for children's schools and child care social work
Dip SW	Diploma in Social Work – the professional qualification for social workers prior to the introduction of the new award in 2003
DH	Department of Health – responsible for adult social care services
EBP	Evidence-based practice – a very important and contested concept for the promotion of research informing practice
ESRC	Economic and Social Research Council – a major provider of research grants
GNC	The General Nursing Council was the forerunner of the Nursing and Midwifery Council responsible for the registration of nurses and nursing programmes
GSCC	General Social Care Council – the registration and regulatory body for social workers and social care due to be disbanded in 2012
HEFCE	Higher Education Funding Council for England – provides funding for higher education
HEI	Higher Education Institution – includes universities and colleges of higher education
IAASW	International Association of Schools of Social Work – an international academic organisation for promoting social work education
IFSW	International Federation of Social Workers – international campaigning organisation for social workers
IPPR	Institute of Public Policy Research is a UK progressive thinktank whose aims include the production of research and innovative policy ideas for a fair, democratic and sustainable world

IRISS   Institute of Research and Innovation in Social Services – in Scotland, to enhance the social services workforce to access and make use of knowledge and research

JAR   Joint Area Reviews – CSCI along with nine other inspectorates' inspection of an areas Children's Services, including those services provided by social workers

JUC SWEC   Joint Universities Council Social Work Education Committee – a membership body of HEI social work programmes

MRC   Making Research Count – a national research development initiative based on a hub-and-spoke principle between universities, local authorities and voluntary agencies

NASW   National Association of Social Workers. In the United States of America is the largest membership organisation of social workers in the world whose aims include the enhancement of the personal development and growth of its members

NHS   National Health Service

NIHR   National Institute of Health Research – this has a separate project under the Department of Health for the School of Social Care Research

NQSW   Newly Qualified Social Worker – supported by both CWDC and Skills for Care specialist programmes in children's and adult's social work, respectively, to promote the development of NQSWs

PAF   Performance Assessment Framework – a programme of key performance measures for measuring social services performance

PQ   Post Qualifying – refers to the social work qualification framework beyond the qualifying degree

QAA   Quality Assurance Agency – there is a specific Quality Assurance Agency for Higher Education whose role is to ensure that higher education courses meet subject benchmarks and are of a suitable standard

RCT   Random Control Trial – specialist and some would say 'gold standard' research method

REF   Research Excellence Framework – has replaced the Research Assessment Exercise (RAE) that used to allocate university research funds

RGF   Research Governance Framework – DH initiative to ensure that local authority social care research is ethical and accountable

RiP   Research in Practice – a national organisation promoting the utilisation of research for practice with a very informative website

RiPfA   Research in Practice for Adults – RiP's sister organisation for promoting research utilisation in adult social care

SCIE   Social Care Institute of Excellence – collects and synthesises up-to-date knowledge about what works in social care and then makes this knowledge available and accessible

SfC   Skills for Care – the employer-led authority on the training standards and workforce development needs of adult social care staff in England

SWRB   The Social Work Reform Board (SWRB) was set up in January 2010 to take forward the recommendations of the Social Work Task Force for the reform of social work. They have a useful website: www.education.gov.uk/swrb/

SWTF   The Social Work Taskforce was established in 2008 by the Labour Government to conduct a 'nuts and bolts' review of social work in England and to advise on the shape and content of a comprehensive reform programme for the future of social work. The final report of the Social Work Task Force was published on Tuesday 1 December 2009, and makes a challenging set of recommendations to the Government for reform

TOPSS   Training Organization for Personal Social Services – has been replaced by Skills for Care, a national employer-led sector skills council

UPIAS   Union of Physically Impaired Against Segregation – a campaigning organisation for people with disabilities

YOT   Youth Offending Team – interagency teams constructed to manage and reduce youth offending; consisting of representatives from social work, probation, police, education and health services personnel

Appendix A

Quasi-Experimental Studies

Please circle the appropriate answers to the questions below.

Screening

1. Were the aims of the research clear?

   Y   N

   Please write in the box what the aims of the research were, or what the research question was. (Everything that is done in the piece of research should relate to this question.)

2. Was a quasi-experimental study the right sort of research design to answer the question?

   Y   N

3. Did the study aim to find out the effectiveness of an intervention or service, but it would have been very complicated or impossible to have conducted a randomised controlled trial?

   Y   N

4. Is it worth continuing?

   Y   N

Methods

5. Do the researchers justify why a randomised controlled trial would not have been possible or desirable?

   Y   To some extent   N

6. Were the participants recruited to the intervention and control group in a way that minimised bias and confounders?

   Y   N

7. Were the intervention and control groups well *matched* at the beginning of the study?

   Y   To some extent   N

8. Was the number of participants in the study justified?

   Y   Not enough detail given   N

9. Were the participants in the intervention and control groups followed up, and the data collected, in the same way?

   Y   To some extent   N

Results

10. Were *all* participants who started off in the study accounted for at the end?

    Y   N

11. Are all the results clearly presented and are they appropriate?

    Y   To some extent   N

Briefly describe the main findings.

12. Have the researchers taken account of potential confounding factors in the analysis?

Y   To some extent   N

Conclusions

13. Are the conclusions drawn supported by the study results?

Y   To some extent   N

Ethics

14. Were the ethical issues addressed?

Y   To some extent   N

Relevance

15. Is this study relevant to your clients and/or practice?

Y   To some extent   N

Appendix B

Qualitative Research

Screening

1. Were the aims of the research clear?

   Y   N

   Please write in the box what the aims of the research were, or what the research question was.

2. Was qualitative research the right sort of approach to use or to answer the research question?

   Y   N

3. Did the researchers aim to interpret or illuminate people's actions and/or their experiences?

   Y   N

4. Is it worth continuing?

   Y   N

Methods

5. Was the research design the most appropriate to address the aims of the study?

   Y   To some extent   N

6. Was the sampling strategy used for the study clear/appropriate?

    Y   To some extent   N

7. Was the number of participants in the study justified?

    Y   To some extent   N

8. Did the way in which the data was collected fit with the aims of the study?

    Y   To some extent   N

9. Was the data collection systematic?

    Y   To some extent   N

10. Was it clear how the data were analysed?

    Y   To some extent   N

Results

11. Are the results clearly presented/appropriate?

    Y   To some extent   N

Briefly describe the main results.

12. Were steps taken to increase the trustworthiness of the study findings?

    Y   To some extent   N

13. Did the researchers critically examine their role, potential bias and influence on the study?

    Y   To some extent   N

Ethics

14. Were the ethical issues addressed?

    Y   To some extent   N

Relevance

15. Is this study relevant to your clients and/or practice?

    Y   To some extent   N

References

Ackroyd, S. and Hughes, J.A. (1981) *Data Collection in Context.* London: Longman.

Adams, R. (1998) *Quality Social Work.* Basingstoke: Macmillan.

Adams, R. (2002) *Social Policy for Social Work.* Basingstoke: Palgrave.

Ahmad, B. (1990) *Black Perspectives in Social Work.* Birmingham: Venture Press.

Antman, E., Lau, J., Kupeltruck, B., Mostellet, F. and Chalmers, I. (1992) 'A comparison of the results of meta-analyses of random controlled trials and recommendations of clinical experts', *Journal of the American Medical Association,* 268 (4): 240–8.

Argyris, C. and Schon, D.A. (1978) *Organisational Learning: A Theory to Action Perspective.* Reading: Addison Welsey.

Arnstein, S. (1971) 'A ladder of citizen participation', *Journal of the Royal Planning Institute,* 35 (4): 216–24.

Aveyard, H. (2010) *Doing a Literature Review in Health and Social Care.* Maidenhead: Open University Press.

Bailey, R. and Brake, M. (1975) *Radical Social Work.* London: Arnold.

Baldwin, M. (2004) 'Optimism and the art of the possible', in N. Gould, and M. Baldwin (eds), *Social Work Critical Reflection and the Learning Organisation.* Aldershot: Ashgate. pp. 161–76.

Balloch, S. and Taylor, M. (2001) *Partnership Working: Policy and Practice.* Bristol: Policy Press.

Banks, S. (1995) *Ethics and Values in Social Work.* Basingstoke: Macmillan.

Barclay, P. (1982) *Social Workers: Their Roles and Tasks.* London: National Institute of Social Work and Bedford Square Press.

Barn, R. (1993) *Black Children in the Public Care System.* London: Batsford.

Barn, R. (1994) 'Black children in the public care system', in B. Humphries, and C. Truman (eds), *Re-Thinking Social Research: Anti-Discrimination Approaches in Research Methodology.* Aldershot: Avebury, pp. 37–58.

Barnes, C. and Mercer, G. (1997) 'Breaking the mould: An introduction to disability research', in C. Barnes and G. Mercer (eds), *Doing Disability Research.* Leeds: Disability Press. pp. 1–14.

Barnes, K. (2002) *Focus on the Future: Key Messages from Focus Groups on the Future of Social Work Training.* London: Department of Health.

Barr, H., Freeth, D., Hammick, M., Koppell, I. and Reeves, S. (1999) *Evaluating Interprofessional Education: A United Kingdom Review for Health and Social Care.* London: BERA and CAIPE.

Barr, H., Koppel, I., Reeves, S., Hammick, M. and Freeth, D. (2005) *Effective Interprofessional Education: Argument Assumption and Evidence.* Oxford: Blackwell Publishing.

Barr, H. and Waterton, S. (1996) *Interprofessional Education in Health and Social Care in the United Kingdom: A CAIPE Survey.* London: CAIPE.

Barratt, M. and Hodson, R. (2006) *Firm Foundations: A Practical Guide to Organisational Support for the Use of Research Evidence.* Dartington: RiP.

BASW (2002) *The Code of Ethics for Social Work.* Available at: www.basw.co.uk/articleld=2fpage=1 (accessed 10 September 2005).

Bateson, G. (1972) *Steps to an Ecology of Mind.* New York: Ballantine.

Bebington, A. and Miles, J. (1989) 'The background of children who enter local authority care', *British Journal of Social Work,* 19 (5): 349–68.

Becker, S. and Bryman, A. (2004) *Understanding Research for Social Policy and Practice: Themes, Methods and Approaches.* Bristol: Policy Press.

Beresford, P. (1994) *Changing the Culture: Involving Service Users in Social Work Education.* London: CCETSW.

Beresford, P. (2000) 'Users' knowledges and social work theory: Conflict or collaboration', *British Journal of Social Work,* 30 (4): 495–503.

Beresford, P. (2005) 'Theory and practice of user involvement in research: Making the connection with public policy and practice', in L. Owes and I. Hulatt (eds), *Involving Service Users in Health and Social Care Research.* London: Routledge. pp. 6–17.

Beresford, P. and Croft, S. (1993) *Citizen Involvement.* London: Macmillan.

Berger, P. and Luckman, T. (1979) *The Social Construction of Reality.* London: Peregrine.

Bhaskar, R. (1979) *The Possibility of Naturalism.* Brighton: Harvester.

Bhatti-Sinclair, K. (2011) *Anti-Racist Practice in Social Work.* Basingstoke: Palgrave Macmillan.

Biestek, F. (1961) *The Casework Relationship.* London: George Allen and Unwin.

Black, T.R. (1999) *Doing Quantitative Research in the Social Sciences: An Integrated Approach to Research Design, Measurement and Statistics.* London: Sage.

Boddy, J. and Oliver, C. (2010) *Research Governance in Children's Service: The Scope for New Advice.* London, Department of Education. Available at: www.education. gov.uk/publications/eOrederingDownload/DFE-RB072.pdf (accessed 1 March 2011).

Booth, T. (1988) *Developing Policy Research*. London: Avebury.

Boushel, M. (1996) 'Vulnerable multi-racial families and early years services: Concerns challenges and opportunities', *Children and Society*, 10: 305–16.

Boushel, M. (2000) 'What kind of people are we? "Race", anti-racism and social welfare research', *British Journal of Social Work*, 30 (1): 71–89.

Bullock, R., Gooch, D., Little, M. and Mount, K. (1998) *Research in Practice: Experiments in Development and Information Design*. Aldershot: Ashgate.

Butler, I. (2002) 'A code of ethics for social work and social care research', *British Journal of Social Work*, 32 (2): 239–48.

Butler, I. (2003) 'Doing good research and doing it well', *Social Work Education*, 33 (1): 19–30.

Butt, J. and O'Neill, A. (2005) *'Let's Move On': Black and Minority Ethnic Older People's Views on Research Findings*. York: Joseph Rowntree Foundation.

Cabinet Office (1990) *Modernising Government*, Cm 4310. London: Stationery Office.

CAIPE (2002) Definition of interprofessional education www.caipe.org.uk/about-us/defining-ipe/

Campbell, D.T. and Fiske, D.W. (1959) 'Convergent and discriminant validation by the multitrait-multimethod matrix', *Psychological Bulletin*, 56 (1): 81–105.

Carpenter, J. and Dickinson, H. (2008) *Interprofessional Education and Training*. Bristol: Policy Press in association with Community Care.

Carpenter, J., McLaughlin, H., Blewett, J., Patsios, D., Platt, D., Scholar, H., Tunstill, J. and Shardlow, S. (2010) *Joint Qualitative and Quantitative Report on the First Year of the Evaluation of the Newly Qualified Social Worker Pilot Programme*. Leeds: CWDC. Available at: www.cwdcouncil.org.uk/research/projects/nqsw-pilot-evaluation (accessed 10 March 2011).

Carr, S. (2004) *Has Service User Participation Made a Difference to Social Care Services?* London: SCIE and Policy Press.

CCETSW (1989) *Rules and Requirements for the Diploma in Social Work*. London: Central Council for the Education and Training of Social Work.

CCETSW (1991a) *Rules and Requirements for the Diploma in Social Work*, Paper No. 30. London: CCETSW.

CCETSW (1991b) *Setting the Context for Change: Anti-Racist Social Work Education*. London: CCETSW.

CCETSW (1995) *Rules and Requirements for the Diploma in Social Work (Revised)*. London: CCETSW.

Chapman, T. and Hough, M. (eds) (1998) *Evidence-Based Practice: A Guide to Effective Practice*. London: Home Office.

Charles, M., Rashid, S. and Thoburn, J. (1992) 'The placement of black children with permanent new families', *Adoption and Fostering*, 16 (1): 13–19.

Christensen, P. and Prout, A. (2002) 'Working with ethical symmetry in social research with children', *Childhood*, 9 (4): 477–97.

Citizens as Trainers, Young Independent People Presenting Educational Entertainment, Rimmer, A. and Harwood, K. (2004) 'Citizen participation in the education and training of Social Workers', *Social Work Education*, 22 (3): 309–23.

Clark, A. (2004) 'The mosaic approach and research with young children', in S. Fraser, V. Lewis, S. Ding, M. Kellett and C. Robinson (eds), *The Reality of Research with Children and Young People*. London: Sage in association with the Open University Press, 142–56.

Clifford, D. (1994) 'Critical life histories: Key anti-oppressive research methods and processes', in B. Humphries and C. Truman (eds), *Re-Thinking Social Research: Anti-Discriminatory Approaches in Research Methodology*. Aldershot: Avebury, pp. 102–22.

Coghlan, D. and Brannick, T. (2001) *Doing Action Research: In Your Own Organization*. London: Sage.

Corrigan, P. and Leonard, P. (1978) *Critical Texts in Social Work and the Welfare State*. London: Macmillan.

Cresswell, J.W. (2003) *Research Design: Qualitative, Quantitative, and Mixed Methods Approaches* (2nd edn). London: Sage.

Cresswell, J.W. (2007) *Research Design: Qualitative, Quantitative and Mixed Methods Approaches*, (2nd edn). London: Sage.

Croft, S. and Beresford, P. (1989) 'User involvement, citizenship and social policy', *Critical Social Policy*, 26 (1): 5–18.

Cronin, A. (2001) 'Focus groups', in N. Gilbert (ed.), *Researching Social Life*, 2nd edn. London: Sage. pp. 164–77.

Crotty, M. (2003) *The Foundations of Social Research*. London: Sage.

CWDC (2008) *The State of the Children's Social Care Workforce: A Critical Review of the Workforce Providing Children's and Families Social Care in England*. Leeds: CWDC. Available at: www.cwdcouncil.org.uk/assets/0000/2257/The_state_of_the_children_s_social_care_workforce_2008.pdf (accessed 20 April 2011).

CYPU (2001) *Learning to Listen: Core Principles for the Involvement of Children and Young People*. London: CYPU.

Dalrymple, J. and Burke, B. (1995) *Anti-Oppressive Practice*. Buckingham: Open University Press.

Davidson, J.O.C. and Layder, D. (1994) *Methods, Sex and Madness*. London: Routledge.

Dawson, A. (1994) 'Professional codes of practice and ethical conduct', *Journal of Applied Philosophy*, 11 (2): 145–53.

Day, L. (1993) 'Women and oppression: race, class and gender', in M. Langan and L.Day (eds), *Women, Oppression and Social Work*. London: Routledge. pp. 12–31.

D'Cruz, H. and Jones, M. (2004) *Social Work Research: Ethical and Political Contexts.* London: Sage.

Deetz, S. (1993) *Communication 2000: The Discipline, the Challenges, the Research, the Social Contribution.* NJ: Rutgers University.

Delanty, G. and Strydom, P. (2003) 'Introduction: What is the philosophy of social science?' in G. Delanty and P. Strydom (eds), *Philosophies of Social Science: The Classic and Contemporary Readings.* Maidenhead: Open University. pp. 1–12.

Denzin, N.K. (1989) *Interpretive Interactionism.* London: Sage.

DETR (1998) *Modern Local Government: In Touch with the People,* Cm 4014. London: Stationery Office.

DH (1991) *Patterns and Outcomes in Child Placements.* London: HMSO.

DH (1995) *Child Protection: Messages from Research.* London: HMSO.

DH (1998a) *Caring for Children Away from Home; Messages from Research.* London: HMSO.

DH (1998b) *Modernising Social Services: Promoting Independence, Improving Protection and Raising Standards,* CM 4169. London: Stationery Office.

DH (1999a) *Framework for the Assessment of Children in Need and their Families.* London: HMSO.

DH (2000a) *A Quality Strategy for Social Care.* London: DH.

DH (2000b) *The NHS Plan: A Plan for Investment, A Plan for Reform.* London: DH.

DH (2001a) *Research Governance Framework for Health and Social Care* London: DH.

DH (2001b) *Mental Health National Service Framework: Full Report by the Workforce Action Team on Workforce Planning, Education and Training.* London: Her Majesty's Stationery Office (HMSO).

DH (2001c) *Working Together, Learning Together: A Framework for Lifelong Working for the NHS.* London: Her Majesty's Stationery Office (HMSO).

DH (2001d) *The Royal Liverpool Children's Inquiry.* Liverpool.

DH (2002) *Listening, Hearing and Responding.* London: Stationery Office.

DH (2004) *The Research Governance Framework for Health and Social Care.* London: DH.

DH, Association of Directors of Adult Services (ADASS), and the Social Services Research Group (SSRG) (2010) *Research Governance Framework: Research Pack for Social Care.* (2nd edn) London: Stationery Office. www.researchregister.org.uk/files/RGFGuidancepack2010.pdf (accessed 07/07/2011).

DH and Department for Education and Skills (2004) *National Service Framework for Children, Young People and Maternity Services: Executive Summary.* London: Department of Health.

DH, Home Office and Department for Education and Employment (1999) *Working Together to Safeguard Children: A Guide to Interagency Working to Safeguard and Promote the Welfare of Children.* London: DH.

DH, RiP and MRC (2002) Quality Protects Research Briefing: Placement Stability, London: DH, RiP, MRC.

Dominelli, L. (1993) *Social Work: Mirror of Society or its Conscience?* Sheffield: Department of Sociological Studies.

Dominelli, L. (1997) *Anti-Racist Social Work.* Basingstoke: Macmillan.

Dominelli, L. (1998) 'Anti-oppressive practice in context', in R. Adams, L. Dominelli and M. Payne (eds), *Social Work: Themes, Issues and Critical Debates.* Basingstoke: Macmillan Press, pp. 3–22.

Dominelli, L. (2005) 'Social work research: Contested knowledge for practice', in R. Adams, L. Dominelli and M. Payne (eds), *Social Work Futures: Crossing Boundaries, Transforming Practice.* Basingstoke: Palgrave Macmillan, pp. 223–36.

Dominelli, L. and McLeod, E. (1989) *Feminist Social Work.* Basingstoke: Macmillan.

Downie, R.S. and Telfer, E. (1969) *Respect for Persons.* London: Allen and Unwin.

Dummett, A. (1991) 'Europe? Which Europe?' *New Community,* 18: 161–75.

Easterby-Smith, M. and Thorpe, R. (1996) *Research Traditions in Management Learning.* London: Sage.

Easterby-Smith, M., Thorpe, R. and Lowe, A. (1991) *Management Research: An Introduction.* London: Sage.

Eborall, C., Fenton, W. and Woodroe, W. (2010) *The State of the Adult Social Care Workforce in England 2010: 4th Report of Skills for Care Research and Analysis Unit.* Leeds: Skills for Care. Available at: http://sfcnational.activclient.com/research/research_reports/annual_reports_SCW.aspx (accessed 20 April 2011).

England, H. (ed.) (1986) *Social Work as Art.* London: Allen and Unwin.

ESRC (2010a) *Framework for Research Ethics.* Available at: www.esrc.ac.uk/_images/Framework_for_Research_Ethics_tcm8-4586.pdf (accessed 1 March 2011).

ESRC (2010b) *Social Science Excellence with Impact.* Swindon: ESRC.

Everitt, A., Hardiker, P., Littlewood, J. and Mullender, A. (1992) *Applied Research for Better Practice.* Basingstoke: Macmillan.

Farmer, E. and Owen, M. (1995) *Child Protection Practice: Private Risks Public Remedies, A Study of Decision-Making, Intervention and Outcomes in Child Protection Work.* London: HMSO.

Ferguson, I. (2008) *Reclaiming Social Work: Challenging Neo-Liberalism and Promoting Social Change.* London: Sage.

Finklestein, V. (1985) Unpublished paper at the World Health Organization, 24–25 June, Netherlands.

Fisher, M. (1999) 'Social work research, social work knowledge and the research assessment exercise', in B. Broad (ed.), *The Politics of Social Work Research and Evaluation.* Birmingham: Venture Press, pp. 91–108.

Folkard, S., Smith, D.E. and Smith, D.D. (1976) *IMPACT Intensive Matched Probation and After-Care Treatment,* Vol. 11. *The Results of the Experiment.* London: Her Majesty's Stationery Office (HMSO).

Fook, J. (2002) *Social Work: Critical Theory and Practice.* London: Sage.

Foster, P. (1990) *Policy and Practice in Multicultural and Anti-Racist Education.* London: Routledge.

Foster, P. (1991) 'Cases not proven: A reply to Cecile Wright', *British Educational Research Journal,* 17 (2): 335–48.

Foster, P. (1992) 'What are Connolly's rules? A reply to Paul Connolly', *British Educational Research Journal,* 18 (2): 149–54.

France, A. (2004) 'Young people', in S. Fraser, J. Lewis, S. Ding, M. Kellett and C. Robinson (eds), *Doing Research with Young People.* London: Sage in association with the Open University, pp. 97–112.

Frost, N. (2005) *Professionalism, Partnership and Joined-Up Working.* Dartington: RiP.

Furedi, F. (2002) 'Don't knock the research boat', *Times Higher Education Supplement,* 11th January :20. Galvani, S. (2008) 'Working together: Responding to people with alcohol and drug problems', in K. Morris (ed.), *Social Work and Multi-Agency Working: Making a Difference.* Bristol: Policy Press. pp. 105–26.

Gardner, A. (2011) *Personalisation in Social Work.* Exeter: Learning Matters.

Garfinkel, H. (1967) *Studies in Ethnomethodology.* Englewood Cliffs, NY: Prentice Hall.

Garrett, P.M. (2000) 'Responding to Irish "invisibility": Anti-discriminatory social work practice and the placement of Irish children in Britain', *Adoption and Fostering,* 24 (1): 23–34.

Garrett, P.M. (2003) *Remaking Social Work with Children and Families: A Critical Discussion on the 'Modernisation' of Social Care.* London: Routledge.

Gibbons, J., Conroy, S. and Bell, C. (1995) *Operating Child Protection Policies in English Local Authorities.* London: Her Majesty's Stationery Office (HMSO).

Gibbons, M., Limoges, C., Nowotny, H., Schwartzman, S. and Scott, P. and Trow, M. (1994) *The New Production of Knowledge: The Dynamics of Science and Research in Contemporary Societies.* London: Sage.

Giddens, A. (1977) *Studies in Social and Political Theory.* London: Hutchinson.

Giddens, A. (2001) *Sociology.* Cambridge: Polity Press.

Gilbert, N. (2001) 'Research theory and method', in N. Gilbert (ed.), *Researching Social Life.* London: Sage, pp. 14–27.

Gillon, R. (1994) 'Medical ethics: Four principles plus attention to scope', *British Medical Journal*, 309: 184–8.

Glasby, J. and Beresford, P. (2006) 'Who knows best? Evidence-based practice and the service user contribution', *Critical Social Policy*, 22 (3): 223–31.

Glasby, J. and Dickinson, H. (2008) *Partnership Working in Health and Social Care*. Bristol: Policy Press in association with Community Care.

Glendinning, C., Powell, M. and Rummery, K. (eds) (2002) *Partnerships, New Labour and the Governance of Welfare*. Bristol: Policy Press.

GNC and CCETSW (1982) *Co-operation in Training*, Part 1. *Qualifying Training*. London: GNC for England and Wales, Scotland and Northern Ireland and the CCETSW.

Goffman, E. (1961) *Asylums*. Garden City, NJ: Doubleday Anchor Books.

Gopineth, C. and Hoffman, C. (1995) 'The relevance of strategy research: Practitioner and academic views', *Journal of Management Studies*, 32 (5): 575–94.

Gould, N. (2004) 'Introduction: The learning organization and reflective practice – the emergence of a concept,' in N. Gould and M. Baldwin (eds), *Social Work: Critical Reflection and the Learning Organization*. Aldershot: Ashgate, pp. 1–9.

Grady, M.D. (2010) 'The missing link: The role of social work schools and evidence-based practice', *The Journal of Evidence-Based Social Work*, 7 (5) 400–11.

GSCC (2002) *Codes of Practice for Employers of Social Care Workers and for Social Care Workers*. London: GSCC.

GSCC (2010) *General Social Care Council Annual Report and Accounts*. London: Stationery Office.

Gutek, G.A. (1978) 'Strategies for studying client satisfaction', *Journal of Social Issues*, 34 (4): 44–55.

Hammersley, M. (1992) *What's Wrong with Ethnography*. London: Routledge.

Hammersley, M. (1995) *The Politics of Social Research*. London: Sage.

Hanley, B. (2005) *Research as Empowerment? Report of a Series of Seminars Organised by the Toronto Group*. York: Joseph Rowntree Foundation.

Hanley, B., Bradburn, J., Barnes, M., Evans, C., Goodare, H., Kelson, M., Kent, A., Oliver, S., Thomas, S. and Wallcraft, J. (2004) *Involving the Public in NHS, Public Health and Social Care: Briefing Notes for Researchers*. Eastleigh: Involve.

Harding, T. and Beresford, P. (1996) *The Standards We Expect: What Service Users and Carers Want from Social Service Workers*. London: National Institute for Social Work.

Hardwick, L. and Worsley, A. (2011) *Doing Social Work Research*. London: Sage.

Harrison, G. and Turner, R. (2011) 'Being a "culturally competent" social worker: Making sense of a murky concept in practice', *British Journal of Social Work*, 41 (2): 333–50.

Harvey, L. (1990) *Critical Social Research*. London: Unwin Hyman.

Hasler, F. (2003) *Users at the Heart: User Participation in the Governance and Operation of Social Regulatory Bodies*. London: SCIE.

Healy, K. (2000) *Social Work Practices*. London: Sage.

Healy, K. (2005) *Social Work Theories in Context: Creating Frameworks for Practice*. Basingstoke: Palgrave Macmillan.

Heath, A., Colton, M. and Aldgate, J. (1994) 'Failure to escape: A longitudinal study of foster children's educational attainment', *British Journal of Social Work*, 24 (3): 241–60.

Heron, J. (1996) *Co-operative Inquiry: Research into the Human Condition*. London: Sage.

Hewson, C., Yule, P., Laurent, D. and Vogel, C. (2003) *Internet Research Methods: A Practical Guide for the Social and Behavioural Sciences*. London: Sage.

Higham, P. (2001) *Integrated Practice: Using Narratives to Develop Theories in Social Care*. Birmingham: Venture Press.

Homan, R. (1991) *The Ethics of Social Research*. Harlow: Longman.

Horner, N. (2006) *What is Social Work? Context and Perspectives*, 2nd edn. Exeter: Learning Matters.

Horner, N. (2003) *What is Social Work? Context and Perspectives*. Poole: Learning Matters.

Howe, Lord (2010) *NIHR Annual Report*. London: DH. Available at: www.nihr.ac.uk/files/pdfs/400891_NIHR_AnnualReport2010_acc3.pdf (accessed: 20 January 2011).

Hudson, B. (2002) 'Interprofessionality in health and social care: The Achilles heel of partnership?', *Journal of Interprofessional Care*, 16 (1): 7–17.

Hughes, J. (1990) *The Philosophy of Social Research*. London: Longman.

Hugman, R. (1991) *Power in Caring Professions*. Basingstoke: Macmillan.

Hugman, R. (2003) 'Going around in circles? Identifying interprofessional dynamics in Australian health and social welfare', in A. Leathard (ed.), *Interprofessional Collaboration: From Policy to Practice in Health and Social Care*. Hove: Brunner-Routledge, pp. 56–68.

Hugman, R. (2010) *Understanding International Social Work: A Critical Analysis*. Basingstoke: Palgrave Macmillan.

Hugman, R. and Smith, D. (1995) 'Ethical issues in social work: An overview', in R. Hugman and D. Smith (eds), *Ethical Issues in Social Work*. London: Routledge, pp. 1–15.

Humphries, B. (1996) 'Contradictions in the culture of empowerment', in B. Humphries (ed.), *Critical Perspectives on Empowerment*. Birmingham: Venture Press, pp. 1–16.

Humphries, B. (2004) 'An unacceptable role for social work: Implementing immigration policy', *British Journal of Social Work*, 34 (1): 93–107.

Humphries, B. (2005) 'From margin to centre: Shifting the emphasis of social work research', in R. Adams, L. Dominelli and M. Payne (eds), *Social Work Futures: Crossing Boundaries, Transforming Practice*. Basingstoke: Palgrave Macmillan, pp. 279–92.

Humphries, B. and Martin, M. (2000) 'Disrupting ethics in social research', in B. Humphries (ed.), *Research in Social Care and Social Welfare: Issues and Debates for Practice*. London: Jessica Kingsley.

Hunt, P. (1981) 'Settling accounts with the parasite people', *Disability Challenge*, 2 (1): 37–50.

Husband, C. (1995) 'The morally active practitioner and the ethics of anti-racist social work', in R. Hugman and D. Smith (eds), *Ethical Issues in Social Work*. London: Routledge, pp. 84–103.

IASSW and IFSW (2004), *Global Standards for Social Work Education*. Berne: IASSW and IFSW. Available at: www.iassw.soton.ac.uk/en/GlobalQualifying Standards/GlobalStandards/.pdf (accessed 28 July 2005).

IFSW (2011) Available at: www.ifsw.org/f38000138.html (accessed 20 April 2011).

Involve (2010) *Payment for Involvement: A Guide for Making Payments to Members of the Public Actively Involved in NHS, Public Health and Social Care Research*. Eastleigh: Involve. Available at: www.invo.org.uk/pdfs/PaymentGuideWEB240510.pdf (accessed 28 January 2011).

IPPR (2010) *August 2010 Migration Statistics: IPPR Briefing*. London: IPPR. Available at: www.ippr.org.uk/publicationsandreports/publications.asp?title=&author=&pubdate=2010&theme=Migration+and+Integration&search=search (accessed 20 March 2011).

IRISS (2011) IRISS main website. Available at: www.iriss.org.uk

Jackson, S. (1987) *The Education of Children in Care*, Bristol Papers in Applied Social Studies No.1. Bristol: University of Bristol.

Jackson, S. (1994) 'Educating children in residential and foster care', *Oxford Review of Education*, 20 (2): 267–79.

Jay Committee (1979) *Report of the Committee of Enquiry into Mental Handicap Nursing and Care*. London: Her Majesty's Stationery Office (HMSO).

Jesson, J., with Matheson, L. and Lacey, F.M. (2011) *Doing Your Literature Review: Traditional and Systematic Techniques*. London: Sage.

Jones, A. (2004) 'Involving young people as researchers', in S. Fraser, J. Lewis, S. Ding, M. Kellet and C. Robinson (eds), *Doing Research with Children and Young People*. London: Sage with the Open University.

Jones, R. (1995) 'Co-opting carers and service users', *ADSS News*, 18–19 April.

Joseph Rowntree Foundation (2011) www.jrf.org.uk

JUC SWEC (2006) *A Social Work Research Strategy in Higher Education 2006–2020*. Nottingham: JUC SWEC. Available at: www.swap.ac.uk/research/strategy.asp (accessed 10 January 2011).

Kadushin, A. (1972) *The Social Work Interview*. London: Columbia University Press.

Kimmel, A.J. (1988) *Ethics and Values in Applied Social Research*. Newbury Park: Sage.

Kirby, P. (2004) *A Guide to Actively Involving Young People in Research: For Researchers, Research Commissioners and Managers*. Eastleigh: Involve.

Kuhn, T. (1970) *The Structure of Scientific Revolutions*, 2nd edn., London: University of Chicago Press.

Laird, S.E. (2008) *Anti-Oppressive Social Work*. London: Sage.

Laming Lord (2003) *The Victoria Climbié Inquiry*, Cm 5730. London: Stationery Office.

Langston, A., Abbott, L., Lewis, V. and Kellett, M. (2004) 'Early childhood', in S. Fraser, J. Lewis, S. Ding, M. Kellett and C. Robinson (eds), *Doing Research with Children and Young People*. London: Sage in association with Open University, pp. 147–60.

Law, S. and Janzon, K. (2005) 'Reaching for the stars: The performance assessment framework for social services', in D. Taylor and S. Bulloch (eds), *The Politics of Evaluation: Participation and Policy Implementation*. Bristol: Policy Press, pp. 57–73.

Leathard, A. (1994) 'Inter-professional developments in Britain: An overview', in A. Leathard (ed.), *Going Inter-Professional: Working Together for Health and Welfare*. London: Routledge, pp. 3–37.

Leathard, A. (2003) 'Introduction', in A. Leathard, *Interprofessional Collaboration: From Policy to Practice in Health and Social Care*. Hove: Brunner-Routledge, pp. 2–10.

Lewis, J. (2002) 'Research and development in social care: Governance and good practice', *Research Policy and Planning*, 20 (1): 3–10.

Lewis, J. (2003) 'Design issues', in J. Ritchie and J. Lewis (eds), *Qualitative Research Practice: A Guide for Social Science Students and Researchers*. London: Sage, pp. 47–76.

Lincoln, Y.S. and Denzin, N. (1998) 'The fifth movement', in N. Denzin and Y.S. Lincoln (eds), *The Landscape of Qualitative Research*. London: Sage, pp. 407–30.

Lockey, R., Sitzia, J., Gillingham, T., Millyard, T., Miller, C., Ahmed, S., Beales, A., Bennett, C., Parfoot, S., Sigrist, J. and Worthing and Southlands Hospitals NHS Trust (2004) *Training for Service Users Involvement in Health and Social Care Research: A Study of Training Provision and Participants Experiences*. Eastleigh: Involve.

Long, T. and Johnson, M. (eds) (2007) *Research Ethics in the Real World: Issues and Solutions for Health and Social Care*. Edinburgh: Elsevier.

Lorde, A. (1984) *Sister Outsider*. New York: Crossing Press.

Lyons, K. (2000) 'The place of research in social work education', *British Journal of Social Work Education*, 30 (4): 433–47.

MacDonald, G. (1999) 'Social work and its evaluation: A methodological dilemma', in F. Williams, J. Popay and A. Oakley (eds), *Welfare Research: A Critical Perspective*. London: UCL Press, pp. 89–103.

MacDonald, G. (2003) *Using Systematic Reviews to Improve Social Care: Report No. 4*. London: SCIE.

MacDonald, G. (2008) 'The evidence-based perspective', in M. Davies (ed.), *The Blackwell Companion to Social Work*, 3rd edn. Oxford: Blackwell, pp. 434–41.

MacDonald, G. and Popay, J. (2010) 'Evidence and practice: The knowledge challenge for social work', in I. Shaw, K. Briar-Lawson, J. Orme and R. Ruckdeschel (eds), *The Sage Handbook of Social Work Research*. London: Sage, pp. 264–80.

MacDonald, G. and Roberts, H. (1995) *What Works in the Early Years*. Ilford: Barnardos.

MacDonald, G., Sheldon, B. and Gillespie, J. (1992) 'Contemporary studies of the effectiveness of social work', *British Journal of Social Work*, 22 (6): 615–42.

Macey, M. and Moxon, E. (1996) 'An examination of anti-racist and anti-oppressive theory and practice in social work education', *British Journal of Social Work*, 26 (3): 297–314.

MacIntyre, A. (1985) *After Virtue*. London: Duckworth.

Mackie, J.L. (1977) *Ethics: Inventing Right and Wrong*. Harmondsworth: Penguin.

Macpherson, Sir William of Cluny (1999) *The Stephen Lawrence Inquiry*. London: Stationery Office.

Macquarie, J. (1973) *Existentialism*. Harmondsworth: Penguin.

Marsh, P. and Fisher, M., in collaboration with Mathers, N. and Fish, S. (2005) *Developing the Evidence Base for Social Work and Social Care Practice*. London: SCIE.

May, T. (2001) *Social Research: Issues, Methods and Process*, 3rd edn. Buckingham: Open University Press.

May, T. (2010) The Home Secretary's Immigration Speech. Available at: www.homeoffice.gov.uk/media-centre/speeches/immigration-speech (accessed 20 March 2011).

May, T. and Williams, M. (2001) 'Social surveys: Design to analysis', in T. May (ed.), *Social Research: Issues, Methods and Process*. Buckingham: Open University Press, pp. 88–119.

Mayer, J.E. and Timms, N. (1970) *The Client Speaks*. London: Routledge and Kegan Paul.

McDonald, P. and Coleman, M. (1999) 'Deconstructing hierarchies of oppression and adopting a 'multi-model' approach to anti-oppressive practice', *Social Work Education*, 18 (1): 19–33.

McGuire, J. (1995) *What Works: Reducing Offending*. Chichester: Wiley.

McLaughlin, H. (2005) 'Young service users as co-researchers', *Qualitative Social Work*, 4 (1): 21–8.

McLaughlin, H. (2006) 'Involving young service users as co-researchers, possibilities, benefits and costs', *British Journal of Social Work*, 36 (8): 1395–410.

McLaughlin, H. (2009) *Service User Research in Health and Social Care*. London: Sage.

McLaughlin, H., Brown, D. and Young, A. (2004) 'Consultation, community and empowerment: Lessons from the deaf community', *Journal of Social Work*, 4 (2): 153–65.

McLaughlin, H. and Shardlow, S. (2009) 'Different cultures, different ethics? Research governance and social care', *Ethics and Social Welfare*, 3 (1): 4–17.

Mental Health Foundation (2011) www.mentalhealth.org.uk

Merrington, S. and Stanley, S. (2004) '"What works?": Revisiting the evidence in England and Wales', *Probation Journal*, 51 (1): 7–20.

Miller, E.J. and Gwynne, G.V. (1972) *A Life Apart*. London: Tavistock.

Mills, D., Jepson, P., Coxon, T., Easterby-Smith, M., Hawkins, P. and Spencer, J. (2006) *Demographic Review of the UK Social Sciences*. Swindon: ESRC. Available at: www.esrc.ac.uk/ESRCIfoCentre/Images/Demographic_Review_tem6-13872.pdf (accessed 6 April 2006).

Molyneux, J. and Irvine, J. (2004) 'Service users and carers involvement in social work training: The long and winding road', *Social Work Education*, 23 (3): 293–308.

Morris, K. (ed.) (2008) *Social Work and Multi-Agency Working: Making a Difference*. Bristol: Policy Press.

Muluccio, A. (1998) 'Assessing child welfare outcomes: The American perspective', *Children and Society*, 12 (2): 161–8.

Mumford, R. and Saunders, L. (2011) 'Embracing the diversity of practice: Indigenous knowledge and mainstream social work practice', *Journal of Social Work Practice*, 25 (1): 63–77.

Murch, S.H., Anthony, A., Casson, D.H. et al. (2004) 'Retraction of an interpretation', *The Lancet*, 364 (9411): 750.

NASW (2001) *Cultural Competence in Social Work Practice*. Washington, DC: NASW.

Newman, T., Moseley, A., Tierney, S. and Ellis, A. (2005) *Evidence-Based Social Work: A Guide for the Perplexed*. Lyme Regis: Russell House Publishing Ltd.

Nolan, M., Hanson, E., Grant, G. and Keady, J. (2007) 'Conclusions: Realizing authentic participatory enquiry', in M. Nolan, E. Hanson, G. Grant and J. Keady (eds), *User Participation in Health and Social Care Research*. Maidenhead: Open University Press, pp. 183–202.

Nutley, S. and Webb, J. (2000) 'Evidence and the policy process', in H.T.O. Davies, S.M. Nutley and P.C. Smith (eds), *What Works? Evidence-Based Policy and Practice in Public Services*. Bristol: Policy Press, pp. 13–41.

Oakley, A. (1981) 'Interviewing women: A contradiction in terms', in H. Roberts (ed.), *Doing Feminist Research*. London: Routledge and Kegan Paul, pp. 30–61.

Oates, R.K. and Bross, D.C. (1995) 'What have we learned from treating physical abuse?' *Child Abuse and Neglect*, 19: 463–73.

Oliver, M. (1990) *The Politics of Disablement*. London: Macmillan.

Oliver, M. (1993) 'Re-defining disability: A challenge to research', in J. Swann, V. Finkelstein, S. French and M. Oliver (eds), *Disabling Barriers: Enabling Research*. London: Sage, pp. 61–7.

Oliver, P. (2003) *The Student's Guide to Research Ethics*. Maidenhead: Open University Press.

Orme, J. (2003) '"Its feminist because I say so!" Feminism, social work and critical practice, in the UK', *Qualitative Social Work*, 2 (2): 218–26.

Orme, J. and Shemmings, D. (2010) *Developing Research-Based Social Work Practice*. Basingstoke: Palgrave Macmillan.

Ovretveit, J. (1993) *Co-ordinating Community Care: Multidisciplinary Teams and Care Management*. Buckingham: Open University Press.

Ovretveit, J. (1997) 'How patient power and client participation affects relations between professions', in J. Ovretveit, P. Mathias and T. Thompson (eds), *Interprofessional Working for Health and Social Care*. London: CCETSW, pp. 79–102.

Paley, J. (2000) 'Paradigms and presuppositions: The difference between qualitative and quantitative research', *Scholarly Inquiry for Nursing Practice*, 14 (2): 143–55.

Parker, R. (1966) *Decisions in Child Care: A Study of Prediction in Fostering*. London: Allen and Unwin.

Parker, R. (1998) 'Evidence, judgment and values', in J. Tunnard (ed.), *Commissioning and Managing External Research: A Guide for Child Care Agencies*. Dartington: Research in Practice, pp. 5–12.

Parker, R., Ward, H., Jackson, S., Aldgate, J. and Wedge, P. (1991) *Looking after Children: Assessing Outcomes in Childcare*. London: Her Majesty's Stationery Office (HMSO).

Pawson, R., Boaz, A., Grayson, L., Long, A. and Barnes, C. (2003) *Types and Knowledge in Social Care*. London: SCIE.

Payne, G. and Payne, J. (2004) *Key Concepts in Social Research*. London: Sage.

Payne, M. (2000) *Anti-Bureaucratic Social Work*. Birmingham: Venture Press.

Payne, M. (2005) *Modern Social Work Theory*, 3rd edn. Basingstoke: Palgrave Macmillan.

Payne, M. and Shardlow, S.M. (eds) (2002) *Social Work in the British Isles*. London: Jessica Kinsley.

Pedler, M., Burgoyne, J. and Boydell, T. (1991) *The Learning Company*. London: McGraw-Hill.

Pew Health Commission (1993) *Critical Challenges: Revisiting the Health Professions for the Twenty-First Century.* San Francisco, CA: Pew Health Professions Commission.

Plomer, A. (2005) *The Law and Ethics of Medical Research: International Bioethics and Human Rights.* London: Cavendish Publishing Ltd.

Popay, J. and Roen, K. (2003) *Using Evidence for Diverse Research Designs: Report No. 3.* London: SCIE.

Popper, K. (1980) *The Logic of Scientific Discovery.* London: Hutchinson.

Preston-Shoot, M. (2002) 'Why social workers don't read', *Care and Health Guide,* 11 March: 11–12.

Pugh, R. (2003) 'Considering the countryside: Is there a case for rural social work?', *British Journal of Social Work,* 33 (1): 67–86.

Punch, M. (1998) 'Politics of ethics in qualitative research', in N. Denzin and Y.S. Lincoln, *The Landscape of Qualitative Research.* London: Sage, pp. 156–84.

QAA (2008) *QAA 236 02/08 Social Work.* Mansfield: Quality Assurance Agency in Higher Education Available at: www.qaa.ac.uk/academicinfrastructure/benchmark/statements/socialwork08.pdf (accessed 7 March 2011).

Qvortrup, J., Bardy, M., Sgritta, G. and Wintersberger, H. (eds) (1994) *Childhood Matters.* Vienna: European Centre.

Ratcliffe, P. (2004) '*Race*', *Ethnicity and Difference: Imagining the Inclusive Society.* Maidenhead: Open University Press.

Raynor, P. (2003) 'Evidence-based practice and its critics', *Probation Journal,* 50 (3): 334–45.

Reason, P. and Rowan, J. (eds) (1981) *Human Inquiry: A Sourcebook of New Paradigm Research.* London: Wiley.

Reynolds, S. (2000) 'The anatomy of evidence-based practice: principles and methods', in L. Trinder and S. Reynolds (eds) *Evidence-Based Practice: A Critical Approach.* Oxford: Blackwell Science. pp. 17–34.

RiP (2011) Available at: www.rip.org.uk

RiPfA (2011) Available at: www.ripfa.org.uk

Ritchie, J. (2003) 'The applications of qualitative methods to social research', in J. Ritchie and J. Lewis (eds), *Qualitative Social Research: A Guide for Social Science Students and Researchers.* London: Sage, pp. 24–46.

Roberts, H. (2004) 'Health and social care', in S. Fraser, J. Lewis, S. Ding, M. Kellett and C. Robinson (eds), *Doing Research with Children and Young People.* London: Sage in association with Open University, pp. 239–54.

Roe, W. (Chair) (2006) *Report of the 21st Century Social Work Review: Changing Lives.* Edinburgh: Scottish Executive.

Rogers, T. (2004) 'Managing in the interprofessional environment: A theory of action perspective', *Journal of Interprofessional Care,* 18 (3): 239–49.

Rosen, M. (1991) 'Coming to terms with the field: Understanding and doing organizational ethnography', *Journal of Management Studies*, 28 (1): 1–24.

Sackett, D.L., Richardson, W.S., Rosenberg, W. and Haynes, R.B. (1977) *Evidence-Based Medicine: How to Practice and Teach EBM*. New York: Churchill Livingstone.

Save the Children (2004) *So You Want to Involve Children in Research? A Toolkit Supporting Children's Meaningful and Ethical Participation in Research Relating to Violence Against Children*. Stockholm: Save the Children.

Schein, E. (1984) 'Coming to a new awareness of organisational culture', *Sloan Management Review*, 25 (2): 3–16.

Schon, D.I. (1971) *Beyond the Stable State*. New York: Random House.

Schutz, A. (1973) *The Phenomenology of the Social World*. Evanstown, IL: Northwestern University Press.

Schutz, A. (1978) 'Concept and theory formation in the social sciences', in J. Brynner and K.M. Stribley (eds), *Social Research: Principles and Procedures*. London: Longman.

SCIE (2004) *Learning Organisations: A Self-Assessment Resource Pack*. London: SCIE.

SCIE (2011) SCIE's main website. Available at: www.scie.org.uk

Seebohm, F. (1968) *Report of the Committee on Local Authority and Allied Personal Social Services* (the Seebohm Report). London: HMSO.

Shah, N. (1989) 'It's up to you sisters: Black women and radical social work', in M. Langan and P. Lee (eds), *Radical Social Work Today*. London: Unwin Hyman, pp. 188–91.

Shaping Our Lives Network (2009) *Definitions*. Available at: www.shapingour lives.org.uk/definitions.html (accessed 11 June 2009).

Shardlow, S. (1989) Changing values in social work education: An introduction', in S. Shardlow (ed.), *The Values of Change in Social Work*. London: Routledge.

Shaw, I. (2003) 'Cutting edge issues in social work research', *British Journal of Social Work Research*, 33 (1): 107–16.

Shaw, I. (2004) 'Evaluation for a learning organization', in N. Gould and M. Baldwin (eds), *Social Work, Critical Reflection and the Learning Organization*. Aldershot: Ashgate, pp. 117–28.

Shaw, I. (2007) 'Is social work research distinctive', *Social Work Education*, 26 (7): 659–69.

Shaw, I. and Lundt, N. (2011) 'Navigating practitioner research', *British Journal of Social Work*, 1–18 advanced access doi:10.1093/bjsw/ber025. Available at: www. bjsw.oxfordjournals.org/content/early2011/03/10/bjsw.bcr025.full.pdf+html (accessed 7 April 2011).

Shaw, I. and Mullender, A. (2004) *ESRC Research, Social Work and Social Care*. Bristol: SCIE.

Shaw, I., Arksey, H. and Mullender, A. (2004) *ESRC Research, Social Work and Social Care.* Bristol: SCIE.

Sheldon, B. (2000) *Prospects for Evidence Based Social Care: An Empirical Study,* Centre for Evidence Based Social Services. Exeter: University of Exeter.

Sheldon, B. and Chilvers, R. (2000) *Evidence-Based Social Care: A Study of Prospects and Problems.* Lyme Regis: Russell House Publishing.

Sheldon, B., Chilvers, R., Ellis, A., Moseley, A. and Tierney, S. (2005) 'A pre-post empirical study of the obstacles to, and opportunities for, evidence-based practice in social care', in A. Bilson (ed.), *Evidence-Based Practice in Social Work.* London: Whiting and Birch, pp. 11–50.

Shepperd, M. (2004) *Appraising and Using Research in the Human Services: An Introduction for Social Work and Health Professionals.* London: Jessica Kingsley.

Silverman, D. (1993) *Interpreting Qualitative Data.* London, Sage.

Smith, J. (2004) *Fifth Report: Safeguarding Patients: Learning the Lessons of the Past – Proposals for the Future,* Cmnd 6394. London: Her Majesty's Stationery Office (HMSO).

Smith, L.T. (1999) *Decolonizing Methodologies: Research and Indigenous People.* London: Zed Books.

Smith, R., Monaghan, M. and Broad, B. (2002) 'Involving young people as co-researchers: Facing up to the methodological issues', *Qualitative Social Work,* 1 (2): 191–207.

Snape, D. and Spencer, L. (2003) 'The foundations of qualitative research', in J. Ritchie and J. Lewis (eds), *Qualitative Research Practice: A Guide for Students and Researchers.* London: Sage, pp. 1–23.

Social Care and Health Workforce Group (2004) *Social Services Workforce Series 2003: Report No. 33.* London. Local Government Association. Available at: www.lg-employers.gov.uk (accessed 2 August 2004).

Social Work and Society (main website) Available at: www.socwork.net/

Social Work Reform Board (2010a) *Building a Safe and Confident Future: One Year On: Progress Report from the Social Work Reform Board.* www.education.gov.uk/publications/eOrderingDownload/Building%20a%20safe%20and%20confident%20future%20-%20One%20year%20on.pdf (accessed 07/07/2011).

Social Work Reform Board (2010b) *Building a Safe and Confident Future: One Year On: Overarching Professional Standards for Social Work in England.* www.education.gov.uk/publications/eOrderingDownload/2%20Overarching%20professional%20standards.pdf (accessed 07/07/2011).

Sociological Research Online (main website) Available at: www.socresonline.org.uk

Solomos, J. (2003) *Race and Racism in Britain.* Basingstoke: Palgrave Macmillan.

Staley, K. (2009) *Exploring Impact: Public Involvement in the NHS, Public Health and Social Care Research.* Eastleigh: Involve.

Steele, R. (2003) *A Guide to Paying Members of the Public who are Actively Involved in Research*. Eastleigh: Involve.

Stein, M. (1997) *What Works in Leaving Care*. Ilford: Barnardos.

Stone, J.A.M., Haas, B.A., Harmer-Beem, M.J. and Baker, D.L. (2004) 'Utilization of research methodology in designing and developing an interdisciplinary course in ethics', *Journal of Interprofessional Care*, 18 (1): 57–62.

Sue, D.W. (2001) 'Multidimensional facets of cultural competence', *Counseling Psychologist*, 29 (6): 790–821.

SWTF (2009) *Building a Safe, Confident Future: The Final Report of the Social Work Taskforce: November 2009*. London: Crown Copyright. Available at: www.education.gov.uk/publications/eOrderingDownload/01114-2009DOM-EN.pdf (accessed 22 April 2011).

Taylor, C. and White, S. (2000) *Practising Reflexivity in Health and Welfare: Making Knowledge*. Buckingham: Open University Press.

Thompson, N. (1997) *Anti-Discriminatory Practice*. Basingstoke: Macmillan.

TOPSS (1999) *Modernising the Social Care Workforce*. Leeds: TOPSS.

TOPSS (2002) *The National Occupation Standards for Social Work*. Leeds: TOPSS England.

Torkington, C., Lymbery, M., Millward, A., Murfin, M. and Richell, B. (2003) 'Shared practice learning: Social work and district nurse students learning together', *Social Work Education*, 22 (2): 165–75.

Trend, M.G. (1979) 'On the reconciliation of qualitative and quantitative analyses', in T.D. Cook and C.S. Reichardt (eds), *Qualitative and Quantitative Methods in Evaluation Research*. Beverly Hills, CA: Sage, pp. 66–86.

Trevillion, S. and Bedford, L. (2003) 'Utopianism and pragmatism in interprofesional education', *Social Work Education*, 22 (2): 215–27.

Trinder, L. (2000a) 'Introduction: The context of evidence-based practice', in L. Trinder and S. Reynolds (eds), *Evidence-Based Practice: A Critical Approach*. Oxford: Blackwell Science, pp. 10–16.

Trinder, L. (2000b) 'Evidence-based practice in social work and probation', in L. Trinder and S. Reynolds (eds), *Evidence-Based Practice: A Critical Appraisal*. Oxford: Blackwell Science, 138–62.

Trinder, L. (2000c) 'A critical appraisal of evidence-based practice', in L. Trinder and S. Reynolds (eds), *Evidence-Based Practice: A Critical Appraisal*. Oxford: Blackwell Science, 212–41.

Tuhiwai Smith, L. (1999) *Decolonizing Methodologies: Research and Indigenous Peoples*. London: Zed Books.

Turner, M. and Beresford, P. (2005) *What User Controlled Research Means: And What it Can Do*. Eastleigh: Involve.

Underdown, A. (1998) *Strategies for Effective Offender Supervision: Report of HMIP What Works Project*. London: Home Office.

United Nations (1989) *Convention on the Rights of the Child.* New York: United Nations.

UPIAS (1976) *Fundamental Principles of Disability.* London: UPIAS.

Walter, I., Nutley, S., Percy-Smith, J., McNeish, D. and Frost, S. (2004) *Knowledge Review 7: Improving the Use of Research in Social Care Practice.* London: SCIE.

Webb, S. (2001) 'Some considerations on the validity of evidence-based practice in social work', *British Journal of Social Work*, 31 (1): 57–79.

What works for children? (2011) www.whatworksforchildren.org.uk

Williams, C. (1999) 'Connecting anti-racist and anti-oppressive theory and practice: Retrenchment or reappraisal?' *British Journal of Social Work*, 29 (2): 211–30.

Wilson, A. and Beresford, P. (2000) '"Anti-Oppressive practice": Emancipation or appropriation?' *British Journal of Social Work*, 30 (5): 553–73.

Wilson, K., Ruch, G., Lymbery, M. and Cooper, A. (2008) *Social Work: An Introduction to Contemporary Practice.* Harlow: Pearson Education Limited.

Young, A., Hunt, R., McLaughlin, H. (2001) 'Exploring models of D/deaf service user involvement in translating quality standards into local practice', *Social Work and Social Science Review*, 1–13 (2): 25–39.

Zwarenstein, M., Atkins, J., Barr, H., Hammick, M., Koppell, I. and Reeves, S. (1999) 'A systematice review of interprofessional education', *Journal of Interprofessional Care*, 13 (4): 417–31.

Zwarenstein, M., Reeves, S. and Perrier, L. (2005) 'Effectiveness of pre-licensure interprofessional education and post-licensure collaborative interventions', *Journal of Interprofessional Care*, 19 (1): 148–65.

Index